GENERAL ENGLISH
FOR AVIATION

Dados Internacionais de Catalogação na Publicação (CIP)
(Câmara Brasileira do Livro, SP, Brasil)

Uemura, Cintia Naomi
   General English for aviation: pilots, cabin crew,
ground staff and ir traffic controller/Cintia Naomi
Uemura. – São Paulo: Cengage Learning, 2014.

   ISBN 978-85-221-1659-1

   1. Inglês - Estudo e ensino I. Título.

14-01105   CDD-420.7

Índices para catálogo sistemático:
   1. Inglês : Estudo e ensino 420.7

General English
FOR AVIATION

PILOTS, CABIN CREW, GROUND STAFF,
AND AIR TRAFFIC CONTROLLER

CINTIA NAOMI UEMURA

WITH ON-LINE AUDIO MATERIAL

Austrália • Brasil • Japão • Coreia • México • Cingapura • Espanha • Reino Unido • Estados Unidos

General English for aviation – Pilots, cabin crew, ground staff, and air traffic controller
    Cintia Naomi Uemura

Gerente editorial: Noelma Brocanelli

Supervisora de produção gráfica: Fabiana Alencar Albuquerque

Editora de desenvolvimento: Viviane Akemi Uemura

Editoras colaboradoras: Gisela Carnicelli e Regina Plascak

Copidesque: Fernanda Troeira Zuchini

Revisão: Sheila Rizzi

Diagramação: Alfredo Carracedo Castillo

Ilustrações: Weber Amendola

Capa: Sérgio Bergocce

Imagem da capa: Sam. C/Shutterstock

Editora de direitos de aquisição e iconografia: Vivian Rosa

Analista de conteúdo e pesquisa: Javier Muniain

Pesquisa iconográfica: Mário Coelho

© 2015 Cengage Learning Edições Ltda.

Todos os direitos reservados. Nenhuma parte deste livro poderá ser reproduzida, sejam quais forem os meios empregados, sem a permissão por escrito da Editora. Aos infratores aplicam-se as sanções previstas nos artigos 102, 104, 106, 107 da Lei nº 9.610, de 19 de fevereiro de 1998.

Esta editora empenhou-se em contatar os responsáveis pelos direitos autorais de todas as imagens e de outros materiais utilizados neste livro. Se porventura for constatada a omissão involuntária na identificação de algum deles, dispomo-nos a efetuar, futuramente, os possíveis acertos.
A Editora não se responsabiliza pelo funcionamento dos links contidos neste livro que possam estar suspensos.

> Para informações sobre nossos produtos,
> entre em contato pelo telefone
> **0800 11 19 39**
> Para permissão de uso de material desta obra, envie seu pedido para **direitosautorais@cengage.com**

© 2015 Cengage Learning. Todos os direitos reservados.

ISBN 13: 9 978-85-221-1659-1
ISBN 10: 85-221-1659-8

Cengage Learning
Condomínio E-Business Park
Rua Werner Siemens, 111 – Prédio 11 – Torre A – Conjunto 12
Lapa de Baixo – CEP 05069-900 – São Paulo – SP
Tel.: (11) 3665-9900 Fax: 3665-9901
SAC: 0800 11 19 39

Para suas soluções de curso e aprendizado, visite
www.cengage.com.br

Impresso no Brasil.
Printed in Brazil.
1 2 3   16 15 14

PREFACE

General English for Aviation has been thought to be a useful tool to help learners with the daily situations in aviation.

The book is aimed for false beginners to intermediate English language learners and provides a range of activities to engage students in a verisimilar communication related to their professional context.

Featuring thirty thematically-based units, this book presents easy-to-use guidelines for teachers with the goals to be achieved by the learners at the beginning of each unit. Then a 'Warm-up and Pre-Listening' activity or a 'Warm-up and Pre-Reading' activity introduces the necessary structures to prepare students for the acquisition of new vocabulary.

Learners will be able to recap the vocabulary and structures presented in the Listening or Reading activity in the sections 'Time to Practice 1' and 'Time to Practice 2'. While advancing, students will feel more comfortable to express themselves after the 'Drill Exercises'. In the sequence, additional exercises will help students to go further and build their writing, listening or communication skills.

Moreover, teachers and students will find symbols to effectively guide them in the usage of the activities in this book. For example, when coming across the symbol, this means that they will begin a listening activity. On the other hand, the symbol will introduce a communicative activity.

Learners journey toward a comprehensive understanding of each unit theme ends up with motivating communicative tasks in the 'Roleplay' or 'Challenge' sections.

This book also includes an on-line audio material for the listening activities and an on-line 'Answer Key' to the exercises proposed with the transcript of the texts used in the fill-in-the-blank activities. This content can be accessed on the book's link through the website: www.cengage.com.br.

In addition to all these features, there is an on-line Teacher's Guide which contains hints and explanations on how to apply the techniques for every activity in order to fully motivate learners during the challenging journey to communicate in a new language.

CINTIA NAOMI UEMURA

The author holds an MBA in General Management and a BA in International Relations. Fluent in English, Spanish and French, she has developed her professional skills for almost 10 years in the Travel Industry while working for two multinational companies.

Moreover, since the beginning of her career she has taught instrumental English with focus on the aviation, tourism and business administration segments.

CONTENTS

Unit 1	At the aviation academy	9
Unit 2	More instructions, yes/no and numbers in aviation	15
Unit 3	Consolidation	20
Unit 4	At the check-in counter	23
Unit 5	Please hold on	29
Unit 6	Consolidation	34
Unit 7	Asking for information	37
Unit 8	At the ticket office	41
Unit 9	Consolidation	46
Unit 10	Are you lost?	49
Unit 11	Security check	54
Unit 12	Consolidation	58
Unit 13	Aviation security	60
Unit 14	Dangerous and prohibited items	63
Unit 15	The future of passport control	67
Unit 16	Carry-on or checked luggage?	70
Unit 17	How's the weather?	75
Unit 18	Consolidation	79
Unit 19	Can I take my pets with me?	83
Unit 20	Flight 274, now boarding	88
Unit 21	Consolidation	93
Unit 22	High level of alertness: bird flu	96
Unit 23	Main airports in the world	99
Unit 24	Consolidation	102
Unit 25	In-flight services	106
Unit 26	VIP passengers	109
Unit 27	Consolidation	114
Unit 28	Baggage claim service	117
Unit 29	Consolidation	121
Unit 30	A funny story in aviation	128
Appendix 1	Countries, capitals, nationalities and currencies	129
Appendix 2	Cities, airports and 3-letter IATA codes	138

UNIT 1

At the aviation academy

FOR TEACHERS' USE

+ Verb To Be, Simple Present, Near Future (Will)
+ Alphabet

GOALS

By the end of Unit 1, students must be able to:

+ Introduce themselves by saying their full names (first name/middle name/last name).
+ Ask other people to introduce themselves.
+ Understand the differences between the common English alphabet and the International Phonetic Alphabet for Aviation.
+ Spell their full names (first name/middle name/last name) in both alphabets.

Bikeriderlondon /Shutterstock

➡ **Warm-up and Pre-Listening**

My name is….
My name's….
My first name is…
My first name's…
My full name is ….
My full name's…

My middle name is …
My middle name's…
My surname is/My family name is …
My surname's…/My family name's…/
What is your full name?
What's your full name?

GENERAL ENGLISH → FOR AVIATION

→ Instructions for Teachers

My full name's…/surname/middle name/first name

> Peter Kern Watson
> Title = Mr.
> Surname/Family Name = Watson
> First name = Peter
> Middle name = Kern
> Nickname = Pete

TRACK 2

 Listening: First Instructions

Mr. Peter Kern Watson is an instructor at Iron Wings Aviation Academy. Today is the first class. Listen:

Mr. Watson: Welcome to Iron Wings Aviation Academy. Let me introduce myself. My full name's Peter Kern Watson and I'll be your instructor during this course. But, you can call me Watson. Please, introduce yourselves and tell me about your future profession.

Anne: My name's Anne Mary Wright and I want to be a flight attendant.

John: Hi, everybody! My name's John Roy Bridge and I'm studying to become a pilot.

Samuel: Hello, guys! My name's Samuel Bold Howard and I'm taking a preparation course to be an air traffic controller. People call me Sam.

Mr. Watson: Great! Let's start our class. Anne, how do you spell your surname?

Anne: W-R-I-G-H-T.

Mr. Watson (laughing): Oh, no! There is a mistake. Here we use a different alphabet!

All (puzzled): Sorry!?

Mr. Watson: At Iron Wings Aviation Academy, we use the International Phonetic Alphabet for aviation. Please, say it again, Anne: Whiskey – Romeo – India – Golf – Hotel – Tango.

Anne: Whiskey – Romeo – India – Golf – Hotel – Tango.

Mr. Watson: Your turn, Sam!

Samuel: H-O-W-A-R-D or using the International Phonetic Alphabet for aviation: Hotel – Oscar - Whiskey – Alpha – Romeo – Delta.

Mr. Watson: Now, you, John! Please, spell your surname.

John: B-R-I-D-G-E.

Mr. Watson: People, note that we can get confused during radio communication if we use the common English alphabet. Is it a 'D' like in 'day' or a 'G' like in 'goat'? Hearing an 'S' for an 'F' or a 'B' for a 'D' and transmitting wrong information can cause accidents. John, let's try it again!

John: Bravo – Romeo – India – Delta – Golf – Echo.

Mr. Watson: Much better! Now, let's practice all together! How do you spell my middle name?

All: Kern – K- E-R-N or Kilo – Echo – Romeo – November!

Mr. Watson: What about my first name?

AT THE AVIATION ACADEMY ← UNIT 1

All: Peter – P- E-T-E-R or Papa – Echo – Tango – Echo – Romeo.

Mr. Watson: Very good! So, people, pay attention! My last name is Watson. Let's practice all together.

All: Whiskey – Alpha – Tango – Sierra - Oscar – November.

Mr. Watson: Much better! Thank you for your participation!

TRACK 3

CHART 1

The International Phonetic Alphabet for Aviation (Audio)

A Alpha	**H** Hotel	**O** Oscar	**V** Victor
B Bravo	**I** India	**P** Papa	**W** Whiskey
C Charlie	**J** Juliet	**Q** Quebec	**X** X-ray
D Delta	**K** Kilo	**R** Romeo	**Y** Yankee
E Echo	**L** Lima	**S** Sierra	**Z** Zulu
F Foxtrot	**M** Mike	**T** Tango	
G Golf	**N** November	**U** Uniform	

Time to Practice 1

Introduce yourself and meet other people.

Example:

A: Let me introduce myself. My full name's Jane Tower Smith.

Now, please, introduce yourself.

B: Let me introduce myself. My full name's Robert Lewis Johnson.

Now, please, introduce yourself.

Time to Practice 2

Ask your colleagues.

Examples:

How do you spell your surname?

J-O-H-N-S-O-N.

How do you spell your middle name?

L-E-W-I-S.

How do you spell your first name?

R-O-B-E-R-T.

Please use the International Phonetic Alphabet for Aviation. How do you spell your surname?

Juliet – Oscar – Hotel – November – Sierra – Oscar – November.

How do you spell your middle name?

Lima – Echo – Whiskey – India – Sierra.

How do you spell your first name?

Romeo – Oscar – Bravo – Echo – Romeo – Tango.

Now it's your turn!

Work in pairs or small groups. Ask other students to spell their names (surname/middle name and first name) using both the common English Alphabet and the International Phonetic Alphabet for Aviation.

GENERAL ENGLISH → FOR AVIATION

🎤 DRILL EXERCISE 1

Example:

Teacher: My *first name* **is** Anne.

Students: My *first name* **is** Anne.

Teacher: Peter.

Students: My *first name* **is** Peter.

Teacher: John.

Students: My *first name* **is** John.

1) My *surname* is Wright. (Bridge/Watson/ Johnson).

2) My *middle name* is Mary. (Kern/Bold/ Lewis/Roy).

3) My *full name* is John Roy Bridge. (Samuel Bold Howard/Robert Lewis Johnson/Anne Mary Wright/Peter Kern Watson).

4) How do you spell your family name? (your surname/your full name/your middle name/your first name/this word).

5) Please, say your full name again. (your first name/your surname/your middle name/your family name/this word).

6) Please, say it again. (spell it/spell your surname/your middle name/family name/ this word).

7) People call me Annie. (Sam/Joey/ Bob/J.R.).

8) I want to be a pilot. (a flight attendant/ an instructor/ an air traffic controller an ATCO).

9) I *will* be a pilot. (a flight attendant/ an air traffic controller/an instructor).

10) I'*ll* be your instructor. (during this course/your colleague/your teacher/your student).

11) My full name's Jane Tower Smith. (but you can call me Jane/Samuel Bold Howard – Sam/Robert Lewis Johnson – Bob/Anne Mary Wright – Annie/John Roy Bridge – J.R.).

12) I *am* studying to be a flight attendant. (a pilot/ an air traffic controller/an instructor).

13) I'*m* studying to become a pilot. (a flight attendant/ an air traffic controller/an instructor).

14) I'*m* taking a preparation course (a prep course) to be a pilot. (an instructor/a flight attendant/an air traffic controller/a flight instructor).

🎤 DRILL EXERCISE 2 (Read and repeat)

Read the sentences below loudly. Pay special attention to the pronunciation and stressed syllables of the underlined words.

a) Please, <u>introduce</u> yourself.

b) Tell me about your <u>future profession</u>.

c) I'm studying to become a <u>flight attendant</u>.

d) I <u>want to</u> be a <u>pilot</u>.

e) Please, <u>spell</u> your <u>full name</u> again.

f) How do you <u>spell</u> your <u>surname</u>?

g) I'm taking a <u>preparation course</u> to be <u>an air traffic controller</u>.

h) Please, spell this word using the <u>International Phonetic Alphabet</u> for aviation.

i) Oh, no! There is a <u>mistake.</u>

j) <u>Transmitting</u> wrong information can <u>cause accidents</u>.

AT THE AVIATION ACADEMY ← UNIT 1   **13**

→ Exercise 1

Now use the words below from the dialogue in Part 1 to complete each short conversation.

~~flight attendant~~ – transmitting – preparation course – surname – radio communication – pilot – better – International Phonetic Alphabet – aviation – practice – air traffic controller – profession – spell – accidents – using – introduce – common – again

a) Instructor: Please, _____ yourself and tell me about your future _____ .

You: *My name's Anne Mary Wright and I want to be a* **flight attendant.**

b) Instructor: How do you spell your _____ ?

Anthony Smith: S-M-I-T-H.

Instructor: Please, use the International Phonetic Alphabet for _____ .

Anthony Smith: Sierra – Mike – India – Tango – Hotel.

c) You: I'm taking a _____ to become a _____ .

Instructor: Great! What about you, Mike?

Mike: I want to be an _____ .

d) Instructor: Please, _____ your middle name _____ the _____ English alphabet.

John: R-O-Y.

Instructor: Now, spell it _____ using the _____ for aviation.

John: Romeo – Oscar – Yankee.

Instructor: Much _____ !

e) Instructor: Let's use the International Phonetic Alphabet for aviation during _____ .

Students: _____ wrong information can cause _____ .

Instructor: Now, let's _____ all together!

TRACK 4

🔊 Exercise 2

You are a new student at Iron Wings Aviation Academy. Mr. Watson is going to interview you. Use your personal information to answer the questions.

Mr. Watson: Welcome to Iron Wings Aviation Academy. Let me introduce myself. My full name's Peter Kern Watson and I'll be your instructor during this course. But, you can call me Watson. Please, introduce yourself and tell me about your future profession.

You: (Option 1) My name's _____ _____ and I want to be (a flight attendant/a pilot/an air traffic controller).

(Option 2) Hi! My name's _____ _____and I'm studying to become (a flight attendant/a pilot/an air traffic controller).

(Option 3) My name's _____

and I'm taking a preparation course to be (an air traffic controller/a pilot/ a flight attendant). People call me_____

Mr. Watson: Great! How do you spell your surname?

You: _____ (*Say your surname and spell it using the common English Alphabet*).

Mr. Watson (laughing): Oh, no! There is a mistake. Here we use a different alphabet!

You : Sorry?

Mr. Watson: At Iron Wings Aviation Academy, we use the International Phonetic Alphabet for aviation. Please, say it again:

GENERAL ENGLISH → FOR AVIATION

You: _____ (Example: Whiskey – Romeo – India – Golf – Hotel – Tango. *Say your surname and spell it using the International Phonetic Alphabet for aviation*).

Mr. Watson: Much better! Now, let's practice! How do you spell your middle name?

 You: (*Spell your middle name using the common English Alphabet*).

Mr. Watson: Let's try it again.

You: (*Spell your middle name using the International Phonetic Alphabet for aviation*).

Mr. Watson: What about your first name?

You: (*Spell your first name using the International Phonetic Alphabet for aviation*).

Mr. Watson: Very good!

UNIT 2

More instructions, yes/no and numbers in aviation

FOR TEACHERS' USE

- Verb To Be, Simple Present, Present Continuous, Near Future (Will), Imperative
- Cardinal and Ordinal Numbers

GOALS

By the end of Unit 2, students must be able to:

- Understand structures with the Verb To Be (negative form), Imperative, Simple Present (affirmative and interrogative forms), Near Future (negative form).
- Interact with the teacher and other colleagues in classroom using English.

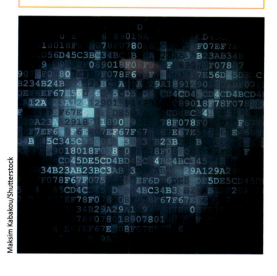

Maksim Kabakou/Shutterstock

➡ Warm-up and Pre-Listening

TRACK 5

	NUMBERS				NUMBERS		
	CARDINAL		ORDINAL		CARDINAL		ORDINAL
1	one	1st	first	8	eight	8th	eighth
2	two	2nd	second	9	nine	9th	ninth
3	three	3rd	third	10	ten	10th	tenth
4	four	4th	fourth	11	eleven	11th	eleventh
5	five	5th	fifth	12	twelve	12th	twelfth
6	six	6th	sixth	13	thirteen	13th	thirteenth
7	seven	7th	seventh	14	fourteen	14th	fourteenth

16

GENERAL ENGLISH ➜ FOR AVIATION

TRACK 5

NUMBERS				NUMBERS			
CARDINAL		**ORDINAL**		**CARDINAL**		**ORDINAL**	
15	fifteen	15th	fifteenth	40	forty	40th	fortieth
16	sixteen	16th	sixteenth	50	fifty	50th	fiftieth
17	seventeen	17th	seventeenth	60	sixty	60th	sixtieth
18	eighteen	18th	eighteenth	70	seventy	70th	seventieth
19	nineteen	19th	nineteenth	80	eighty	80th	eightieth
20	twenty	20th	twentieth	90	ninety	90th	ninetieth
21	twenty-one	21st	twenty-first	100	one hundred	100th	one hundredth
22	twenty-two	22nd	twenty-second	200	two hundred	200th	two hundredth
23	twenty-three	23rd	twenty-third	300	three hundred	300th	three hundredth
24	twenty-four	24th	twenty-fourth	400	four hundred	400th	four hundredth
25	twenty-five	25th	twenty-fifth	500	five hundred	500th	five hundredth
26	twenty-six	26th	twenty-sixth	600	six hundred	600th	six hundredth
27	twenty-seven	27th	twenty-seventh	700	seven hundred	700th	seven hundredth
28	twenty-eight	28th	twenty-eighth	800	eight hundred	800th	eight hundredth
29	twenty-nine	29th	twenty-ninth	900	nine hundred	900th	nine hundredth
30	thirty	30th	thirtieth	1,000	one thousand	1,000th	one thousandth

TRACK 5

🔊 Listening: Yes/No and Numbers in Aviation

Today is Mr. Watson's second class at Iron Wings Aviation Academy. As you all know, he is the instructor. Let's listen to him:

Mr. Watson: Welcome to our second class. As you all already know, I'm Watson and I'll be your instructor for this semester. Now, please, open your books and pay attention to me.

TRACK 5

CHART 2

The International Phonetic Alphabet Numerals (Audio)

0 - zero
1 - one
2 - two
3 - three
4 - (fow – er) = four

5 - five
6 - six
7 - seven
8 - eight
9 - (ni – ner) = nine

Pasko Maksim/Shutterstock

Anthony Smith raises his hand because he wants to ask one question to the instructor.

Mr. Watson: Yes, Mr. Smith! Can I help you?

Anthony Smith: Sorry, Mr. Watson, but this is my first class at Iron Wings Aviation Academy. All my colleagues have a badge with their names, but I don't, sir. How can I get one for me?

Mr. Watson: Please, go to the reception after the class.

Anthony Smith: Okay! Thank you, Mr. Watson.

Mr. Watson: Smith, you can call me Watson like everybody.

Now students are learning about radio communication.

Mr. Watson: Any other question?

Anthony Smith: Positive, sir.

MORE INSTRUCTIONS, YES/NO AND NUMBERS IN AVIATION ← UNIT 2

Mr. Watson: Smith, please proceed.

Smith: Our next break will be in five minutes, right?

Mr. Watson: Negative. Let's continue our class!

Now, it's your turn!

Listening

Fill in the gaps with the missing words.

Today is Mr. Watson's second _____ at Iron Wings _____ Academy. As you all know, he is the _____. Let's listen to him:

Mr. Watson: _____ to our _____ class. As you _____ already know, I'm Watson and I'll be your instructor for this semester.

Anthony Smith raises his _____ because he wants to _____ one question to the instructor.

Mr. Watson: Yes, Mr. Smith! _____ _____?

Anthony Smith: Sorry, Mr. Watson, but this is my _____ class at Iron _____ Aviation Academy. All my colleagues _____ a badge with their names, but I don't, sir. _____ can I get _____ for me?

All: Yes, sir.

Mr. Watson: Do not close your books.

Mr. Watson: You _____ to the _____ after the class.

Anthony Smith: Okay! Thank you, Mr. Watson.

Mr. Watson: Smith, you can call me Watson like everybody.

Now students are learning about _____ .

Mr. Watson: Any other _____ ?

Anthony Smith: Positive, sir.

Mr. Watson: Smith, please _____ .

Smith: Our next break will be in _____ minutes, right?

Mr. Watson: Negative. Let's _____ our class!

All: Yes, sir.

Mr. Watson: Do not close your books.

Time to Practice 1

Negative form

Exercise 1 – Transform the sentences.

Example:

Today is Mr. Watson's second class at Iron Wings Aviation Academy. (not)

Today is not Mr. Watson's second class at Iron Wings Aviation Academy.

Today isn't Mr. Watson's second class at Iron Wings Aviation Academy.

1) I will be your instructor for this semester. (not)

2) He is the instructor. (not)

3) I'm Watson. (not)

4) This is my first class at Iron Wings Aviation Academy. (not)

5) I can help you. (not)

6) Our break will be in five minutes. (not)

7) Let's continue our class. (not)

8) Let's listen to him. (not)

9) You can call me Watson like everybody. (not)

18 GENERAL ENGLISH → FOR AVIATION

Exercise 2 – Transform the sentences.

Example:

Please open your books.

a) Please do not open your books.
   (= for emphasis)

b) Don't open your books.

1) Please raise your hands.
   a) _____
   b) _____

2) Please close your books.
   a) _____
   b) _____

3) Please go to the reception after the class.
   a) _____
   b) _____

Time to Practice 2

Form a circle. Then, practice like this: Student 1 reads the sentence; student 2 needs to mimic (thumbs up or down). Student 3 will confirm the answer by saying 'yes' or 'no' accordingly to student's 2 mime. Student 4 will repeat the previous question and mimic (thumbs up or down) on his/her choice. This time, the answer will be 'positive' or 'negative'. After some while, students must change positions to be able to practice more.

Example:

Student 1: Now the students are learning about radio communication.

Student 2: Are the students learning about radio communication? (**Yes**)

Student 3: (Normal answer): Yes, the students are learning about radio communication.

Student 4: Are the students learning about radio communication? (**Positive or negative, depending on student's choice**).

Student 5: Positive.

Student 1: Now the students are learning about radio communication.

Student 2: Are the students learning about radio communication? (**No**)

Student 3: (Normal answer): No, the students aren't learning about radio communication.

Student 4: Are the students learning about radio communication? (**Positive or negative, depending on student's choice**).

Student 5: Negative.

1) Now students are learning about aircraft.
2) Now students are opening their books.
3) Now students are learning about numbers.
4) Now students are closing their books.

MORE INSTRUCTIONS, YES/NO AND NUMBERS IN AVIATION ← UNIT 2

DRILL EXERCISE 1

Divide the class in two groups A and B.

Example:

Teacher: I'm Watson. (not/affirmative – He)

Students – Groups A and B: I'm Watson.

Teacher: (Group A) not

Students – Group A: I'm not Watson.

Teacher: (Group B) affirmative – He

Students – Group B: He is Watson.

1) Today is my second class at Iron Wings Aviation Academy. (not/affirmative – first)
2) Let's listen to him. (not/affirmative – her)
3) Let's open the books. (not/affirmative – notebooks)
4) Watson will be our instructor. (not/negative – Smith)
5) Anne wants to be a flight attendant. (doesn't want/affirmative – an ATCO – an air traffic controller)
6) John doesn't want to be a pilot. (wants/doesn't want – Samuel)
7) Let's listen to her. (not/negative – them)
8) Our next break will be in five minutes (not/affirmative – fifteen).

DRILL EXERCISE 2

You raise your hand because you want to ask one question to the instructor.

Mr. Watson: Can I help you?

You: Sorry, Mr. Watson, but this is my _____ class at Iron Wings Aviation Academy. All my _____ have a _____ with their names, but _____ , sir. _____ ?

Mr. Watson: You can go to the reception after the class.

Anthony Smith: Okay! Thank you, Mr. Watson.

 Challenge

Spelling Contest.

Pick up one of the words below. Choose a colleague to guess the word. Spell the chosen word only once using the International Phonetic Alphabet for aviation.

Example: Alpha – Victor – India – Alpha – Tango – India – Oscar - November.

The word is *aviation*.

international – flight attendant – air traffic controller – mistake – different – pilot – communication – radio – preparation

UNIT 3

Consolidation

Time to Practice 1

a) How much time do you need to go to the airport?
   I need ten minutes.
b) How much time does he need to go to the airport?
   He needs twenty minutes.
c) How much time does she need to go to the airport?
   She needs twenty-five minutes.
d) How much time do we need to go to the airport?
   We need fifteen minutes to go to the airport.

e) How much time do they need to go to the airport?
   They need two hours.

Example:
(we/go to the airport/15 minutes)
(a) How much time do we need to go to the airport? (15 minutes)
(b) We need fifteen minutes.

1) (she/go to the reception/7 minutes)
   (a) _____
   (b) _____

CONSOLIDATION ← UNIT 3

2) (the students/open their books/5 seconds)
(a) _____
(b) _____

3) (Samuel/ close his book/3 seconds)
(a) _____
(b) _____

4) (we /do this exercise/28 minutes)
(a) _____
(b) _____

5) (you/come to the aviation academy/45 minutes)
(a) _____
(b) _____

Time to Practice 2

Read and repeat.

Who is he?

He is Mr. Peter Kern Watson. So, his surname/family name is Watson. His middle name is Kern and his first name is Peter. He has a nickname. People call him Pete. He'll be our instructor during this semester.

Now use the information in Part 1 to complete the information for Anne Mary Wright and Samuel Bold Howard.

Who is she?

She is Anne Mary Wright. So, her surname/family name is Wright. _____ middle name is Mary and _____ first name is Anne. She has a nickname. People call _____ Annie. She wants to be a flight attendant.

Who is he?

He is _____. So, _____ surname/family name is _____ . _____ middle name is _____ and his _____ is _____ . He has a _____. People call _____ Sam.

Use Parts 1 and 2 to complete the information.

Who are they?

The first student is John Roy Bridge and he _____ to become a pilot. _____ surname/family name is _____ .
_____ middle name is _____ and his _____ is _____ . He has a _____. People call _____ Roy.

The second student is Anthony Smith. Today is Anthony's first class at Iron Wings Aviation Academy. His _____ is Smith. He doesn't have a badge like the other students. He will need to go to the _____ to get one. _____ is Roy's best friend.

GENERAL ENGLISH ➔ FOR AVIATION

 Exercise 1

Read and repeat.

1a) Do you have a badge?
1b) I have a badge.
1c) I don't have a badge.

2a) Does Anne have a badge?
2b) Anne has a badge.
2c) She doesn't have a badge.

3a) Does Anthony have a badge?
3b) Anthony has a badge.
3c) He doesn't have a badge.

4a) Do John and Samuel have badges?
4b) John and Samuel have badges.
4c) John and Samuel don't have badges.

 Exercise 2

Follow the example.

1) Anne/flight attendant/yet.
Teacher:
(a) Is Anne a flight attendant?
(b) Anne is **not** a flight attendant **yet**.
(c) Anne **isn't** a flight attendant **yet**.

2) John and Anthony/pilots/yet.
Teacher:
(a) _____
(b) _____
(c) _____

3) Samuel/an ATCO/yet.
Teacher:
(a) _____
(b) _____
(c) _____

4) John and Anne/ in the classroom/yet.
Teacher:
(a) _____
(b) _____
(c) _____

 Exercise 3

Pay attention to the teacher. Then, make questions like in the example below.

Teacher: Anne needs to go to the reception.
Student: Does Anne need to go to the reception?

1) Sam wants to raise his hand to ask a question.
2) Roy needs to go to the airport today.
3) John and Anne want to start the course today.
4) Anthony needs a badge.

 Exercise 4

Now write a small paragraph about you like the examples in *Time to Practice 2*.

 Roleplay

Choose a colleague at random. First, interview your colleague by asking him/her questions about his/her full name and nickname. After finishing the interview he/she must introduce you to the other colleagues by reading the paragraph. You'll do the same about him/her.

The class will have to ask the following questions:

• Who is he?   • Who is she?   • Who are they? (for groups of 3 students)

UNIT 4

At the check-in counter

FOR TEACHERS' USE

+ Verb To Be, Simple Present, Present Continuous, Near Future (Will): interrogative and negative forms
+ Modal (can)
+ Plural
+ Pronouns subject and pronouns object

GOALS

By the end of Unit 4, students must be able to:

+ Understand the check-in procedures.

 Warm-up and Pre-Listening

airport – aircraft – airplane – passenger terminal – check-in counter – departure entrance – embarkation – debarkation – flight – boarding area – information counter – luggage – baggage – passport – visa – wallet – car keys – purse – suitcase – many – various – how many – lady – ladies – woman – women – man – men – boy – boys – guy – guys – girl – girls – naughty – tall – short – smiley – strange

I am getting worried. They are getting anxious.
He is getting nervous. We are getting stressed.
She is getting tired.

Listening: Queueing up for the check-in

John Roy Bridge and Anthony Smith want to become pilots. They are not pilots yet, but today they are going to travel from New York to Dallas for two days. Though it's a domestic flight, they will need a valid document for identification. It will be a business trip. Listen.

John Roy Bridge: I'm getting anxious because I don't travel much, Smith.

Anthony Smith: Don't worry, Roy. Everything will be fine. Take a look! I can see various aircraft from here.

Roy: Which documents of identification do we need to travel?

Smith: We usually need the passport and a visa if it's an international travel. For domestic flights in the USA we can hold a U.S. passport or a state-issued driver's license. However, it's always better to contact the airline first, because each one can have specific identification requirements.

Roy and Smith are now heading to the check-in counter.

Roy: The queue is getting too long.

Smith: We are the twenty-seventh and the twenty-eighth, in fact, for the check-in.

Roy: Oh, no! Where is my passport? I can't find it!

Smith: Without your passport, you can't check in or embark.

B: Just a minute. I'll go on looking for my passport in my hand luggage.

Smith: Okay. Look over there! I think we know the lady who is coming towards us…

Roy: Really? I can see many ladies before us and behind us in the queue.

Smith: So, take a look again!

Roy: What?

Smith: Don't look at your right side. Look at your left side and behind you.

Roy: My wife? I can't believe it! What are you doing here at the airport?

Janet Bridge: Roy, I guess you forgot your passport at home. Here it is.

Roy: Thank you, my dear!

Janet Bridge: You're welcome!

AT THE CHECK-IN COUNTER ← UNIT 4

 Time to Practice 1

Follow the example.

I'm getting anxious because I don't travel much. (Roy)

Roy is getting anxious because he doesn't travel much.

1) I'm getting worried because I don't travel much. (nervous)
2) She is getting tired because she doesn't travel much. (Peter)
3) Roy and Smith are getting stressed because they don't travel much. (We)
4) Samuel is getting nervous because he doesn't travel much. (They)

Follow the example.

(get worried)

Don't get worried. Everything will be fine.

5) (get nervous).
6) (get stressed).
7) (get anxious).

 Time to Practice 2

Substitute the terms and make the correct grammatical modifications when necessary.

Example:

Roy: Which documents of identification do we need to travel?

Smith: We usually need the passport and a visa if it's an international travel.

1) Roy and Smith
2) Anne Mary
3) Mr. Watson
4) Mr. Samuel Bold Howard

Example:

Take a look! I can see an aircraft from here. (various)

Take a look! I can see various aircraft from here.

Attention: There is no plural for aircraft.

5) (one lady)/many
6) (a strange guy) / two
7) (a naughty boy)/ ten
8) (a tall woman)/ five
9) (a smiley girl)/twelve
10) (a short man)/three

Example:

What can he see? He can see … from here.
What can she see? She can see … from here.
What can they see? They can see … from here.

11) (she)/the passenger terminal
12) (they) /the check-in counter
13) (he)/ the departure entrance
14) (Mary)/ the information counter
15) (John)/many suitcases
16) (Mike and Tom)/ the boarding area

GENERAL ENGLISH → FOR AVIATION

 DRILL EXERCISE 1

Practice Cardinal and Ordinal numbers.

Example:

How many passengers are there in line for the check-in? (256)

There are two hundred fifty six passengers in line for the check-in.

1) How many passengers are there in line for the check-in? (78)

2) How many passengers are there at the departure entrance? (39)

3) How many passengers are there for embarkation? (167)

4) How many passengers are there on flight 132? (206)

5) How many passengers are there in the boarding area? (145)

Example:

The queue is getting too long. (We/27th and 28th /for the check-in)

We are the twenty-seventh and the twenty-eighth, in fact, for the check-in.

6) The queue is getting too long. (I/43rd/at the departure entrance).

7) The queue is getting too long. (Anne Mary/34th/in the embarkation area).

8) The queue is getting too long. (Smith and Roy/11th and 12th/at the information counter).

9) The queue is getting too long. (Samuel/51st/for debarkation).

 DRILL EXERCISE 2

**Where is…? I can't find it.
Here it is.
Where are…? I can't find them.
Here they are.**

Complete the short dialogues.

Example:
(my/passport)

A: *Where is my passport? I can't find it!*

B: *Just a minute. Let's go on looking for your passport.*

C: *Here it is.*

AT THE CHECK-IN COUNTER ← UNIT 4

Example:

(her/keys)

A: *Where are her keys? She can't find them!*

B: *Just a minute. Let's go on looking for her keys.*

C: *Here they are.*

1) (his/car keys). He can't find _____!

2) (her/purse). She can't find _____!

3) (my/hand luggage). I can't find _____!

4) (their/documents). _____ can't find _____!

5) (his/wallet). _____ can't find _____!

6) (our/ suitcases). _____ can't find _____!

A: *Where is Mr. Howard? We can't find him!*

B: *Just a minute. Let's go on looking for him.*

C: *There he is. He's near the check-in counter.*

A: *Where is Miss Jones? We can't find her!*

B: *Just a minute. Let's go on looking for her.*

C: *There she is. She's at Gate 26.*

A: *Where are Mr. and Mrs. Smith? We can't find them!*

B: *Just a minute. Let's go on looking for them.*

C: *There they are. They're at the information counter.*

7) (the Johnsons/in passenger terminal 2).

8) (Mrs. Janet White/at the check-in counter).

9) (Mr. Carl Bright/near Gate 73).

10) (the Yorks/near the information counter).

11) (Mr. William Banks/near the departure entrance).

→ ## Exercise 1

Write interrogative sentences by following the example.

Example:

I can't believe it! (you/at the airport) What are you doing here at the airport?

1) I can't believe it! (she/at the departure entrance).

2) I can't believe it! (they/at the information counter).

3) I can't believe it! (he/in the passenger terminal).

4) I can't believe it! (John Roy and Anthony/in the embarkation area)

5) I can't believe it! (Anne Mary/at the check-in counter)

TRACK 6

Exercise 2

Listen to the dialogue again and fill in the gaps with the missing words.

John Roy Bridge and Anthony Smith want to become pilots. They are not pilots yet, but today they are going to travel from New York to Dallas for two days. It will be a business trip. Listen:

John Roy Bridge: I'm getting _____ because I don't travel much, Smith.

Anthony Smith: Don't worry, Roy. _____ . Take a look! I can see various _____ from here.

Roy: Which _____ of identification do we need to travel?

Smith: We usually need the _____ and a _____ if it's an _____ travel.

GENERAL ENGLISH → FOR AVIATION

For domestic flights in the USA we can hold a U.S. passport or a state-issued driver's license. However, it's always better to contact the _____ firs t, because each one can have _____ identification _____ .

Roy and Smith are now heading to the _____ .

Roy: The _____ is getting too long.

Smith: We are the _____ and the _____, in fact, for the check-in.

Roy: Oh, no! Where is my passport? _____ !

Smith: Without your passport, you can't check in or embark.

Roy: Just a minute. I'll go on _____ my passport in my hand luggage.

Smith: Okay. Look over there! I think that we know the lady who is coming towards us…

Roy: Really? I can see many ladies before us and behind us in the queue.

Smith: So, take a look again!

Roy: What?

Smith: _____ at your right side. _____ at your left side and behind you.

Roy: My wife! _____ ! What are you doing here at the airport?

Janet Bridge: Roy, I guess you forgot your passport at home. Here it is.

Roy: Thank you, my dear!

Janet Bridge: You're welcome!

UNIT 5

Please hold on

FOR TEACHERS' USE

+ Verb To Be, Simple Present, Present Continuous, Near Future (Will): Interrogative and Negative forms
+ Modal (can, could)
+ Will/Would
+ Plural
+ Pronouns subject and pronouns object
+ Question tag

GOALS

By the end of Unit 5, students must be able to:

+ Understand the check-in procedures.
+ Solve problems at the check-in counter.

 Warm-up and Pre-Listening

unbelievable – long queue – episode – a little bit – My goodness! – door – window – delayed – cancelled – engine – air conditioner – lavatory – gentleman – gentlemen – destination – flight number – to assign seats – to confirm – e-tickets – scale – pieces of luggage

I hope we won't miss the flight.

I have an idea./Follow me.

GENERAL ENGLISH → FOR AVIATION

 Listening: Problems at the check-in counter

John Roy Bridge: I'm getting stressed because of this long queue!

Anthony Smith: I guess you are stressed because of the passport episode, aren't you?

Roy: Yes, a little bit.

Smith: Don't worry. Now we are the fifth and the sixth for the check-in.

After some minutes, Roy and Smith are the first and the second in the queue for the check-in.

Ticket agent: Good afternoon, gentlemen!

Roy and Smith: Good afternoon!

Ticket agent: I'm sorry to inform you that the check-in system is out of order now.

Roy: Unbelievable! Now that is our turn, the system is off!

Ticket agent: A technician is coming soon to solve the problem. I really apologize.

Smith: My goodness! It would be so easy to check-in.

Ticket agent: You are right, sir. I would only need to ask you for a document of identification. Second, I would check the names on your passports and on the e-tickets. Then, I would verify the destination, the flight numbers and assign your seats or confirm your seat numbers if you were already pre-checked on the airlines' website. After this, I would weigh your pieces of luggage by putting then on the scale. Finally, I would print the boarding passes.

Roy: How much time will it take to fix the check-in system?

Ticket agent: For now, we don't have this information, sir. Please, hold on.

Roy: I hope we won't miss our flight.

Smith: I have an idea! Let's look for a self check-in kiosk.

Roy: A what?

Smith: Follow me.

 Time to Practice 1

Example:

(You/stressed/because of the passport episode).

<u>Affirmative</u>: **I guess** you are stressed.

<u>Interrogative</u>: Are you stressed?

<u>Negative</u>: You aren't stressed.

<u>Interrogative</u>: Why are you stressed?

I guess you are stressed because of the passport episode.

1) You/anxious/ because you don't fly much.
2) He/nervous/because he doesn't travel much.
3) She/stressed/ because she can't find her purse.
4) He/nervous/because he can't find his wallet.
5) They/stressed/because they can't find their documents.

PLEASE HOLD ON ← UNIT 5

Example:
They fly a lot.
Interrogative: Do they fly a lot?
Negative: They don't fly much.
They fly a lot, don't they?

6) He travels a lot.
7) She flies a lot.
8) They speak English.
9) He speaks French.
10) She speaks Portuguese.
11) They have a Spanish passport.
12) Grace has a German passport.

Example:
They don't fly much.
They don't fly much, do they?

13) He doesn't travel much.
14) She doesn't fly much.
15) They don't speak English.
16) He doesn't speak French.
17) She doesn't speak Portuguese.
18) They don't have a Spanish passport.
19) Grace doesn't have a German passport.

 Time to Practice 2

Example:
Unbelievable! Now that is **our** turn, the system is off! (our)

1) his turn
2) her turn
3) your turn
4) their turn
5) our turn/the flight is cancelled
6) our turn/the flight is delayed

 **DRILL EXERCISE 1**

Example:
(you/stressed). Yes, a little bit.
Are you stressed? Yes, a little bit.
1) (she/worried). Yes, a little bit.
2) (he/nervous). Yes, a little bit.
3) (they/stressed). Yes, a little bit.
4) (you/anxious). Yes, a little bit.

Example:
(you/stressed).
You aren't stressed, are you?
5) (she/worried).
6) (he/nervous).
7) (they/stressed).
8) (you/anxious).

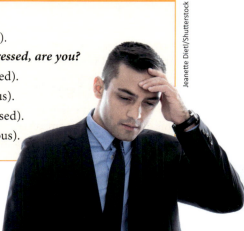

DRILL EXERCISE 2

Example:
(to check-in) My goodness! It would be so easy to check-in.

1) (to open the doors)
2) (to fix the lavatory door)
3) (to close the windows)
4) (to go to the check-in counter)
5) (to close the door)
6) (to fix the air conditioner)
7) (to go to the reception)

DRILL EXERCISE 3

Example:

How much time will it take to fix the check-in system?
(to fix the check-in system/20 minutes)
It will take **20 minutes** *to fix the check-in system.*

1) (to fix the lavatory door/45 minutes). It will take …
2) (to fix the window/2 hours). It will take…
3) (to fix the engine/48 hours). It will take…
4) (to fix the lavatory/50 minutes). It will take…
5) (to fix the air conditioner/ 1 hour and 45 minutes). It will take…
6) (to go to the information counter/9 minutes). It will take…
7) (to go to the airport/35 minutes). It will take…
8) (to go to the other passenger terminal/13 minutes). It will take…

 Exercise 1

Take a look at this example. A ticket agent is giving explanations on the check-in procedures. Read the text silently.

Ticket agent: You are right, sir. I would only need to ask you for a document of identification. Second, I would check the names on your passports and on the e-tickets. Then, I would verify the destination, the flight numbers and assign your seats or confirm your seat numbers if you were already pre-checked on the airlines' website. After this, I would weigh your pieces of luggage by putting then on the scale. Finally, I would print the boarding passes.

Now you have to tell your colleague what she (the ticket agent) would have to do.

She would only need to…

PLEASE HOLD ON ← UNIT 5

Now you have to tell your colleague what he (the ticket agent) would have to do.

He would only need to…

Now there are two ticket agents at the check-in counter. Tell your colleague what they would have to do.

They would only need to…

Check-in checklist

Now complete with the correct verbs:

Step 1: _____ for a document of identification. _____ the names on the passports and on the e-tickets.

Step 2: _____ the destination.

Step 3: _____ the flight numbers.

Step 4: _____ the seat numbers to each passenger. Or _____ the seat numbers if passengers were already pre-checked.

Step 5: _____ the pieces of luggage by _____ them on the scale.

Step 6: _____ the boarding passes.

Exercise 2

Listen to the dialogue again and fill in the blanks with the missing words.

John Roy Bridge: I'm getting stressed because of this long queue!

Anthony Smith: I guess you are stressed because of the passport _____, aren't you?

Roy: Yes, _____.

Smith: Don't worry. Now we are the _____ and the _____ for the check-in.

After some minutes, Roy and Smith are the first and the second in the queue for the check-in.

Ticket agent: Good afternoon, gentlemen!

Roy and Smith: Good afternoon!

Ticket agent: I'm sorry to _____ you that the check-in _____ is _____ now.

Roy: Unbelievable! Now that is our turn, the system is off!

Ticket agent: A _____ is coming soon to solve the problem. I really apologize.

Smith: My goodness! It would be so easy to check-in.

Ticket agent: You are right, sir. I would only need to ask you for a document of identification. Second, I would _____ the names on your passports and on the e-tickets. Then, I would verify the _____, the _____ and assign your seats or _____ your seat numbers if you were already _____ on the airlines' website. After this, I would _____ your pieces of _____ by putting then on the _____. Finally, I would print the _____.

Roy: How _____ will it take to fix the check-in system?

Ticket agent: For now, we don't have this _____, sir. Please, hold on.

Roy: I hope we won't miss our _____.

Smith: I have an _____! Let's look for a self check-in kiosk.

Roy: A what?

Smith: _____ me.

Unit 6

Consolidation

Listening: Self check-in kiosks

1) What is the text about?
a) ATM machines
b) text messaging
c) mobiles
d) self check-in kiosks

2) Why are self check-in kiosks different from ATM machines?

3) Complete the sentences:
a) Forget about _____ , long _____ , lots of people waiting in _____ for hours.
b) Self Check-in Kiosks screens are very _____ to those of the ATM _____ .
c) Some airlines allow you to _____ , including the confirmation of your _____ and the printing of your _____ through their _____ sites.
d) Technology is _____ everything to make _____ lives _____ , easier and faster.

4) What do more modern check-in systems allow passengers to do?

5) What do you get when checking in through your mobile?
a) nothing
b) a paper
c) a confirmation message
d) a boarding pass

Time to Practice 1

Example:
I/my/mine
a) *I have an idea.*
b) *This is my idea.*
c) *This idea is mine.*

1) She/her/hers
2) He/his/his
3) We/our/ours
4) They/their/theirs

CONSOLIDATION ← UNIT 6

 Time to Practice 2

Which one is correct?

Example:

Follow *I/mine/my/me*.

Correct: Follow *me*.

1) Follow she/her/hers.
2) Follow his/him/he.
3) Follow ours/us/we/our.
4) Follow they/theirs/them/their.

 Exercise 1

Choose the correct alternative.

1) I need to follow *he/his/him* to the check-in counter.

2) She *need/needs* to follow *we/ours/us/our* to the other passenger terminal.

3) *Us/Our/We* needs/need to follow *he/his/hers/she/him* to the information desk.

4) Anne Mary needs *help/to help/helps I/me/my/mine* with my baggage.

5) They are nervous because *them/theirs/they/their* are looking for *they/theirs/them/their* lost baggage.

 Exercise 2

Example:

I'm looking for my purse. The purse is mine.

1) Peter is looking for _____ car keys. The car keys are _____ .

2) Anne Mary is looking for _____ bag. The bag is _____ .

3) Anthony Smith is looking for _____ wallet. The wallet is _____ .

4) Peter and I are looking for _____ documents. The documents are _____ .

5) Smith and Roy are looking for _____ passports. The passports are _____ .

 Exercise 3

Unscramble the sentences.

1) guess/episode/of/the/are/stressed/passport you/because/I.

2) now/is/to/inform/sorry/out of/order/I'm/you/the/that/system/check-in.

3) soon/a/coming/technician/is/solve/problem/the/to.

4) need/check/would/e-tickets/I/and/only/the passports/on/the/names/on/your/to.

5) to/fix/system/the/check-in/time/it/much/will/how/take?

6) information/we/this/have,/now/don't/for,/sir.

7) flight/miss/hope/I/won't/we/our.

GENERAL ENGLISH → FOR AVIATION

 Exercise 4

Put the text in the correct order.

(A) More modern check-in systems allow passengers even to check in through their mobiles. In this case, instead of printing your boarding pass, you'll receive your personal confirmation of your check-in by text messaging.

(B) Self Check-in Kiosks screens are very similar to those of the ATM machines, but instead of getting cash, you can assign your own seat and get your boarding pass printed.

(C) Technology is changing everything to make our lives better, easier, and faster.

(D) Some airlines allow you to pre-check in, including the confirmation of your seat number, and the printing of your boarding pass through their web sites.

(E) Check-in procedures are changing. Forget about check-in counters, long queues, lots of people waiting in line for hours.

 Roleplay

You are at the check-in counter. When it's your turn, something happens to the check-in system. Roleplay the situation with a colleague.

UNIT 7

Asking for information

FOR TEACHERS' USE
- Simple Past
- Could
- Rules/enforcement

GOALS
By the end of Unit 7, students must be able to:
- Ask for information on hand luggage.
- Confirm information with airport agent.

 Warm-up and Pre-Listening

could – queue up – maybe – great – self check-in kiosk – to proceed – procedures – airlines' ground staff – security check point – malfunctioning – regulation – dimension – weight – to weigh – by himself – by herself – by yourself – by ourselves – by yourselves – by themselves – easy – difficult – to wait – still – tiresome – to watch – movie – boring – complex – manual – go away – to leave – to enter – later – to take – without

 Listening: Asking for information

John Roy Bridge: Do you think the passengers from the other flights could check-in?

Anthony Smith: I think they are still queueing up there!

Roy: Maybe the technicians could fix the check-in system. Your idea was really great!

Smith: Using the self check-in kiosk was very easy.

Roy: Do you think that we still have to go back to the check-in counter?

Smith: Why can't we just proceed to the security check point? We are carrying only our hand luggage. Let's ask the airlines' ground staff.

After some minutes, Roy and Smith could find an agent near the information counter.

Agent: Can I help you, gentlemen?

Smith: Yes, please. Due to the check-in system malfunctioning, we had to use the check-in kiosk.

Agent: We apologize for the inconvenient.

Roy: We already have our boarding passes. We could find a self check-in kiosk, confirm our seat numbers, and print our boarding passes.

Smith: As we only have our hand luggage, do we need to go back to the check-in counter before going to the security check?

Roy: Are there any other procedures that we need to follow?

Agent: Yes, airlines have specific regulation for hand luggage and weight. One piece of cabin baggage is allowed for adult and the weight is limited to 5kg (or 11 pounds) and it may not exceed the following dimensions:
45cm × 30cm × 20cm.

Smith: I guess that the dimensions of our hand luggage comply with the regulation.

Agent: Good! Now you can proceed to the security check.

Smith: Thanks a lot for the information!

Agent: You're welcome! Have a nice trip!

 Time to Practice 1

Do you think...?

Example:

Do you think the passengers from the other flights could check-in?

1) he/go to the reception
2) she/arrive at the airport
3) the students/go to the aviation academy
4) Roy and Smith/check-in
5) they/find their bags
6) she/find her purse
7) he/find his wallet

 Time to Practice 2

Example:

Maybe the technicians could fix the check-in system by themselves.

1) he/go to the reception/by himself
2) she/arrive at the airport/by herself
3) the students/go to the aviation academy/by themselves
4) Roy and Smith/check-in/by themselves
5) they/find their bags/ by themselves
6) she/find her purse/by herself
7) he/find his wallet/by himself

 DRILL EXERCISE 1

Example:

Your idea was really great! Using the check-in kiosk was very easy.

You did it by yourself.

1) Her/by herself
2) His/by himself
3) Our/by ourselves
4) Your (plural)/by yourselves
5) Their/by themselves

ASKING FOR INFORMATION ← UNIT 7

DRILL EXERCISE 2

Example:
(to use/self check-in kiosk/very easy)
Using the self check-in kiosk was very easy.

1) (to go/to the reception/by myself/very easy).
2) (to wait in line/for hours/very tiresome).
3) (to do/ the exercises/by ourselves/very difficult).
4) (to find/the information desk/by themselves/very difficult).
5) (to look for/her purse/by herself/very difficult).
6) (to watch/the movie/ by himself/very boring).
7) (to read/the manual/by yourselves/very complex).

→ Exercise 1

Example:
(to proceed/to the security check point)
A: *Why can't we just proceed to the security check point?*
B: *Because there are some procedures that we need to follow.*

1) (to leave our bags/here)
2) (to leave the classroom/now)
3) (to enter the embarkation area/without a boarding pass)
4) (to queue up/there/to check in)
5) (to enter here/without a badge)
6) (to check in/later)
7) (to go to the security check point/without taking our hand luggage)

filmfoto/Shutterstock

Exercise 2

Listen to the dialogue again and fill in the blanks with the missing words.

John Roy Bridge: Do you think that the passengers from the other flights could check-in?

Anthony Smith: I think they are still queueing up there!

Roy: Maybe the _____ could fix the check-in system. Your idea was really great!

Smith: _____ the self check-in kiosk was very _____ .

Roy: Do you think that we still have to go _____ to the check-in _____ ?

Smith: Why can't we just proceed to the security check point? We are carrying only our hand _____ . Let's ask the airlines' ground staff.

After some minutes, Roy and Smith could find an agent near the information counter.

Agent: Can I help you, gentlemen?

Smith: Yes, please. Due to the check-in system _____ , we had to use the check-in kiosk.

Agent: We apologize for the inconvenience.

Roy: We already have our _____ passes. We could find a self check-in kiosk, confirm our _____ and print our boarding passes.

Smith: As we only have our hand luggage, do we need to go back to the check-in counter _____ going to the _____ check?

Roy: Are there any other _____ that we need to follow?

Agent: Yes, airlines have specific _____ for hand luggage and weight. One piece of cabin baggage is allowed for adult and the _____ is limited to 5 kg (or 11 pounds) and it may not exceed the following _____ : 45 cm × 30 cm × 20 cm.

Smith: I guess that the dimensions of our hand luggage comply with the _____ .

Agent: Good! Now you can _____ to the security check.

Smith: Thanks a lot for the _____ !

Agent: You're welcome! Have a nice trip!

Unit 8

At the ticket office

FOR TEACHERS' USE
+ Simple Past
+ Will and going to

GOALS
By the end of Unit 8, students must be able to:
+ Find out a problem with the e-ticket.
+ Give information on how to reissue a ticket (rules/procedures).

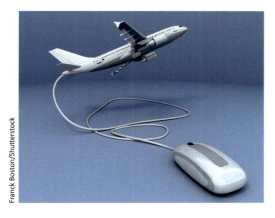

→ **Warm-up and Pre-Listening**

to notice – to head to – on vacation – relatives – to solve a problem – would – nothing – right – wrong – maiden name – different – married – nothing – moreover – any – anything – else – restrictive – to find out – to understand – to spell – to apologize – booked – Economy class – promotional fare – available – reservation – to calculate

TRACK 10   **Listening: Solving a problem**

Anne Mary Wright is on vacation. So, she decided to go to Spain to visit some relatives. Now she is at the airlines' ticket office to solve a problem.

Anne: Good morning!

Agent: Good morning, ma'am (madam). Can I help you?

Anne: Yes, please. I found out that my e-ticket has my maiden name on it and now my last name is different on my passport because I got married.

Agent: Let's see. Here on your e-ticket your last name is Gonzales.

Anne: But now my last name on my passport is Wright!

Agent: I'm sorry, ma'am. If your surname is right, there is nothing I can do for you.

Anne: No, no…You didn't understand. I'll spell my last name for you: W-R-I-G-H-T.

Agent: I really apologize, ma'am.

Anne: That's okay. Moreover, there is another problem: I'm heading to Barcelona, not to Madrid.

Agent: On your e-ticket you are booked on a direct flight to Madrid. Just a moment, please. As you have a ticket in Economy Class, I'll have to check if there is any seat available. The fare basis is quite a restrictive one as it is a promotional fare. A reimbursement is allowed if you pay a fifty-dollar (US$ 50) fee.

Anne: So, you are telling me that I'll have to pay for the reimbursement of this e-ticket?

Agent: This is the rule, ma'am. And you'll have to buy another ticket. I am going to cancel this reservation which contains your maiden name and make another one with the surname Wright: W-R-I-G-H-T. Then, I'm going to calculate the new fare for you. Please hold on.

Anne: Is it the only solution?

Agent: Yes, ma'am. You can't travel if your e-ticket and passport don't have exactly the same information when it refers to names.

Time to Practice 1

Example:
Can I help you?
1) he/her
2) you/them
3) she/him
4) you/us

Example:
(he/us/to find/our documents)
Can he help us to find our documents?
5) (she/him/his/wallet)
6) (they/her/her/purse)
7) (you/us/our/passports)
8) (he/them/their/lost baggage)

Time to Practice 2

Example:
Could you help me?
1) she/us
2) he/them
3) you/him
4) they/her

Example:
(he/them/to find/their documents)
Could he help them to find their documents?
5) (she/us/our/wallets)
6) (they/him/his/passport)
7) (you/her/her/purse)
8) (he/them/their/boarding passes)

Time to Practice 3

Example:
Excuse me. I was wrong.
1) her/she
2) him/he
3) us/we
4) them/they

Choose the correct answer, then read the sentences.

5) Their names (was/were) wrong on the e-ticket.

6) My destination (were/was) wrong on the e-ticket.

7) Our seats (was/were) wrong on our boarding passes.

AT THE TICKET OFFICE ← UNIT 8

DRILL EXERCISE 1

Example:

I found out that my e-ticket has my maiden name on it and now my last name is different on my passport because I got married.

1) I/to find out (simple past)/that/my last name/to be (simple past)/wrong/on the e-ticket.

2) She/to find out (simple past)/that/her middle name/to be (simple past)/wrong/on the e-ticket.

3) He/to find out (simple past)/that/ his destination/to be (simple past) wrong/on the e-ticket.

4) They/to find out (simple past)/that/their destination/to be (simple past) wrong/on the e-tickets.

5) We/to find out (simple past)/that/our names/to be (simple past) wrong/on the e-tickets.

Transform the sentences.

I'm heading to Barcelona, not to Madrid.

I was heading to Barcelona, not to Madrid.

6) She can understand me.

7) Can she understand you?

8) Excuse me, you can't understand him. He's heading to London, not to Liverpool.

9) They can't understand us. We're heading to Brasilia, not to São Paulo.

10) Can't he understand you? His surname is wrong on the e-ticket.

11) He can't understand her. Her destination is wrong on the e-ticket.

12) Moreover, there is another problem: Mrs. Wright is heading to Barcelona.

13) On your e-ticket you are booked on a direct flight to Madrid.

14) The fare basis is a restrictive one as it is a promotional fare.

15) The reimbursement is allowed.

16) There are some seats available.

Now put the sentences below in the negative form.

I'm heading to Barcelona.

I'm not heading to Barcelona.

I wasn't heading to Barcelona.

17) Moreover, there is another problem: Mrs. Wright is heading to Barcelona.

18) On your e-ticket you are booked on a direct flight to Madrid.

19) The fare basis is a restrictive one as it is a promotional fare.

20) The reimbursement is allowed.

21) There are seats available.

DRILL EXERCISE 2

Read and repeat.

1) This is the rule, ma'am. And you'll have to buy another ticket.

2) Is it the only solution?

3) Please hold on.

4) Then, I'm going to calculate the new fare for you.

5) Moreover, there is another problem: I'm heading to Barcelona, not to Madrid.

6) No, no… You didn't understand. I'll spell my last name for you: W-R-I-G-H-T.

GENERAL ENGLISH ➔ FOR AVIATION

Now, substitute the underlined words in the sentences. Then, read the sentences again.

Example:
Is it the only *solution*?
a) *(was)* Was it the only solution?
b) *(problem) Is* it the only problem?/*Was* it the only problem?

1) I was telling him that he won't have to buy another ticket.
a) (her/she)
b) (will)

2) I'm going to calculate the new fare for you.
a) (him)
b) (was)
c) (them)

3) No, no…You didn't understand us.
a) (don't/me)
b) (can't)
c) (couldn't)

4) On your e-ticket you are booked on a direct flight to Madrid.
a) (her/she is)
b) (his/he is)
c) (Barcelona)

5) The fare basis is restrictive.
a) (promotional)
b) (isn't)
c) (wasn't)

 Exercise 1

Unscramble the sentences.

1) to/Madrid/on/a/booked/on/e-ticket/your/flight/are/direct/booked/you.
2) ma'am,/apologize/I/really.
3) buy/to/ticket/another/and/have/you'll.
4) fee/is/allowed/a/reimbursement/pay/if/a/fifty-dollar/you.
5) there/is/as/you/have/any/seat/a/Economy ticket,/if/to/check/have/available/in/Class/I'll.

 Exercise 2

Listen to the dialogue again and fill in the blanks with the missing words.

Anne: Good morning!

Agent: Good morning, ma'am. Can I help you?

Anne: Yes, please. I found out that my e-ticket has my _____ on it and now my last name is _____ on my passport because I got_____ .

Agent: Let's see. Here on your e-ticket your _____ name is Gonzales.

Anne: But now my last name on my passport is Wright!

Agent: I'm sorry, ma'am. If your surname is right, there is _____ I can do for you.

Anne: No, no…You didn't understand. I'll _____ my last name for you: W-R-I-G-H-T.

Agent: I really _____ , ma'am.

Anne: That's okay. _____ , there is another problem: I'm _____ to Barcelona, not to Madrid.

AT THE TICKET OFFICE ← UNIT 8

45

Agent: On your e-ticket you are _____ on a direct flight to Madrid. Just a moment, please. As you have a ticket in Economy Class, I'll have to check if there is any seat _____ . The fare basis is quite a restrictive one as it is a _____ fare. A _____ is _____ if you pay a fifty-dollar (US$ 50) fee.

Anne: So, you are _____ me that I'll have to pay for the reimbursement of this e-ticket?

Agent: This is the rule, ma'am. And you'll have to buy another ticket. I am going to cancel this _____ which contains your maiden name and make another one with the _____ Wright: W-R-I-G-H-T. Then, I'm going to calculate the new fare for you. Please hold on.

Anne: Is it the only solution?

Agent: Yes, ma'am. You can't travel if your e-ticket and passport don't have exactly the same _____ when it refers to names.

→ Roleplay

You are going to Spain to visit some relatives. But, suddenly you find out there is something wrong (surname, departure date or arrival date). How will you solve this problem?

Unit 9

Consolidation

→ Warm-up and Pre-Listening

conveyor belt – to place – piece of baggage – to weigh (weighed) – to scan – barcode – details – security – to attach – to press – label – flight details

🔊 Listening: Baggage drop-off

🎤 Time to Practice 1

Read and repeat.

1) Baggage Drop-Off machines were invented, basically, for automatic baggage detection.
2) On the screen, a message will appear.
3) You'll have to choose one of the buttons ('Yes' or 'No').
4) You'll read a 'Printing Label' message on the screen.
5) On the screen, you'll have to answer 'Yes' to the question 'Ready?' to confirm attached label.

CONSOLIDATION ← UNIT 9   47

Time to Practice 2

Part 1: Look at the picture below. What can you see? Could you identify and understand some of the words written on the picture?
Use them to make sentences.

Example:
(holiday/cheap/hotel)

Next month I'll be on holiday, so I'm going to look for a cheap hotel.

Part 2: Now listen to the recorded text and complete the blanks with the missing words.

Steps

First: Place your baggage on the _____ .
Second: Your piece of baggage will be _____ .
Third: _____ your boarding pass _____.
Fourth: Confirm your flight _____ .
Fifth: You'll have to answer the _____ details.
Sixth: _____ and press the label on itself.
The compartment will close _____ .

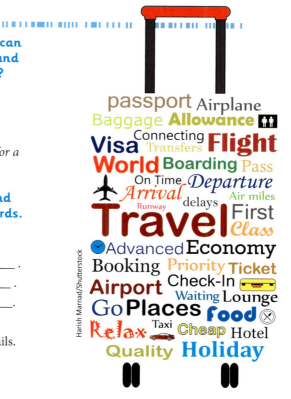

Exercise 1

Pay attention to the pronunciation of these words.

machine – choose – answer – attached – label – ready

Now complete the sentences.

1) The machine is _____.
2) The label was _____.
3) She had to _____ an _____.

Exercise 2

Mark which of these options can be considered 'flight details'.

a) destination
b) seat number
c) last name
d) date of departure
e) surname
f) address
g) date of arrival
h) departure time
i) middle name
j) flight number
k) arrival time

 Exercise 3

What is considered 'security details' according to the instructions?

a) a passenger's full name
b) two standard questions
c) two marks
d) a name in the passport

 Exercise 4

After answering the two standard questions on security details, to print the label you'll have to:

a) open the compartment
b) close the compartment
c) press ready
d) press continue

 Exercise 5

The message 'checking bag' appears on the screen after you:

a) attached the label to the baggage
b) attached the self-sticking label to the baggage and pressed it to itself
c) had attached the self-sticking label to the baggage and pressed it to itself, then press 'Yes' after the question 'Ready?'.
d) press continue

 Exercise 6

The last document the machine will print is:

a) your claim tag
b) your passport with a barcode
c) your boarding pass
d) your self-sticking label

 Challenge

Do you think that automatic check-in and baggage handling will substitute the contact with human beings? Exchange information with your colleagues about the future of check-in and baggage processing.

Unit 10

Are you lost?

FOR TEACHERS' USE

+ Simple Past
+ To be supposed to
+ Airport facilities

GOALS

By the end of Unit 10, students must be able to:

+ Give information on how to get to a place.
+ Understand the airport plant and give directions.

→ Warm-up and Pre-Listening

a little bit – lost – information desk – flight information board – on time – shy – courage – earlier – specific – famous – exactly – similar – facilities – between – next to – beside – on the other side – on the right – on the left – near – far from – first aid – restrooms – to pick up – parking lot – refueling facilities – dangerous – to ring (rang) – to break (broke) down – upstairs – downstairs – duty-free shop – to park (parked)

Listening: Are you lost?

Carl is Instructor Watson's friend. They are supposed to meet at the airport, but Carl is lost. So, Carl is at the information desk to try to find the correct direction and meet his friend Pete. Listen.

Carl: Excuse me. I'm a little bit lost. Could you help me, please?

Agent 1: Yes, of course! What can I do for you, sir?

Carl: I was supposed to meet my friend Pete, but I got lost. I saw at the flight information board that his flight is on time. We could only book seats in different flights, so I arrived earlier than him.

Agent 1: I understand, sir. But where exactly were you supposed to meet?

Carl: My friend Pete mentioned a famous café called Rembrandt. We were supposed to meet there.

Agent 1: If you look up in the map, this café is at Arrival 1.

Carl is a little bit shy. He needed more specific information to find the café, but didn't have courage to ask. Fortunately, his mobile rings and Pete is talking to him now.

Carl: Hi, Pete. Did you have a nice trip?

Pete: Yes, I did. And you?

Carl: Some turbulence during the flight, but it was okay.

Pete: Where are you now?

Carl: I'm lost, Pete! I asked for information at the information desk, but the agent's explanation didn't help much.

Pete: Okay. Are you upstairs or downstairs?

Carl: I'm upstairs.

Pete: Oh, no, Carl. You must go downstairs.

Carl goes downstairs and asks again for information.

Agent 2: Can I help you, sir?

Carl: Yes, please. I was upstairs, but my friend will wait for me downstairs, near Arrival 1, in front of a café called Rembrandt.

Agent 2: On this floor where we are now, there are bars with food and beverage facilities which are open 24 hours a day. Also, downstairs, there are similar stores and shops to those found upstairs. The café you're looking for is between the department store and the flower shop, not so far from here.

Carl: Thank you for all the explanations! They were very helpful.

Agent 2: You're welcome, sir.

Carl finally could meet Pete.

Carl: It's good to see you again.

Pete: Good to see you too.

Carl: Where are we going now?

Pete: If you prefer, we can go to one of those coffee bars near the exit. I also need to find a cash machine. From there, you can exit the airport and get a bus, a taxi or a train.

Carl: What about you?

Pete: A friend of mine will pick me up. He'll park his car at P3, that is, Parking Lot number 3.

ARE YOU LOST? ← UNIT 10

 Time to Practice 1

Part 1: Look at the charts below. Then, play the role of the airport agent at the information desk. Your colleagues will play the part of the passengers.

Examples:
Airport agent: Can I help you, sir? (madam/gentlemen/ladies)

Passenger: Yes, please. I was upstairs, but my friend will wait for me downstairs, near Arrival 1, in front of a café called Rembrandt.

Airport agent: Downstairs, you'll find the arrival gates and the café.

Downstairs
- Bar (between the Café and the Book Store)
- Restaurant (next to the Book Store)
- Parking Lot (in front of the exit)
- Book Store
- Arrival Gates (turn left)
- Passport Control (on your right)
- Café (near the bar)

Upstairs
- Cash dispenser (between the telephones and the Baggage Claim).
- Departure gates (next to the Duty-free shop).
- Telephones (near the Restrooms).
- Baggage Claim
- Duty-free shop (in front of the Baggage Claim)
- Restrooms (WC) (go ahead and turn right).

Part 2: Now, follow the example and make sentences to give information.

Example:
(café/between the department store and the flower shop).

*The café you're looking for is **between** the Department Store and the flower shop.*

1) (restaurant/next to/Arrival 3)

2) (The first aid/on the other side/near the restrooms)

3) (delicatessen/in front of /the chocolate & candies shop)

4) (bijoux & accessories shop/on your right side)

5) (gift & souvenirs shop/on your left side)

6) (electronics shop/between/the gift shop and the jewelry)

7) (toy shop/next to/the electronics shop)

8) (the bar/near/the airport exit)

GENERAL ENGLISH → FOR AVIATION

Time to Practice 2

Example:
I am supposed to be at work at 8 a.m. every day.

1) She
2) He
3) Everybody
4) They
5) We

DRILL EXERCISE 1

Transform the sentences.

Example:

I'm supposed to meet my friend in front of a famous café called Rembrandt. (but I got lost).

I was supposed to meet my friend in front of a famous café called Rembrandt, but I got lost.

1) She is supposed to work from 8 a.m. to 6 p.m. (when she was hired, but now she works overtime).

2) He is supposed to do his homework in the afternoon (when he was a kid).

3) The excursion group is supposed to leave at 4 p.m. (but the bus broke down).

4) Peter is supposed to buy gifts and souvenirs for his family. (but he lost his wallet).

5) Passengers are not supposed to be at the refueling facilities. (because it was dangerous).

DRILL EXERCISE 2

Pair work.

Example:

A: *But where exactly were you supposed to meet?*

B: *My friend Pete mentioned a famous café called Rembrandt. We were supposed to meet there.*

A: *If you look up in the map, this café is at Arrival 1. The café you're looking for is between the department store and the flower shop.*

Choose the place where you were supposed to meet your friend and use: in front of, next to, between, beside, on the right, on the left, to give the correct location. Don't forget to say if you are upstairs or downstairs.

But where exactly were you supposed to meet?

ARE YOU LOST? ← **UNIT 10**

53

TRACK 12

Exercise 1

Fill in the blanks with the missing words.

Carl goes downstairs and asks again for information.

Agent 2: Can I help you, sir?

Carl: Yes, please. I was _____ , but my friend will wait for me _____ , near Arrival 1, in front of a café _____ Rembrandt.

Agent 2: On this floor where we are now, there are bars with food and beverage facilities which are open 24 hours a day. Also, _____ , there are similar stores and _____ to those found upstairs. The café you're looking for is _____ the _____ and the _____ , not so far from here.

Carl: Thank you for all the explanations! They were very helpful.

Agent 2: You're welcome, sir.

TRACK 12

Exercise 2

Listen to the dialogue again and fill in the blanks with the missing words.

Carl finally could meet Pete.

Carl: It's _____ to see you again.

Pete: Good to see you too.

Carl: Where are we going now?

Pete: If you prefer, we can go to one of those _____ near the exit. I also _____ to _____ a cash machine. From there, you can exit the airport and get a _____ , a _____ or a _____ .

Carl: What about you?

Pete: A friend of mine will _____ . He'll park his car at P3, that is, _____ number 3.

UNIT 11

Security check

FOR TEACHERS' USE
- Simple Past
- Active and passive voices
- Security check and immigration control

GOALS
By the end of Unit 11, students must be able to:
- Know how to go through the security check

Warm-up and Pre-Listening

screening bin – watch – to set off – in a rush – to get on a flight – to happen – belt buckle – to take off – to put on – pockets – loose change – coins – jewelry – keys – metal object – clumsy – late – to catch a flight – irritated – afraid – tight – to sit down – coat – trench coat – raincoat – earrings – cell phone – a pair of scissors – gloves – boots – to miss the flight

SECURITY CHECK ← UNIT 11

Listening: Security check

Samuel Bold Howard is traveling on business, so he is in a rush to get on his flight. But something is happening at the security check point.

Security officer: I'm sorry, sir, but the alarm was set off.

Samuel: Oh, excuse me. It must be my belt buckle.

Security officer: So, please, take off your belt and put it on the screening bin.

Samuel: You asked me to take my belt off and put it on the screening bin, so I did it. Why was the alarm set off again?

Security officer: This time it must be your watch, sir.

Samuel: So, I'll have to take it off and put it on the bin too.

Security officer: Exactly, sir. The queue behind you is getting longer, sir. So, I kindly ask you to verify your pockets.

Samuel: Okay, I'm verifying my pockets.

Security officer: Please remove coins, loose change, heavy jewelry, keys and cell phones.

Samuel: Now the alarm wasn't set off by any metal object.

Security officer: Just one more thing, sir. Do you happen to have a laptop in your hand baggage?

Samuel: Yes, I do have a laptop with me.

Security officer: Sir, we'll have to screen it too. And your shoes, sir. We'll also need to have your shoes screened.

Samuel: Sorry, I'm a little clumsy because I'm late to catch my flight. My shoes are a bit tight because they are new. Can I sit down here on this chair to take them off?

Security officer: For sure. And thank you for your cooperation, sir.

Samuel: I guess now everything is right.

Security officer: I'm afraid you still have to give us your coat and scarf… and your boarding pass to be screened.

Samuel: Here they are.

Security officer: Thank you, sir.

Samuel: I'm sorry for the inconvenient. The queue is really getting longer and longer…

Security officer 2: I could identify a small package in your luggage, sir.

Samuel: It's a gift for my client: a desk clock with a paper pad.

Security officer 2: I'm sorry to tell you, but you'll have to unwrap it to show it to us.

Samuel unwraps the gift and shows it to the security agents.

Samuel: Okay. Here it is.

Security officer 1: Now you can put on your shoes, coat and scarf, sir.

Security officer 2: You can pass, sir. Have a nice trip.

Samuel: Thanks. I'm glad I didn't have to go through hand-screening or a pat-down.

 Time to Practice 1

Follow the pattern.

The alarm was set off by…

1) (Samuel's belt buckle)
2) (Sam's watch)
3) (his coins and loose change)
4) (Samuel's heavy jewelry)
5) (Sam's shoes buckles)
6) (his keys)
7) (Samuel's cell phone)

Time to Practice 2

I'm afraid you still have to give us your coat and scarf… and your boarding pass to be screened.
I'm afraid you…

1) can't stay here.
2) can't work here.
3) can't enter here.
4) still have to give us your trench coat to be screened.
5) still have to give us your raincoat to be screened.
6) still have to give us your shoes to be screened.
7) still have to give us your gloves to be screened.
8) still have to give us your boots to be screened.

DRILL EXERCISE 1

I'm a little clumsy because I'm late to catch my flight.

1) anxious
2) nervous
3) worried
4) stressed
5) irritated
6) afraid

DRILL EXERCISE 2

Active voice: Any metal object sets off the alarm.
Passive voice: The alarm is set off by any metal object.

1) Active voice: The X-ray machine screens the laptop.
   Passive voice: _____
2) Active voice: The X-ray machine screens the passengers' shoes.
   Passive voice: _____
3) Active voice: The X-ray machine screened Samuel's laptop.
   Passive voice: _____
4) Active voice: The X-ray machine screened the passenger's coat.
   Passive voice: _____
5) Active voice: Samuel put off the shoes because the security officer asked him to do it.
   Passive voice: _____
6) Active voice: Samuel put off the coat because the security officer asked him to do it.
   Passive voice: _____
7) Active voice: The security officer asked the lady to put her earrings in the screening bin.
   Passive voice: _____
8) Active voice: The security officer asked the gentleman to put his watch in the screening bin.
   Passive voice: _____

SECURITY CHECK ← UNIT 11

57

→ Exercise 1

Follow the pattern.

Please…

1) Put your belt on the screening bin.

2) Put your shoes on the screening bin.

I kindly ask you (to verify your pockets).

3) to take off your coat.

4) to take off your shoes.

5) to take off your watch.

6) to take off your gloves.

Do you happen to have (a laptop) in your hand baggage?

7) A pair of scissors.

I'm glad I didn't (have to go through hand-screening or a pat-down).

8) arrive late.

9) miss the flight.

Be polite! Memorize:

I'm sorry for the inconvenient.

I'm sorry to tell you…

🔊 Exercise 2

TRACK 13

Listen to the dialogue again and fill in the blanks with the missing words.

Security officer: I'm sorry, sir, but the alarm was set off.

Samuel: Oh, excuse me. It _____ be my belt _____ .

Security officer: So, please, _____ your belt and put it on the _____ .

Samuel: You asked me to take my belt off and put it on the screening bin, so I did it.

Why was the alarm set off again?

Security officer: This time it must be your _____ , sir.

Samuel: So, I'll have to take it off and put it on the bin too.

Security officer: Exactly, sir. The queue _____ you is getting longer, sir. So, I kindly ask you to verify your _____ .

Samuel: Okay, I'm verifying my pockets.

Security officer: Please _____ coins, loose change, heavy jewelry, keys and cell phones.

Samuel: Now the alarm wasn't set off by any _____ .

Security officer: Just one more thing, sir. Do you _____ to have a laptop in your hand baggage?

Samuel: Yes, I do have a laptop with me.

Security officer: Sir, we'll have to _____ it too. And your shoes, sir. We'll also need to have your shoes screened.

Samuel: Sorry, I'm a little _____ because I'm late to catch my flight. My shoes are a bit _____ because they are new. Can I _____ here on this chair to take them off?

Security officer: For sure. And thank you for your cooperation, sir.

Samuel: I guess now everything is right.

Security officer: _____ you still have to give us your _____ and _____ … and your boarding pass to be screened.

Samuel: Here they are.

Security officer: Thank you, sir.

Samuel: I'm sorry for the _____ .

The queue is really getting longer and longer…

Security officer 2: I could _____ a small package in your luggage, sir.

Samuel: It's a gift for my client: a desk _____ with a paper pad.

Security officer 2: I'm sorry to tell you, but you'll have to _____ it to show it to us.

Samuel unwraps the gift and shows it to the security agents.

Samuel: Okay. Here it is.

Security officer 1: Now you can put on your shoes, coat and scarf, sir.

Security officer 2: You can pass, sir. Have a nice trip.

Samuel: Thanks. I'm glad I didn't have to pass through hand-screening or a pat-down.

UNIT 12

Consolidation

→ **Warm-up and Pre-Listening**

Ask students if they know what to do at the security checkpoint.

TRACK 14

🔊 **Listening: How not to get caught in the airport security line**

Read the text. There are some verbs missing. Listen to the dialogue and match the verbs below with the sentences.

give – take off – wanted – guarantees – taking – to get – didn't take – unpack – passes – pack – pay – dressing – need – put – buying – remove – obstructed – won't – see

Samuel was in a rush to get on his flight and the last thing he _____ was _____ caught in the security line.
But, he _____ time to _____ attention to what he was _____ on or to the rules.
Let's _____ how not to get caught in the airport security line like Sam.
First:
_____ your stuffs in layers. For example, a layer of clothes, a layer with electronics, then more clothes. This will _____ a clear view of your luggage to inspectors when it _____ through the X-Ray machine.

Second:
Consider _____ a security friendly case for your laptop. This special case _____ that vision won't be _____ . Then, you _____ be obliged to _____ your baggage to show your laptop to security officers and have it screened.
Third:
Do not wrap gifts you're _____ to friends, relatives or clients as a security officer can ask you to unwrap them.
Fourth:
_____ coins or loose change, keys, heavy jewelry, watches, cell phones. _____ your

CONSOLIDATION ← UNIT 12

belt because of its buckle, otherwise it will set the alarm off.

Fifth:

Don't forget to take off your shoes or boots and _____ them in the screening bin.

Sixth:

There are some pieces of clothing that also _____ to be screened: hats, gloves, caps, coats, scarves etc.

Exercise 1

Rewrite the passage using *must* and *mustn't*.

Must – strong obligation

Musn't – prohibition

Exercise 2

Unscramble the words and form sentences.

1) was on his flight caught in a rush Samuel wanted to get he the was and thing last to get line in the security.
2) some scarves pieces coats also need gloves are there of clothing caps, that: hats etc to screened be.
3) can not relatives officer you're do a security taking or as wrap ask to friends clients gifts you to them unwrap.
4) take off forget your shoes bin and them in the to screening or boots don't put.

Challenge

Roleplay the scene from Unit 11 with your colleagues. Use the pictures below to help you.

UNIT 13

Aviation security

FOR TEACHERS' USE	GOALS
✦ Simple Past ✦ Passive voice (Present Perfect)	By the end of Unit 13, students must be able to: ✦ Talk about a new technology concerning aviation security

Zern Liew/Shutterstock

➤ Warm-up and Pre-Listening

Ask students if they know what biometrics is about or if they know anything about aviation security.

TRACK 15 **Listening: Biometric authentication or identification**

Read the text. There are some words missing. Listen to the audio material and match the words from Exercise 1 with the paragraphs.

1) After 9/11 (September 11ᵗʰ), many _____ were _____ to prevent terrorists from acting. Various _____ have been thought to make people feel _____ since then.

2) Nevertheless, people want to _____ safer but have the right to _____ and to keep the _____ about their own bodies.

3) But what is biometrics about?

4) A common and simple _____ for biometrics states that some physiological or behavioral _____ of a human being can be used as a means of _____ or verification of _____ . It is believed, for example, that the iris, the fingerprints, and some facial characteristics can distinguish one _____ from another. A person's voice and signature are considered behavioral traces.

AVIATION SECURITY ← UNIT 13

5) Biometrics can be _____ in aviation _____ in _____ manners, considering the applications _____ today in other _____ .

6) If _____ in _____, biometrics can _____ governments – which would share data, like in the case of Interpol – passengers, the airport _____ , airlines as well as the Federal Border Guard.

7) Theoretically, federal _____ and border control would have to acquire the data (iris, fingerprints, retinal, _____ or face recognition) from each traveler, then, create the master characteristics and _____ about the storage of all the data that could be used in a wrong way if in the hands of _____ .

8) As one US official said the names of _____ suspects identified by the U.S. _____ will continue to be _____ on security watch lists and airlines will continue to have no-fly _____ in the same sense.

9) The _____ at airports to _____ all individuals of a particular _____ or all individuals using a particular passport is not very _____ , as it leads to _____ and is counterproductive.

10) After a Nigerian man, _____ a _____ of a jetliner _____ to Detroit on Christmas day in 2009, anyone traveling to the U.S. will receive extra screening under a new policy that is based on specific _____ about _____ threats on _____ of _____ . That is, the border _____ will make a traveler go through the extra _____ , accordingly to these characteristics: Nigerian man, aged between 22 and 32 years old. Then, all men who match the _____ will face extra screening.

11) Before this _____ , there was another _____ under which anyone from, or traveling through Afghanistan, Algeria, Cuba, Iran, Lebanon, Libya, Nigeria, Pakistan, Saudi Arabia, Somalia, Sudan, Syria, and Yemen would be _____ to go through extra screening.

→ Exercise 1

For each paragraph there are missing words. Match the words to the text. Then, use the words below to form sentences and discuss the issue with your colleagues.

1) adopted, technologies, safer, measures
2) privacy, data, feel
3) This question is the same as:
   a) Who is biometrics?
   b) What is biometrics for?
   c) Where is biometrics?
4) identification, characteristics, identity, definition, person
5) various, industries, applied, security, available
6) aviation, administration, affect, used
7) criminals, worry, police, hand
8) government, terrorism, lists, included
9) nationality, rational, policy, stop, discrimination
10) en route, potential, bombing, anonymity, attempted, information, condition, description, authorities, screening
11) episode, required, policy

Axstokes/Shutterstock
Franck Boston/Shutterstock

GENERAL ENGLISH → FOR AVIATION

→ Exercise 2

Match the verbs to the nouns and vice versa.

1) to create   a) to require
2) to inform   b) to communicate
3) request   c) information
4) communication   d) creation
5) to identify   e) identification

→ Exercise 3

Rewrite the text in one or two paragraphs with your own words.

→ Exercise 4

Explain what you wrote to a colleague.

UNIT 14

Dangerous and prohibited items

FOR TEACHERS' USE	GOALS
✦ Vocabulary on dangerous and prohibited items	By the end of Unit 14, students must be able to: ✦ Talk about dangerous and prohibited items in aviation

 Warm-up and Pre-Listening

Ask students if they know which items are dangerous and prohibited to take to an aircraft. Motivate them to speak about it before starting this Unit.

 Listening: Prohibited items

Patricia Sanders works at the airport. She is a transportation security officer. Now she is orienting and giving instructions on dangerous and prohibited items to the students at the aviation academy. Listen.

Patricia Sanders: Good morning! I'm Patricia Sanders, a TSO, that is a transportation security officer.

All: Good morning!

Patricia: As you all know, the Transportation Security Administration prepares a prohibited items list. This list is not all-inclusive and is updated when necessary. For example, a TSO, to ensure traveler's security can even determine that an item on the permitted chart is dangerous and therefore may not be brought through the security checkpoint. If passengers are not well instructed, they can put their lives at risk.

Mr. Watson: They are aware of how much security is important in aviation and agree that everybody must contribute to everybody's safety.

All: Yes!

Patricia: Now, let's see. The first important items when we talk about security are: explosive materials, flammable items and chemicals. And why are they at the top of our list? Because these items are not allowed in both carry-on or checked baggage. The exception are small compressed gas cartridges which can be in both carry-on and checked baggage, but are restricted to up to 2 in life vests and 2 spares. The life vest must be accompanied by the 2 spares and presented as one unit. On the charts I've handed to you, these items are specified. Please read them silently.

(Pause)

GENERAL ENGLISH → FOR AVIATION

CHART 1

Explosive materials

Item	Carry-on Baggage	Checked Baggage
Dynamite	No	No
Fireworks	No	No
Hand grenades	No	No
Realistic replicas of explosives	No	No

CHART 2

Flammable items

Item	Carry-on Baggage	Checked Baggage
Aerosol (any except for personal care or toiletries in limited quantities)	No	No
Gasoline	No	No
Lighter fluid	No	No
Torch lighters (for pipes and cigars)	No	No

Patricia: Now, let's pay close attention to the sharp objects, guns and firearms. Although there are some general procedures, each airline company can have its own policy concerning these items. Most of sharp objects, guns and firearms can be taken as checked luggage. The exception here is gun powder that is considered an explosive and prohibited as carry-on and checked luggage.
(Pause)

CHART 3

Sharp objects

Item	Carry-on Baggage	Checked Baggage
Box cutters	No	Yes
Knives (except for plastic or round bladed butter knives)	No	Yes
Blades (such as box cutters and razor blades not in a cartridge)	No	Yes

DANGEROUS AND PROHIBITED ITEMS ← UNIT 14

CHART 4

Guns & Firearms

Item	Carry-on Baggage	Checked Baggage
Ammunition	No	Yes
Firearms	No	Yes
Gun powder	No	No
Parts of guns or firearms	No	Yes
Realistic replicas of firearms	No	Yes

Patricia: I hope you have had an overview on prohibited items. Thank you for your attention!

Time to Practice 1

Read and repeat

1) Ammunition is a prohibited item only for carry-on luggage.
2) Box cutters are allowed for checked luggage.
3) Gun powder is prohibited for both carry-on and checked luggage.
4) Aerosol items are prohibited for both carry-on and checked luggage.
5) Small compressed gas cartridges are allowed for both carry-on and checked luggage.

Time to Practice 2

Torch lighter

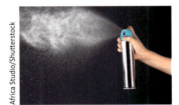
Aerosol

Box cutters

Now it's your turn! Practice with a partner. Say if items are prohibited or not. Look at the charts from the dialogue. Use the sentences from *Time to Practice 1* to help you.

1) dynamite   2) aerosol   3) lighter fuel   4) knives   5) ammunition
6) torch lighters 7) gun powder   8) box cutters   9) parts of guns or firearms
10) razor blades

➔ Exercise 1

Answer the questions:

a) Who's Patricia Sanders?
b) What does she do?
c) Why is she at the Aviation Academy today?

➔ Exercise 2

Was the information about prohibited items useful for you? Why?

➔ Exercise 3

A passenger wants to take a pepper spray with him, as a self-defense item. Do you think it's a prohibited item. Why? Or why not?

➔ Exercise 4

There is a baseball team embarking. How do you think they would be able to take their baseball bats?

UNIT 15

The future of passport control

FOR TEACHERS' USE
+ Vocabulary building
+ New technologies

GOALS
By the end of Unit 15, students will be:
+ Aware of new technologies in passport control

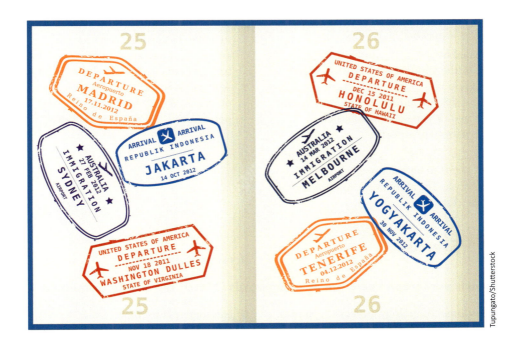

 Warm-up and Pre-Listening

border protection – to disappear – quicker – painless – trusted – prompted – fingerprints – scanner – scanning – traveler – receipt – customs – processes – procedures

Listening: Passport control

Read the text. There are some words missing. Listen to the audio material and match the words from Exercise 1 with the paragraphs.

1) _____ has been posing us a lot of _____ , especially if the _____ or procedures we think of are _____ and take a lot of _____ to be completed or done.

2) _____ moving _____ and a _____ governmental official asking a lot of questions today could be replaced by other _____ in the future.

3) Passport _____ is still a _____ security step and isn't going _____ , but if we take a look at technology, in the future, it may be _____ and _____ .

4) Created by _____ and border _____ needs, the Global Entry Trusted Traveler Program is _____ at 7 major _____ in the U.S., including Washington, Dallas, Chicago O´Hare and San Francisco International Airport.

5) You _____ by _____ your passport that needs to be machine _____ _____ at a kiosk. The automate kiosk guides you to the rest.

6) The second _____ uses _____ , that is, your _____ are required to verify your _____ . You only have to place four of your _____ of your _____ or _____ hand on the green _____ .

7) The _____ step is _____ customs questions without having _____ forms.

8) If _____ is in _____ , the kiosk _____ a _____ the traveler takes to an exit point. From there, the _____ goes to customs.

9) Unfortunately, the program is not _____ to _____ and there are a few barriers to entry. To enroll, travelers must _____ an _____ , pay a USD 100 _____ , pass a background check and submit an interview with a customs and border protection officer. And only U.S. _____ and permanent _____ may apply.

Exercise 1

For each paragraph there are missing words. Match the words to the text.

1) questions, technology, processes, painful, time
2) serious, procedures, lines, slow
3) quick, to disappear, control, necessary, painless
4) airports, protection, customs, available
5) readable, scanning, start
6) left, fingerprints, biometrics, identity, fingers, right, procedure, scanner
7) to fill in, third, answering
8) prints, traveler, order, everything, receipt
9) fee, citizens, open, submit, residents, interview, application, everyone

THE FUTURE OF PASSPORT CONTROL ← UNIT 15

 Exercise 2

Answer the questions.

1) What's the first step?
2) What's the second step?
3) What's the third step?
4) What are the procedures to apply for Global Entry Trusted Traveler?
5) Who can apply for the program?

 Exercise 3

How is passport control done nowadays in your country? Use the words from Exercise 1 to help you describing it.

 Exercise 4

How to expand your vocabulary.

Examples:

1) By using antonyms:
   a) slow (paragraph 2) and quick (paragraph 3)
   b) painful (paragraph 1) and painless (paragraph 3)

2) By using a verb and a noun or adjective
   a) to read – readable
   b) to print – printable
   c) to interview – an interview

Now it's your turn!

a) to communicate
b) to identify
c) to exit
d) to scan
e) to screen
f) to apply
g) to protect

Unit 16

Carry-on or checked luggage?

FOR TEACHERS' USE
✦ Should/Shouldn't

GOALS
By the end of Unit 16, students must be able to:
✦ Understand the difference of carry-on and checked luggage
✦ Comprehend the rules about baggage allowance

➜ Warm-up and Pre-Listening

call center – doubts – departure date – frequent flyer programa – to permit – company's policy – to pack – to carry – to load – to unload – password – baseball match – validity – expiry date – member – to access – to enroll

CARRY-ON OR CHECKED LUGGAGE? ← UNIT 16

Listening: Call center

Karin Whistle works at the call center of an airline company called Appalachian Airlines*. Many passengers have doubts about what they should take or not with them in the airplane. Listen.

*Appalachian Airlines is a fictitious air company.

Karin: Appalachian Airlines, good morning! Karin speaking.

Gentleman: Good morning, Karin! I have a flight booked to Alaska because the grizzly bear hunting season is open. It's the first time I'm flying with Appalachian Airlines and I don't know the company's policy concerning ammunition and firearms.

Karin: May I ask your name, sir?

Gentleman: My name's Robert Kurt.

Karin: How do you spell your last name, please?

Gentleman: K-U-R-T.

Karin: Mr. Kurt, what's your departure date?

Gentleman: September 3rd.

Karin: Mr. Kurt, would you please take note of your 6-letter reservation code?

Gentleman: Sure!

Karin: It's ZB3P78. Well, ammunition is permitted, but it must be in your checked luggage. Also, ammunitions must be securely packed in a fiber, wood or metal box. The firearm, carried as checked luggage, must be unloaded and packed in a locked hard-sided container. Both ammunition and firearm must be declared to the airline at the check-in.

Gentleman: Thank you for the clarification!

Karin: Just a minute, please. I'll register some observations in your reservation about the ammunition and the firearm. Also, some fees apply in this case, sir. The fees totalize USD 350. And I'll need your credit card number and validity date.

Gentleman: Could you confirm the amount, please?

Karin: You'll be charged in USD 350. If you want to become a member of our frequent flyer program, please access our website and enroll. Any other question?

Gentleman: No, no. Thank you very much.

Karin: You're welcome, sir.

Time to Practice 1

I have a flight booked to Alaska because the grizzly bear hunting season is open.

1) She/to have/a flight booked to Washington/her mom is sick.
2) He/to have/a flight booked to New York/he/to have an important meeting.
3) The baseball team/to have/a flight booked to New Jersey/they have an important match.
4) Mr. Vishneva/to have/a flight booked to Bangalore/to visit an important client.
5) The Taylors/to have/a flight booked to Indonesia/they are on vacation.

Now ask your colleague why he/she has a flight booked to a certain city or country.

Why do you have a flight booked to ...?

72

GENERAL ENGLISH → FOR AVIATION

 Time to Practice 2

Follow the example.

Would you please take note of *your 6-letter reservation code*?

1) the 8-letter surname?
2) the 5-letter middle name?
3) the 7-letter first name?
4) the 4-letter provisional password?
5) the 6-letter login?

 DRILL EXERCISE 1

And I'll need *your* credit card number and validity date. *You'll be charged in USD 350*.

1) her/she
2) his/he
3) their/they
4) her/she/ USD 567.50
5) his/he/USD 1,876.30

 DRILL EXERCISE 2

You'll be charged in …
USD 567.50 = five hundred, sixty-seven dollars and fifty cents.
USD 1,876.30 = one thousand, eight hundred seventy-six dollars and thirty cents.

1) USD 56.22
2) USD 68.99
3) USD 2,351.76
4) USD 10,876.55
5) USD 4,675.10

Vladyslav Starozhylov/Shutterstock

→ **Exercise 1**

Pay attention:

a) a locked hard-sided container: the container is locked and has a hard side.
b) a 6-letter reservation code: the reservation code is composed of 6 letters.
c) a tall 42-year-old gentleman: the gentleman is tall and his age is 42.
d) a 350-dollar fee will be charged in your credit card: the fee is 350 dollars and it will be charged in your credit card.

Now it's your turn!

1) the box is big and has a hard side.
2) the box is small and has a hard side.
3) the girl is thin and she is 11 years old.
4) the lady is short and she is 63 years old.
5) the fee is 452 dollars and it will be charged in your credit card.
6) the fee is 786 dollars and it will be charged in your credit card.

CARRY-ON OR CHECKED LUGGAGE? ← UNIT 16

 Exercise 2

Listen to the dialogue again and fill in the blanks with the missing words.

Karin: Appalachian Airlines, good morning! Karin _____ .

Gentleman: Good morning, Karin! I have a flight _____ to Alaska because the grizzly bear hunting season is open. It's the first time I'm _____ with Appalachian Airlines and I don't know the company's _____ concerning ammunition and firearms.

Karin: May I ask your name, sir?

Gentleman: My name's Robert Kurt.

Karin: How do you _____ your _____ , please?

Gentleman: K-U-R-T.

Karin: Mr. Kurt, what's your _____ date?

Gentleman: September 3rd.

Karin: Mr. Kurt, would you please take _____ of your 6-letter reservation code?

Gentleman: Sure!

Karin: It's ZB3P78. Well, _____ is permitted, but it must be in your checked _____. Also, ammunitions must be securely _____ in a fiber, wood or metal box. The firearm, carried as _____ luggage, must be unloaded and packed in a locked hard-sided container. Both ammunition and firearm must be declared to the airline at the check-in.

Gentleman: Thank you for the clarification!

Karin: Just a minute, please. I'll register some _____ in your reservation about the ammunition and the firearm. Also, some fees apply in this case, sir. The fees totalize USD 350. And I'll need your credit card _____ and _____ date.

Gentleman: Could you confirm the amount, please?

Karin: You'll be charged in USD 350. If you want to become a _____ of our _____ , please access our website and enroll. Any other question?

Gentleman: No, no. Thank you very much.

Karin: You're welcome, sir.

→ Exercise 3

Advise people using 'should' or 'shouldn't':

Example:
You look pale. (see a doctor)
You should see a doctor.

1) Andrew looks pale. (see a doctor)
2) Sally can't see very well. (have an appointment with an eye doctor).
3) His children don't eat well. (have some vitamins)
4) Mark had a burnout and is stressed. (work overtime)
5) Your daughter has a fever. (go out in the cold weather)
6) Patricia will travel. (have a travel insurance).

Now practice with a partner!

Example:

Andrew looks pale. Should he see a doctor?
You will give your own opinion about it.

GENERAL ENGLISH → FOR AVIATION

→ Roleplay

Now you are at the Call Center and pick up a call. Your colleague will be the passenger. Look back at the charts from Unit 14. The passenger will ask you information about what he/she *must* or *mustn't* take in carry-on or checked luggage.

Should I take… in carry-on luggage or checked luggage?

You must take… in carry-on.

You must take… in checked luggage.

You mustn't take… in carry-on, but in checked luggage.

You mustn't take… in checked luggage, but in carry-on luggage.

UNIT 17

How's the weather?

FOR TEACHERS' USE
+ Weather forecast

GOALS
By the end of Unit 17, students must be able to:
+ Understand the weather forecast
+ Comprehend how the weather conditions impact aviation

→ Warm-up and Pre-Reading

interdisciplinary – atmosphere – phenomenon – phenomena – variables – interactions – dynamic – dependent – air pressure – water vapor – to impact – air transportation – heavy rain – drizzle – sunny –rainy – windy – stormy – geographic features – altitude – drought – tornado – hurricane

→ Reading: The Weather Forecast

Meteorology can be defined as the interdisciplinary scientific study of the atmosphere. Meteorological phenomena are observable events and are bound by the variables that exist in Earth's atmosphere like: temperature, air pressure, water vapor. There are interactions of each variable and they are dynamic, that is, they change in time and are dependent on the geographic features and altitude.

How do weather conditions impact air transportation?

Meteorology:

- can help pilots to fly their planes safer;
- can help pilots to know where storms are, so they can fly around them;
- can help pilots to be sure about where other planes are, so they won't crash with them;
- can help pilots to understand where the ground is, so they won't have difficult emergency landings.

All of these measures will help to maintain planes better, so they won't have engine problems or cracks in the wings or electronic set fail.

Meteorologists are supposed to tell us what the weather is going to be like. They watch local climate patterns and try to predict how the weather will change.

Scientists predict that, with climate change, we are going to experience more extreme weather conditions.

The United States is subject to one of the most diversified weather conditions. During the course of a normal year, this country may experience high temperatures, jungle humidity, severe cold, drought conditions, as well as being the world leader in tornado activity, not to mention an occasional east coast hurricane.

Aviation is strongly impacted by weather conditions, as 75% of flight delays, diversions or cancellations are related to the weather.

 Time to Practice 1

   sunny   rainy   stormy   cloudy   windy

How's the weather today? The weather is… or It's …

1) sunny
2) rainy
3) windy
4) stormy
5) cloudy

**How was the weather yesterday?
The weather was… or It was …**

1) sunny
2) rainy
3) windy
4) stormy
5) cloudy

**Now practice with a partner:
How was the weather…?**

The weather was… or It was…

1) yesterday
2) last week
3) two days ago
4) last month

HOW'S THE WEATHER? ← UNIT 17

 Time to Practice 2

The pilot is facing…

1) a difficult situation.
2) severe icing conditions.
3) freezing winds.
4) a thunderstorm.
5) snow.
6) heavy rain.
7) drizzle.

Now practice with a partner:
***Two days ago*, the pilot faced _____ .**

1) last week/a difficult situation
2) 10 days ago/severe icing conditions
3) in 2008/freezing winds
4) 3 years ago/a thunderstorm
5) last month/snow
6) 5 days ago/heavy rain
7) a week ago/drizzle

 DRILL EXERCISE 1

Read and repeat

1) Meteorology can be defined as the interdisciplinary scientific study of the atmosphere.
2) Aviation is strongly impacted by weather conditions.
3) The United States is subject to one of the most diversified weather conditions.
4) The United States is the world leader in tornado activity.
5) Occasional east coast hurricanes occur in the United States.

Now think of the weather conditions in your own country and tell your colleagues about it.

DRILL EXERCISE 2

Read and repeat

1) Meteorologists are supposed to tell us what the weather is going to be like.
2) Meteorology helps pilots to fly their planes safer.
3) Meteorology can help pilots to know where storms are.
4) Meteorology can help pilots to be sure about where other planes are.
5) Meteorology can help pilots to understand where the ground is.
6) 75% of flight delays, diversions or cancellations are related to the weather.

Exercise 1

Match the number and the letter to form a sentence:

1) Meteorology can help pilots to be sure about where other planes are…
2) Meteorology can help pilots to know where storms are…
3) Meteorology can help pilots to understand where the ground is…
4) All of these measures will help to maintain planes better…
5) Meteorologists are supposed to tell us what…

a) the weather is going to be like.
b) so they won't have difficult emergency landings.
c) so they won't crash with them.
d) so they won't have engine problems or cracks in the wings or electronic set fail.
e) so they can fly around them.

Exercise 2

Read the text again and fill in the blanks with the missing words.

Meteorology can be defined as the _____ scientific study of the atmosphere. Meteorological _____ are observable events and are bound by the variables that exist in Earth's _____ like: temperature, air _____, water _____. There are _____ of each variable and they are _____, that is, they change in time and are dependent on the geographic features and _____.

How do weather _____ impact air transportation?

Meteorology:

- can help pilots to fly their planes _____;
- can help pilots to know where _____ are so they can fly around them;
- can help pilots to be sure about where other planes are, so they won't _____ with them;
- can help pilots to _____ where the ground is, so they won't have difficult emergency _____.

All of these measures will help to maintain planes better, so they won't have engine problems or cracks in the wings or electronic set fail.

Meteorologists are _____ to tell us what the _____ is going to be like. They watch local climate patterns and try to predict how the weather will change.

Scientists predict that, with climate _____, we are going to experience more extreme weather conditions.

The United States is subject to one of the most diversified weather conditions. During the course of a normal year, this country may experience high _____, jungle humidity, severe _____, drought conditions as well as being the world leader in _____ activity, not to mention an occasional east coast _____.

Aviation is strongly impacted by weather _____, as 75% of flight delays, diversions or cancellations are related to the weather.

Challenge

How can the weather conditions affect aviation? First, debate this issue with your colleagues. Then, write three short paragraphs on the impact of meteorology in aviation.

UNIT 18

Consolidation

FOR TEACHERS' USE
✦ Weather forecast for aviation

GOALS
By the end of Unit 18, students must be able to:
✦ Understand the weather forecast for aviation

➡ **Warm-up and Pre-Reading**

forecast – acronym – occasionally – to report – largest – airfields – identifier – valid – validity – to issue – wind speed – visibility – direction – degrees – to report – to describe – mandatory

Reading: How to read a TAF

Aviation is totally dependent on the weather forecast. Predicting the weather conditions for aviation seems to be more complicated. It's not enough to know if it will rain or be sunny tomorrow because weather conditions can affect the security of passengers.

A TAF is an acronym for Terminal Aerodrome Forecast and it's a specific weather forecast for aviation. Though the validity time may vary, most of TAFs are valid for 9 hours or 18-hour periods.

For the largest airfields, since November 5th 2008, the TAF format changed from 24 hours to 30 hours.

What's reported in a TAF?

The following eight items are mandatory in a TAF:

- location
- date/time
- validity period
- wind
- visibility
- weather
- cloud
- significant changes

Location

Location is expressed by a 4-letter ICAO airport code. Example: EGLL (Heathrow).

Sometimes the airfield identifier may be prefixed with FC or FT (Forecast), as in FCEGLL that means forecast for Heathrow.

Hint: For more 4-letter ICAO airport codes, you can consult the website:

http://www.airport-technology.com/icao-codes/

Date & Time

The Date & Time field gives the exact date and time the TAF was issued.

Example: 051633z

This means that the forecast report was issued on the 5th of the month at 16:33 zulu.

Validity period

This is the period that the TAF is valid for.

The date along with the first hour and the last hour forecast are given.

Example 1: 0621/0706

This is a nine-hour TAF. Why?

Because it was issued on the 6th of the month at twenty-one hundred hours (2100, that is 9:00 p.m.) and it's valid until the 7th of the month at zero six hundred hours (0600, or 6:00 am). That's how hours are said in aviation.

Example 2: 0218/0318

Wind

The wind direction is given in degrees true (nearest 10°).

VRB is used if this condition is variable and in a clock wise direction.

This variable may not be mentioned if the wind isn't coming from one specific direction or won't change at any point.

A letter **G** will be used for gusting conditions.

The speed of the wind is in knot (KT) and is given using the average of the last 10 minutes.

Example 1: 17011KT

The wind is coming from one seven zero degree true at eleven knots (11KT).

Example 2: 090VRB12008G18KT

The wind is coming from zero nine zero degrees, but it's variable (VRB) between zero eight and one two zero degrees and the speed is gusting (G) eighteen knots (18KT).

Visibility

Visibility is given in meters.

- Above 10km, visibility will be reported as '9999' or 'all nines'.
- For less than 50 meters, visibility will be reported as '0000' (zero, zero, zero, zero).

Example 1: 5000.

In this case, visibility is 5,000 (five thousand) meters.

CONSOLIDATION ← UNIT 18

If visibility is greater in one direction, this is shown as in the example:

Example 2: 3000N5000E

Visibility is three thousand North and five thousand East.

Weather

There are two letters to identify the forecast of significant weather. Up to three groups may be used at once.

Examples: **DZ = drizzle**

BR = mist

The severity of each phenomenon is described by a + (plus sign) to mean *heavy* and a – (minus sign) that means *light*. If there is no + or – it means *moderate*.

Example: **+TSRAGR = heavy thunderstorms, rain and hail.**

TS also implies that in heavy thunderstorms, pilots will face moderate turbulence and icing.

2-letter codes	Phenomena
FG	Fog
DZ	Drizzle
RA	Rain
SN	Snow
SG	Snow grains
IC	Ice crystals
PL	Ice pellets
GR	Hail
GS	Small hail
UP	Unknown precipitation
BR	Mist
TS	Thunderstorm
SH	Showers
FU	Smoke
VA	Volcanic ashes
SS	Sandstorm
DS	Duststorm

Cloud

The amount of cover (= amount of clouds in the sky) is given in *oktas* and the cloud base height above the aerodrome level is given in *feet*.

For more information on the measure of amount of clouds in the sky, you can consult the website: www.worldweather.org/oktas.htm

Significant changes
Probability

The probability that the weather phenomena will occur can be measured as:

Example: PROB30 (0%-30%) or PROB40 (30%-50%).

And the time indicates the beginning and the end of the forecast period.

Example: 1520, that is, between 3 p.m. or 1500 (fifteen hundred hours) and 8 p.m. or 2000 (twenty hundred hours).

Change indicator

Change indicator or TEMPO indicates that a weather phenomenon will take place temporarily, that is, there will be a temporary change.

Example: TEMPO 1820 170G22KT

There will be a change in the weather between 6 p.m. (or 1800= eighteen hundred hours) and 8 p.m. (or 2000 = twenty hundred hours), when the wind will be one seven zero degrees gusting twenty-two knots.

Exercise 1

a) What does the TAF acronym stand for?
b) What is a TAF?
c) What items are mandatory to be reported in a TAF?
d) What does Zulu time mean?

Exercise 2

1) Look at the *Example 2* in the Validity item. What is the validity period of this TAF? When was it issued?
2) How is the wind speed measured?
3) Why is a letter G used?
4) In the *Example 2* in the Wind item, why VRB and G are used? What is the wind speed in knots?

Exercise 3

1) How is visibility given?
2) What does '9999' or 'all nines' mean?
3) What does '0000' mean?

Exercise 4

1) Match the two-letter codes with the description of the weather condition:

a) RA   ( ) showers
b) GR   ( ) snow
c) SH   ( ) ice crystals
d) SG   ( ) volcanic ashes
e) SN   ( ) hail
f) IC   ( ) rain
g) VA   ( ) snow grains

2) What does - RA mean?
3) What does +RAFG mean?
4) What does TSGS mean?

UNIT 19

Can I take my pets with me?

FOR TEACHERS' USE	**GOALS**
✦ If Clause	By the end of Unit 19, students must be able to: ✦ Communicate with passengers ✦ Give information on baggage allowance and transportation of pets

 Warm-up and Pre-Listening

allowance – dimensions – doubts – crutches – assistive devices – kennel – to exceed – length – width – hight – umbrella – hat – located – requirements – restrictions

GENERAL ENGLISH → FOR AVIATION

Listening: Baggage Allowance

Karin Whistle is working at the Call Center this evening. She is talking to a passenger. Let's listen to them.

Karin: Appalachian Airlines, good evening! Karin speaking.

Sarah Park: Good evening!

Karin: How can I help you, madam?

Sarah: My name's Sarah Park and I have some doubts about baggage allowance.

Karin: Yes, Miss Park…What would you like to know exactly?

Sarah: It's Mrs. Park.

Karin: I'm sorry… Mrs. Park …

Sarah: What are the dimensions for carry-on luggage? Also, I broke my right foot, so I'll need to take my crutches with me.

Karin: Baggage may not exceed 45 linear inches (or 114 cm) in combined length, width and height. Also, it must fit easily in the Carry-on Baggage Check, which is located near the check-in counters. If your carry-on luggage doesn't fit, you'll have to take it as checked luggage and probably pay a fee. Though crutches are not considered special items, they are considered assistive devices, just like wheelchairs, for example, so they are not charged.

Sarah: And if it rains, my husband will need to take his hat and umbrella.

Karin: Besides a carry-on luggage, a passenger can take approved additional items, like an umbrella or a jacket, which are not considered as personal items. So, in your husband's case, the umbrella and hat will be freebies. And besides the umbrella and the hat, he can take a personal item.

Sarah: What are the objects considered as personal items?

Karin: In his case, a camera bag, a briefcase or a laptop could be considered personal items. And remember that computers cannot be checked!

Sarah: Just one more question. Can I take my pets with me?

Karin: What kind of pet would you like to take with you?

Sarah: Well, I have a parrot, two cats, a dog and a hamster.

Karin: I'm sorry to tell you, madam, but Appalachian Airlines only accepts to transport cats or dogs and one per passenger. We can neither transport birds nor rodents.

Sarah: Gosh! It will be a very difficult choice!

Karin: I understand, Mrs. Park, this will be a difficult choice for you. And we can only allow pets to be transported under certain requirements and restrictions.

Sarah: What requirements and conditions?

Karin: Your pet can't be taken as checked baggage and it will be transported as a cargo. You'll need a shipper and a health certificate issued and signed by a licensed veterinarian. Also, make sure that you have a list of administered inoculations for your pet and a statement that the animal is in good health.

Sarah: What about the kennel?

Karin: It will depend on the breed of dog or cat that we're talking about.

Sarah: Suppose that I have just decided to take my Shi Tzu dog.

Karin: Well, it's a small pet. So, if the kennel weighs around 6 lbs, you'll pay fifty dollars.

Sarah: Thank you for the information.

Karin: You're welcome.

CAN I TAKE MY PETS WITH ME? ← UNIT 19

 Time to Practice 1

What would you like to *know* exactly?

1) take
2) do
3) ask
4) request

 Time to Practice 2

It will depend on *the breed of dog or cat* (that) we're talking about.

1) the situation
2) the dimension of the bag
3) the departure date
4) the arrival date
5) the flight

 DRILL EXERCISE 1

Substitute the words:

Suppose that I have just decided to take my *Shi Tzu dog*.

1) umbrella
2) raincoat
3) crutches
4) briefcase
5) laptop computer
6) jacket
7) camera bag
8) purse

 DRILL EXERCISE 2

Examples:

If your carry-on luggage doesn't fit, you'll have to take it as checked luggage and probably pay a fee.

And if it rains, my husband will need to take his hat and umbrella.

1) If/you (negative) put gasoline in your car/it (negative) start.
2) If/you (affirmative) take your pet with you/you (affirmative) need a kennel.
3) If/it (affirmative) to rain/you (affirmative) need an umbrella.
4) If/it (negative) to rain/you (negative) need an umbrella.
5) If/you (negative) hurry up/you (affirmative) miss your flight.
6) If/you (affirmative) to be early/you (negative) miss your flight.

GENERAL ENGLISH → FOR AVIATION

 Exercise 1

Look at the chart below and practice with a colleague.

1 pound(1 lb) = 453.5 grams
Example:
If the kennel weighs 6 lbs (pounds), how much will I have to pay?
If the kennel weighs around 6 lbs (pounds), you'll pay fifty dollars.

Kennel Type	Kennel Weight	Cost of Kennel
SML	6 lbs.	U$ 50.00
MED	12 lbs.	U$ 65.00
MED	18 lbs.	U$ 75.00
LRG	24 lbs.	U$ 85.00
XLG	31 lbs.	U$ 100.00
GIANT (accepted as cargo only)	51 lbs.	U$ 180.00

SML = small/MED = medium/LRG= large/XLG=extra-large

1) 12 lbs.
2) 18 lbs.
3) 24 lbs.
4) 31 lbs.
5) 51 lbs.

TRACK 19 Exercise 2

Listen to the dialogue again and fill in the blanks with the missing words.

Karin Whistle is working at the Call Center this evening. She is talking to a passenger. Let's listen to them.

Karin: Appalachian Airlines, good evening! Karin speaking.

Sarah Park: Good evening!

Karin: How can I help you, madame?

Sarah: My name's Sarah Park and I have some _____ about _____ .

Karin: Yes, Miss Park…What would you like to know _____ ?

Sarah: It's Mrs. Park.

Karin: I'm sorry…Mrs. Park…

Sarah: What are the _____ for carry-on luggage? Also, I broke my right foot, so I'll need to take my _____ with me.

Karin: Baggage may not exceed 45 linear inches (or 114 cm) in combined _____ , _____ and _____ . Also, it must _____ easily in the Carry-on Baggage Check, which is _____ near the check-in counters. If your carry-on luggage doesn't fit, you'll have to take it as _____ luggage and probably pay a fee. Though crutches are not considered special items, they are considered assistive devices, just like wheelchairs, for example, so they are not _____ .

Sarah: And if it rains, my husband will need to take his hat and _____ .

Karin: Besides a carry-on luggage, a passenger can take approved _____ items, like an umbrella or a jacket, which are not considered

CAN I TAKE MY PETS WITH ME? ← UNIT 19

as _____ items. So, in your husband's case, the umbrella and hat will be freebies. And besides the umbrella and the hat, he can take a personal item.

Sarah: What are the objects considered as personal items?

Karin: In his case, a camera bag, a briefcase or a laptop could be _____ personal items. And remember that computers cannot be checked!

Sarah: Just one more question. Can I take my pets with me?

Karin: What kind of pet would you like to take with you?

Sarah: Well, I have a parrot, two cats, a dog and a hamster.

Karin: I'm sorry to tell you, madame, but Appalachian Airlines only accepts to _____ cats or dogs and one per passenger. We can neither transport birds nor rodents.

Sarah: Gosh! It will be a very difficult _____ !

Karin: I understand, Mrs. Park, this will be a _____ choice for you. And we can only allow pets to be transported under certain _____ and _____ .

Sarah: What requirements and conditions?

Karin: Your pet can't be taken as checked baggage and it will be transported as a _____ . You'll need a shipper and a health certificate issued and signed by a licensed veterinarian. Also, make sure that you have a list of administered inoculations for your pet and a statement that the animal is in good health.

Sarah: What about the kennel?

Karin: It will depend on the _____ of dog or cat that we're talking about.

Sarah: Suppose that I have just decided to take my Shi Tzu dog.

Karin: Well, it's a _____ pet. So, if the kennel weighs around 6lbs, you'll pay fifty dollars.

Sarah: Thank you for the information.

Karin: You're welcome.

UNIT 20

Flight 274, now boarding

FOR TEACHERS' USE
+ Present Perfect
+ Should

GOALS
By the end of Unit 20, students must be able to:
+ Get information on flight schedules

➔ Warm-up and Pre-Listening
Ask students if something has ever gone wrong when they were traveling.

FLIGHT 274, NOW BOARDING ← UNIT 20

🔊 Listening: Last call

The Taylors and the Parks have been friends for more than a decade. They have decided to go to China together, but some incidents have happened. The Taylors are coming from Boston to meet the Parks at the airport in Europe.

John Park: You shouldn't have brought the crutches and the wheelchair just because you broke your right foot.

Sarah Park: I have called the Call Center and the assistant told me that I could bring the crutches too as they are considered assistive devices.

John Park: But I couldn't bring my umbrella with me because I have to carry your crutches. I'm so glad that you haven't decided to bring all the pets with us!

Sarah Park: Come on, John! This is our first long haul flight! We're celebrating our 25th anniversary and traveling with the Taylors who are celebrating their 16th anniversary! We couldn't cancel everything just because I broke my right foot!

John: Let's see at the flight information board if the Taylors' flight is on time.

Sarah: I remember they said they would fly with Appalachian Airlines and their flight number is 259.

John: I guess they will have to take a shuttle from Terminal 1 to Terminal 4 where we are.

Sarah: Here it is. Flight 259 with Appalachian Airlines. It's on time. They will be landing in 45 minutes.

John: As the Taylors are on a connecting flight, they won't have to check-in again. Don't you think we should check in for the flight, right away?

Sarah: I have already checked in through the company's website. I've also confirmed our seat numbers and printed our boarding passes. Now we only have to find one of those drop-off machines.

John: You're unbelievable! It's the first time we're traveling abroad in a long haul flight and you know everything!

Sarah: I'll stay here and you go to one of the drop-off machines with our two pieces of luggage. I have already printed the instructions from the website for you. And don't forget to print our claim tag and keep it with you in case we need to claim for our baggage.

Some minutes later, John Park returned.

John: I've had some difficulties in dealing with that drop-off machine, but I got to do it.

Sarah: Good! Let's go to the debarkation area to wait for the Taylors.

Sylvia Taylor: Nice to see you again!

Josh Taylor: We have arrived in time to our connecting flight to China!

Sylvia Taylor: I can't wait to see The Great Wall, the Forbidden City and the Imperial Palace Museum in Beijing, the Silk Road, Shangai and Hong Kong!

John: Listen! The loudspeakers are announcing the last call to our flight!

Loudspeakers: Last call to flight 274 to Beijing with Appalachian Airlines. Flight 274 now boarding. Passengers must embark immediately at gate 11.

GENERAL ENGLISH → FOR AVIATION

 Time to Practice 1

1) Sarah has broken her right foot.
2) John has had difficulties with the drop-off machine.
3) The Parks and the Taylors have been friends for more than a decade.
4) The loudspeakers have just announced the last call to our flight.
5) Sarah has already checked in on the airlines website.
6) Sarah has already printed the instructions from the website.
7) Sylvia and Josh Taylor have arrived in time to their connecting flight to China.
8) Sarah has called the Call Center because she had some doubts.

 Time to Practice 2

1) Sarah broke her right foot (last week).
2) John had difficulties with the drop-off machine (ten minutes ago).
3) The Parks and the Taylors have been friends for more than a decade.
4) The loudspeakers announced the last call to our flight (five minutes ago).
5) Sarah already checked in on the airlines website (yesterday afternoon).
6) Sarah printed the instructions from the website (this morning).
7) Sylvia and Josh Taylor have arrived in time to their connecting flight to China.
8) Sarah called the Call Center (three days ago) because she had some doubts.

 DRILL EXERCISE 1

Tell Peter and his wife what they should have done.

Example:
Peter had some of his things stolen from his luggage. (to lock his luggage with a padlock)
You should have locked your luggage with a padlock.

1) Now it's raining and Peter doesn't have an umbrella with him. (to bring/an umbrella with him).

Hint: to bring – brought – brought

2) It's raining and Peter doesn't have a raincoat with him. (to bring/a raincoat with him).

3) Peter wanted to go to Hawaii but now there aren't tickets available. (to book a flight earlier).

Hint: to book – booked – booked

4) Peter's wife forgot to bring a dress for a party in her luggage. (She/to bring/a dress for a party in her luggage)

5) They arrived at the airport five minutes before the last call announcement. (They/to arrive/earlier/at the airport).

Hint: to arrive – arrived – arrived

FLIGHT 274, NOW BOARDING ← UNIT 20

DRILL EXERCISE 2

Josh and Sylvia Taylor had some problems during their last trip.

Example:
They could only book their seats separately.
Josh and Sylvia shouldn't have forgotten to book their seats together.

1) As they were traveling to the beach they had to take sunscreen lotion.
2) As they were traveling to a tropical country they had to wear light clothes.
3) As they were traveling to a tropical country they had to be vaccinated.
4) As they were traveling to a tropical country they had to take flip flops.
5) As they were traveling to a tropical country they had to drink a lot of water.

→ Exercise 1

Here are the instructions Sarah has printed to her husband John. Suppose that you were near him when he was having difficulties with the drop-off machine. Instruct him by saying 'must'. Then, write down the new instructions.

Steps

First: Place your baggage on the conveyor belt.
Second: Your piece of baggage will be weighed.
Third: Scan your boarding pass barcode.

Fourth: Confirm your flight details.
Fifth: You'll have to answer the security details.
Sixth: Attach and press the label on itself.
The compartment will close automatically.

Exercise 2

Listen to the dialogue again and fill in the blanks with the missing words.

The Taylors and the Parks have been friends for more than a decade. They have decided to go to China together, but some incidents have happened. The Taylors are coming from Boston to meet the Parks at the airport in Europe.

John Park: You shouldn't have brought the _____ and the _____ just because you broke your right foot.

Sarah Park: I have called the Call Center and the assistant told me that I could bring the crutches too as they are _____ assistive devices.

John Park: But I couldn't bring my umbrella with me because I have to carry your crutches. I'm so glad that you haven't decided to bring all the pets with us!

Sarah Park: Come on, John! This is our first _____ _____ flight! We're celebrating our 25th anniversary and traveling with the Taylors who are _____ their 16th anniversary! We couldn't have cancelled everything just because I broke my right foot!

John: Let's see at the flight information board if the Taylors' flight is on time.

Sarah: I remember they said they would fly with Appalachian Airlines and their flight number is _____.

John: I guess they will have to take a _____ from Terminal 1 to Terminal 4 to arrive where we are.

Sarah: Here it is. Flight 259 with Appalachian Airlines. It's on time. They will be landing in 45 minutes.

John: As the Taylors are on a connecting flight, they won't have to check-in again. Don't you think we should check in for the flight, right away?

Sarah: I have already checked in through the company's website. I've also _____ our seat numbers and _____ our boarding passes. Now we only have to find one of those drop-off machines.

John: You're _____! It's the first time we're _____ abroad in a long haul flight and you know everything!

Sarah: I'll stay here and you go to one of the drop-off machines with our two pieces of luggage. I have already _____ the _____ from the website for you. And don't forget to print our claim tag and keep it with you in case we need to claim for our baggage.

Some minutes later, John Park returned.

John: I've had some _____ in dealing with that drop-off machine, but I got to do it.

Sarah: Good! Let's go to the _____ area to wait for the Taylors.

Sylvia Taylor: Nice to see you again!

Josh Taylor: We have arrived in time to our _____ flight to China!

Sylvia Taylor: I can't wait to see The Great Wall, the Forbidden City and the Imperial Palace Museum in Beijing, the Silk Road, Shangai and Hong Kong!

John: Listen! The _____ are announcing the last call to our flight!

Loudspeakers: Last call to flight _____ to Beijing with Appalachian Airlines. Flight 274 now _____ . Passengers must _____ immediately at gate 11.

UNIT 21

Consolidation

FOR TEACHERS' USE
✦ The life of an air traffic controller

GOALS
By the end of Unit 21, students must be able to:
✦ Understand what an air traffic controller does

→ Warm-up and Pre-Listening

responsibility – toward – complex – lifetime – to happen – priority – to control – runway – taxing – take off – route – landing – directions – points – destination gate – monitored

GENERAL ENGLISH → FOR AVIATION

TRACK 21

🔊 Listening: The life of an air traffic controller

Philip Cage is an air traffic controller.
He is telling something about his job routine:

1) In our area of responsibility, planes come from all directions and leave at the same time toward those points. It's something quite complex.

( ) If you start thinking that in those airplanes there are people, you lose focus. You have to start thinking of each plane as a person.

( ) As a traffic agent, you choose which one can fly closest, which one is the fastest, and which one has the best chance to clear space quickly. In other words, you treat the airplanes in order of priority.

( ) A challenging situation can be when you have a lot of aircraft inbound with only one runway available. That's a difficult moment because you have to manage a situation in which many aircraft need to land and you can only offer them a very limited space.

( ) An aircraft is controlled from the time it starts taxing toward the runway, then after taking off, when it's flying along its route, during the landing phase until the plane reaches its destination gate. It's always monitored by an ATCO.

( ) I don't know if in a controller's lifetime you get to control twice the Air Force One, that is, the president of the United States of America's aircraft. I don't think it will happen again. I felt a bit nervous, but his aircraft was treated like any other. Of course that it was given priority because it gets priority over other aircraft.

→ Exercise 1

Listen to the text and put the paragraphs in the right order.

→ Exercise 2

Complete the sentences with the missing words.

1) Planes come from all _____ and leave at the same _____ . It's something quite _____ . (complex – time – directions).

2) I don't _____ it will _____ again. I felt a bit _____ , but his _____ was treated like any other. (nervous – happen – know – aircraft).

3) An aircraft is _____ from the time it starts _____ toward the _____ , then after _____ , when it's _____ along its _____ during the _____ phase until the plane _____ its destination _____ . (landing – route – gate – flying – runway – taking off – reaches – monitored – taxing).

4) A _____ situation can be when you have a lot of aircraft _____ with only one runway _____ . (inbound – available – challenging).

CONSOLIDATION ← UNIT 21

→ Exercise 3

Match the words.

1) to fly   ( ) complexity
2) to land   ( ) flying
3) to take off   ( ) taking off
4) to monitor   ( ) landing
5) complex   ( ) monitoring

Now circle the correct word and complete the sentence.

1) The (complex/complexity) of the task made us nervous.
2) (To fly/Flying) during thunderstorms can be dangerous.
3) An ATCO task is (to monitor/monitoring) the planes (to land/landings) and (to take off/ taking offs).
4) (To take off/taking offs) and (To land/landings) are very (complexity/complex).

→ Exercise 4

Suppose you are an ATCO (air traffic controller) and you are being interviewed. Tell a colleague about your job routine. Then, write a paragraph about it.

UNIT 22

High level of alertness: bird flu

FOR TEACHERS' USE
+ Reading Comprehension of an article

GOALS
By the end of Unit 22, students must be able to:
+ Talk about a situation of high level of alertness at airports

➔ Warm-up and Pre-Reading

bird-flu – swine flu – pig flu – hog flu – local governments – pandemic – influenza – uncounted dead people – preventive measures – to stockpile supplies

Discussion in groups on what happened at the airports in 2009 with the influenza pandemic, called the pig flu, hog flu or swine flu.

Reading: Bird flu alert in Asia

Airports and the local governments of the cities where they are located must be prepared for any kind of pandemic. Since the 2009 influenza pandemic, airlines and airports all around the world have developed strategies to be ready for such contingencies.

This influenza H_1N_1-type called popularly the swine-flu, the hog-flu or the pig-flu, must have killed, experts agreed, an estimated 294,500 people. However, this number could be higher if we consider that many of those without access to health facilities who died went uncounted.

Airports administration must work in cooperation with the local sanitary and health authorities to provide flu inspection on the flights arriving from the influenza hotspots. Such inspection must provide thermal imaging camera and screen, as thermal imaging can detect elevated body temperature, one of the signs of influenza.

At the time of the pandemic, people started stockpiling medical supplies as the World Health Organization (WHO) and governments discussed worst-case scenarios in which anybody couldn't leave their homes.

In such a severe scenario, who hadn't been infected would have to stockpile supplies, from paper masks and hand sanitizer to food and water.

The following symptoms constituted what experts have called "emergency warning signs" and anyone was advised seeking immediate care if a person experienced these signs: confusion, sudden dizziness, severe or persistent vomiting, pain or pressure in the chest or abdomen. Note that these symptoms are different from the typical signs of other types of influenza, such as, headache, fever, muscle or joint pain, sore throat, cough, chills, fatigue and runny nose.

As it occurs with the seasonal flu transmission, the spread of the H_1N_1 virus occurred through coughing or sneezing by people with influenza. People at the time of the pandemic used to avoid places with agglomeration of people, wear paper masks, wash their hands frequently and also avoided touching their noses, eyes and mouths due to contamination. A vaccine was obtained by scientists and health authorities declared the outbreak over in 2010.

 Exercise 1

Read the text and say if the statement is true (T) or false (F).

1) Another influenza pandemic has already started. (   )
2) All governments around the world were in alert. (   )
3) The spread of the H_1N_1 virus occurred through coughing or sneezing by people with influenza. (   )
4) There isn't any treatment or vaccine for the H_1N_1 influenza type. (   )
5) Airport administration and airlines must cooperate with sanitary and health authorities in case of an endemic or pandemic. (   )

GENERAL ENGLISH → FOR AVIATION

→ Exercise 2

Unscramble the words and find out the symptoms of a simple flu:

1) lusmce or itnjo aipn
2) chgou
3) veefr
4) unnyr onse
5) hacheead
6) lilhcs
7) orse thtora
8) atiugef

→ Exercise 3

a) What are thermal imaging cameras for?
b) What were the "emergency warning signs"?

→ Exercise 4

a) At what airports preventive measures have been taken since 2009?
b) How could people prevent the contamination during the pandemic?
c) What does WHO stand for?

→ Challenge

You work at the airport and have been to a lecture about the H_1N_1 influenza pandemic. Now you have to explain to others what you've learned.

Unit 23

Main airports in the world

FOR TEACHERS' USE	GOALS
✦ Nationalities and currencies	By the end of Unit 23, students must be able to: ✦ Talk about names of airports, identify names of airports, cities and countries

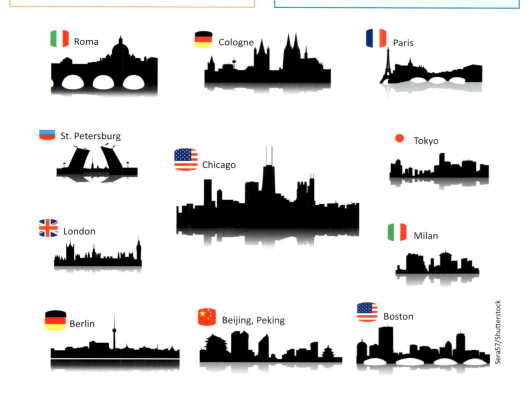

 Warm-up and Pre-Listening

Tell students to take a look at the chart with countries, nationalities and currencies (Appendix 1) to discuss if they know where the country is or not. Also, they need to talk about something they know about the local culture of the chosen country.

GENERAL ENGLISH → FOR AVIATION

Listening: Air transport and travelers

1) During the winter air transport is severely _____ .
   Airport _____ , cancellations, _____ , flight diversion and other _____ are unavoidable.

   (1) problems, closure, affected, delays

2) Experts around the _____ have been alerting countries about the rising cost of _____ , _____ debate the global climate change, but even with the growing awareness of carbon _____ by the air _____ industry, it seems people go on traveling as much as, or even more than before.

   (2) emission, globe, governments, travel, oil

3) People are exposed to different travel _____ as they have different _____ , _____ and _____ . Travellers affect the local people of the place they are visiting and are affected by the local _____ , gastronomy, manners and can even learn the local _____ .

   (3) experiences, language, aspirations, culture, expectations, needs

4) Most of people are likely to travel _____ class. They travel for various reasons and on different _____ : to visit their family, for _____ , on vacation, for business purposes, during national _____ and _____ .

As _____ is usually tight for this group of travelers, they will usually book in advance to get the lowest air fares.

(4) dates, economy, leisure, money, holidays, festivals

5) With this amount of people _____ , airport _____ must focus on _____ .

(5) administration, security, circulating

Finally, if the contextual trends are analyzed, global travel will continue for the next decade no matter of what happens, driven by any of these forces: social, cultural, political or economic.

PARIS   MOSCOW   LONDON   ROME

Danussa/Shutterstock

→ Exercise 1

Listen to the text and complete the paragraphs with the missing words. The words are not in the correct order.

Exercise 2

Write sentences or a paragraph with the words taken from the text above. The words don't have to be necessarily in the same order.

Example:
(5) administration, security, circulating

The <u>administration</u> of this airport has given little importance to <u>security</u>, if we consider the number of people <u>circulating</u> here.

 Exercise 3

What are the factors that could affect the air travel industry?

 Exercise 4

How can the travel experience affect a person?

 Challenge

Look at the chart with the countries, nationalities, capitals and currencies in Appendix 1. Choose one of them. Your colleague must guess from where you are.

Example:
In my country the currency is the rupee. Where am I from?

(But there are many countries in which the currency is the rupee).

My country name is a 5-letter word, starting with the letter N. It ends with the letter L.

Where do I come from?

Answer: Nepal

UNIT 24

Consolidation

FOR TEACHERS' USE
+ Air traffic phraseology
+ If clauses
+ Formal and informal communication

GOALS
By the end of Unit 24, students must be able to:
+ Practice a little bit of air traffic phraseology

This incident happened in real life, on May 7th 2010. As we can't use the airlines names or brands, we are using fictitious names: Appalachian Airlines (AP), Blue Skies (BS) and Space Airlines (SP).

The situation

A B767-200 from Appalachian Airlines is operating Flight AP 245 (Alpha Papa two fower five). (Remember that in aviation we say "fower" instead of "four"). There is a significant crosswind component on 22L (twenty-two Lima). The wind reported 320 (three two zero) at 23 knots, with gusts up to 35 knots, coupled with low fuel.

Also, runways 22L (twenty-two Lima) and 22R (twenty-two Romeo) were in use instead of 31R (thirty-one Romeo) and 31L (thirty-one Lima) because the latter was closed for maintenance. The Tower had to authorize flight AP 245 to land on 31R due to low fuel instead of 22L. But besides Appalachian Airlines (Flight AP 245), there was intense air traffic as Blue Skies (BS 62) and Space Airlines (SP 12) had required authorization to land

too. All the three aircraft had to receive new instructions from the Tower, as they could collide anytime. Note that, at the beginning of the communication, AP 245 had alerted that the Tower's localizer wasn't on, as AP 245 could detect another aircraft coming to them in the same direction.

Listen to the recording.

→ **Warm-up and Pre-Listening**

Ask students if they can describe an incident in air transportation. They must read the item *The situation* before starting to listen to the recording.

CONSOLIDATION ← UNIT 24

 Listening: Appalachian Airlines and Tower

Tower (TWR): Appalachian 245 heavy, 22L, you're cleared to land.

Appalachian 245 (AP 245): Cleared to land, 22L. Your localizer is not on.

TWR: Ok. I will double check it.

TWR: AP 245 heavy, I've just reset it, it should be coming back up in a little while.

TWR: Wind now 320 at 23 knots, gusting to 35 knots.

AP 245: We can't land on 22. We're breaking off the approach due to low fuel and if you don't give us runway 31R, we're gonna declare an emergency.

TWR: Alright! I'll pass it along. Fly runway heading for now.

AP 245: Ok. We're declaring emergency. We're gonna land on 31R. We're going to the left and then we're coming around.

TWR: AP245 heavy just fly runway heading. Ok, you're saying you're declaring an emergency AT THIS POINT?

AP 245: Three times I've told you that. THREE TIMES we've declared an emergency.

TWR: Ok, I just wanted to verify it and now you tell me that if you didn't get 31R you would have to declare an emergency. Ok, I understand: fly runway heading and I gotta get you a turn.

TWR: Blue Skies 62, go left on A and monitor ground to the ramp.

Blue Skies 62 (BS62): Left on A, monitor ground, Blue Skies 62.

AP245: Holding short, Appalachian 245.

TWR: Fly heading 180 (one eight zero).

AP245: AP 245 heavy, we're turning around to left here and landing at 31. Remove everybody from our way, we're declared an emergency. We're on a visual.

TWR: All right, AP 245 heavy, 31R cleared to land. Wind 320 at 23 knots, gusting 35 knots.

AP245: Thank you. Cleared to land on runway 31R, Appalachian 245 heavy.

TWR: Space 12, maintain 2,000 feet, cancel approach clearance.

SP12: Maintain 2000, cancel approach clearance, Space 12.

TWR: Space 12, just fly runway heading, maintain 2,000 (two thousand).

SP12: Maintain runway heading, sir, Space 12.

TWR: Appalachian 245 hold position.

AP 376: Appalachian 245 holding position.

TWR: Appalachian 245, are you passed the hold bars?

AP 376: Yes, we are, Appalachian 245.

TWR: All right, AP 245, I need you to move. I've got traffic inbound, so make the left turn, I said LEFT TURN, no delay, on runway 31R.

AP 245: Ok. Left turn on 31R, Appalachian 245.

TWR: Space 12, you can turn left heading 180 (one eight zero), maintain 3,000 feet.

TWR: Appalachian 245 heavy, left K, right B, ground is .65 (point sixty-five).

AP 245: Ok. We're turning left here, and you want us to go left K, right on B, AP 245 heavy.

TWR: Right on B, ground is .65.

AP 245: .65 (point sixty-five) for ground, right on B, Appalachian 245 heavy.

Time to Practice 1

Informal versus formal

Informal: We're gonna declare an emergency.
Formal: We're going to declare an emergency.

The same happens with wanna:

Informal: We're wanna declare an emergency.
Formal: We want to declare an emergency.
Mistake: Spelling mistake. Though 'alright' is being accepted lately in daily informal writing, the correct spelling would be 'all right'.
Informal: I gotta get you a turn.
Formal: I got to get you a turn.
Informal: 'cause
Formal: because
Ok = okay

1) Informal: I wanna talk to you.
   Formal: _____

2) Informal: She wanna talk to us.
   Formal: _____

3) Informal: We're gonna travel soon.
   Formal: _____

4) Informal: He's gonna wait for us.
   Formal: _____

5) Informal: They wanna travel on the holiday.
   Formal: _____

6) Informal: I gotta get you a coat, 'cause it's cold.
   Formal: _____

7) Informal: I gotta get you an umbrella, 'cause it's raining.
   Formal:
   _____

 Time to Practice 2

1) You're cleared to land./ to take off
2) I will double check it./check it again
3) I've told you three times./ten times/five times
4) We're turning left/right.
5) We can't land on 22L/on 31L.
6) I just wanted to verify it./double check it.

 Exercise 1

Transform the sentences:
Example:
I've just reset it. (= I have just reset it)
(ten minutes ago) → I reset it ten minutes ago.
to reset – reset – reset

1) We've just called him. (2 days ago)
   to call – called – called

2) They've just seen Jane with her boyfriend. (yesterday)
   to see – saw – seen

3) We've just given way to a B747 passing on our right. (5 minutes ago)
   to give – gave – given

4) They've already reported a flat tire. (15 minutes ago)
   to report – reported – reported

5) The pilot has already declared emergency twice. (3 minutes ago)
   to declare – declared – declared

CONSOLIDATION ← UNIT 24

 Exercise 2

Example 1:
And now you tell me that if you didn't get 31R, you would have to declare an emergency.

If you don't get 31R, you will have to declare an emergency.

Example 2:
If it/to rain (present), we won't go with you.
If it rains, we won't go with you.

If it/to rain (present/negative), we'll stay home.
If it doesn't rain, we'll stay home.

1) If you/to study (simple past) more/would be a better student.
2) If you/to get (simple past/negative) your umbrella/would be soaked now.
3) You wouldn't be soaked now/if you/to get (simple past) your umbrella.
4) If the tower/to answer (simple present negative) our request/we will have to declare emergency.
5) If the ATCO/to speak (simple present) louder/we will hear him.
6) If the ATCO/to speak (simple past) slower/ we would understand him.

 Exercise 3

a) Analyzing this recording, how many aircraft were in contact with the same ATCO (air traffic controller) at that time?

b) List some of the verbs from the recording. Now ask your teacher about the past and the past participle of the verbs.

to land
to p _ _ s
to f _ y
to d_ c _ _ _e
to s_ y
to te _ l
to t_ rn
to ca_c_l
to h _ld
to re_o_e
to ma_nt_ _n
to v_r_fy

 Exercise 4

Choose the best alternative to answer the following question:

Why was the pilot of Appalachian 245 requesting immediate clearance for 31R?

a) The pilot was having a bad day and wanted to remove everyone from his way.
b) Appalachian 245 was too close and had to hold position.
c) Blue Skies 62 was just in front of AP 245 and runway heading.
d) There was a traffic inbound.
e) Because of the significant crosswind component on 22L and due to low fuel.

UNIT 25

In-flight services

FOR TEACHERS' USE	GOALS
✦ Superlative ✦ Comparative	By the end of Unit 25, students must be able to: ✦ Offer in-flight services to passengers

 Warm-up and Pre-Reading

Ask students if they can remember anything about the in-flight services from their trips. It can be a positive or a negative comment. Divide the class in six groups (if possible) and each of them will read a paragraph silently. Then, there will be a rotation of groups until everybody reads the whole text. Every time there is a rotation, the readers must take notes of some words they can remember.

 Reading: In-flight services

Passengers are more and more demanding about services. As passengers become more independent, they compare prices and the quality of the services offered. Depending on the passengers needs or, better, depending on their budget to travel, their expectations can be higher or lower.

Most of the airlines offer the same range of in-flight services when we talk about entertainment: music (classical, jazz, rock, international pop etc), movies (blockbusters or not), TV shows and games. What might change in this case is if you're going to have a wider screen in front of you or personal entertainment screens for every seat. Booking in different classes, you get different levels of servicing.

I could find only one carrier in which one person booked in Economy class can have fun watching a movie or playing a game in real large seatback screens. The same carrier offered up to 1,400 channels for passengers' entertainment available in every seat, no matter the cabin in which they were accommodated. Also, mainscreen movie programs change depending if you are flying eastbound, westbound, northbound or southbound, that is, it will also depend on your destination.

One American carrier, for some domestic flights, offer passengers traveling in Business or First class – on selected flights only – what they call their own entertainment system: a tablet, besides the rest of entertainment options. Not to mention the technology

IN-FLIGHT SERVICES ← UNIT 25

achievements in communication when the aircraft is *en route*, offered by another carrier on most aircraft: satellite phones, the possibility of sending e-mails and SMS in every seat due to AeroMobile services.

When we consider legroom and comfortable seating, we have to think about cabin features and configuration, as well as about the fare price we're paying. Don't expect flat-bed seats with direct aisle access, individual lightening, power outlet and USB port, in-flight Wi-fi Internet, built-in mini-bar in your seat or a private suite if you're not traveling Business or First Class. The same with the on-board food served. Food is served, in general, only to passengers in flights which are longer than four hours. So, for short and medium haul flights, you will receive no more than a package of dry roasted peanuts or a cold, paid sandwich for the cheapest fare you could find on Internet.

Some domestic flights don't offer food services or passengers can't choose special meals such as muslim, kosher, vegetarian, veagan meals or meal for diabetics, if they have any dietary restrictions. Be ready to be offered paid food in some flights and take exact change with you. That's why smart travelers buy their food at the airport or bring their own on the plane, when it's allowed.

 Time to Practice 1

1) Passengers are more and more demanding about services.
2) As passengers become more independent, they compare prices and the quality of the services offered.
3) Most of the airlines offer the same range of in-flight services when we talk about entertainment.
4) Booking in different classes, you get different levels of servicing.

 Time to Practice 2

Compare:

Passengers are more and more **demanding** (adjective) about services.

People are **demanding** (verb) more quality in services.

When we consider legroom and comfortable **seating** (noun), we have to think about the fare price we're paying.

They are **seating** (verb) in comfortable seats in the Business cabin.

The localizer needs to be **reset** (verb).

The localizer needs a **reset** (noun).

→ **Exercise 1**

Associate words or expressions from the text with the categories below. Try not to back to the text.

Example:
Entertainment: movies, wider screen
Cabin: _____

Food: _____
Travel: _____
Technology: _____

Exercise 2

What did you understand about the different cabins (First Class, Business Class, and Economy Class)?

Examples:

Passengers are more independent now than they were in the past, because they compare prices and the quality of the services offered.

The best thing about traveling in the First Class is _____ .

VIP passengers are more demanding than other passengers.

If you are taller than the average people ____ _____ .

If a person is shorter than the average people _____ .

Traveling in _____ Class is more comfortable than in _____ Class.

The worst thing about traveling in Economy Class is _____ .

Entertainment in Economy Class is less interesting than in _____ Class, because _____ .

As John was the tallest passenger on that flight, he asked for an aisle seat.

Exercise 3

Comment about the food services mentioned in the text and compare the situation with one of your real experiences.

Example:

It was the tastiest food I've ever eaten on board.

Food in Airline 1 is better than in Airline 2.

Food in Airline 2 is worse than in Airline 1.

Food in Airline 3 is the best of all.

Food in Airline 4 is the worst of all.

Exercise 4

You are the marketing manager of an airline. Write a paragraph promoting the in-flight services that the airline offers.

UNIT 26

VIP passengers

FOR TEACHERS' USE	GOALS
✦ Colors ✦ Clothing	By the end of Unit 26, students must be able to: ✦ Describe suspect people

  Warm-up and Listening

Ask your students if they have already seen any celebrity or someone suspect at the airport.

  Listening: The suspect

The Stuarts are going to travel to Dubai. They are VIP passengers, as Mr. Richard Stuart is one of the wealthiest men in his country and he'll be the major speaker at an event that will be held in Dubai. His wife, Mrs. Alice Stuart always accompanies him, even on his business trips. They are traveling with Mr. Laurent Dupré and his wife Sylvie Dupré. Every time the Stuarts' travel, they need to be closely observed by their own body guards at the airport before departure. Their trips take a lot of preparation.
Now the two couples are at the VIP lounge. Listen:

Alice Stuart: Sylvie, don't you think that the man we saw outside was strange?

Sylvie Dupré: Which one?

Alice Stuart: The one in handcuffs and sided by two other men.

Richard Stuart: He's probably a deportee.

Alice Stuart: I feel so insecure with that man circulating at the airport.

Laurent Dupré: I heard this morning on TV that an international drug dealer had been identified, but as he can't be judged by his crimes in this country, he'll be deported.

Richard Stuart: Don't worry, my dear, our body guards are outside.

Sylvie Dupré: I saw the deportee on TV this morning, but he seemed shorter to me.

Alice Stuart: He seems to be taller and stronger to me. I wonder why the two men who were taking him away weren't dressed like federal agents.

Richard Stuart: They have to wear like that not to scare everybody who will be on the same flight as the deportee.

Sylvie Dupré: He seems to be more dangerous now to me.

Laurent Dupré: Don't worry, he'll be on another flight.

Alice Stuart: I guess I could memorize what clothes they were wearing…

Sylvie Dupré: Me too…

Alice Stuart: The deportee was wearing a blue cap, a black jacket, denim pants, a green T-shirt and brown shoes.

Sylvie Dupré: The man on his right side looked like one of your body guards, but he had blond hair and was wearing sunglasses. He was wearing a white shirt, gray pants and black shoes.

Alice Stuart: The other man on his left was the shortest among the three of them and was wearing sunglasses too. He had a blue shirt on, black pants and shoes. And I've seen some police officers with sniff dogs nearby.

Laurent Dupré: You two stop with this paranoia. We're safe.

Richard Stuart: Laurent is right. You two will have a lot of fun and go shopping in Dubai while Laurent and I will be at the event. We still have to arrange the last details of the event during the flight and I need to get ready for my speech. Come on, relax and let's have an agreeable trip.

Alice Stuart: Sylvie, one of my best friends, Sophie, has already been to Dubai. She said this airline has offered her real premium services. The food was prepared by a famous chef and the wines were paired with the dishes by a well-known sommelier.

Sylvie Dupré: I can't wait to board! Dubai, here we go!

Alice Stuart: And we'll have a limousine waiting for us with champagne, of course!

Sylvie Dupré: I'm sure we'll enjoy the best of Dubai.

Time to Practice 1

1) Laurent is right. (wrong/tall/short)
2) We're safe. (don't feel/are feeling/can't be)
3) Sophie has already been to Dubai. (Shangai/ Hong Kong/the Seychelles Islands)
4) I can't wait to board! (to be at our destination/to arrive at our destination)
5) I'm sure we'll enjoy the best of Dubai. (Paris/Frankfurt/Munich/Rome/Barcelona/Hong Kong)

Now practice with a colleague:

I would feel **safer** if…

People would feel **more comfortable** if they traveled in…

People usually feel **safer** when…

Everybody feels **more insecure** when…

Most of the passengers look for **the cheapest** fares because…

Traveling to (Dubai) is **more expensive than** traveling to…

VIP PASSENGERS ← UNIT 26

 Time to Practice 2

	DARK	LIGHT
BLUE	DARK BLUE	LIGHT BLUE
GREEN	DARK GREEN	LIGHT GREEN

Clothing	Accessories	Shoes
T-shirt	belt	boots
shirt	tie	ankle boots
polo shirt	necklace	sandals
dress	earrings	shoes
blazer	bracelete	trainers
blouse	wrist watch	sneakers
suit	cap	high-heeled shoes
pants	hat	
trousers	beret	
trench-coat		
waist coat		
skirt		
mini-skirt		
shorts		
gloves		
scarf		
vest		

YELLOW
WHITE
BLACK
RED
GREY or GRAY
PINK
BROWN
PURPLE

Clothes and colors

First, practice the colors by matching them to the clothes.

Examples:

blue shirt *red scarf*
brown boots *dark green T-shirt*

Then, describe your colleague's clothes.

Example:

She's wearing…

He's wearing…

GENERAL ENGLISH → FOR AVIATION

 Now suppose that you've seen a suspect person at the airport. A police officer will interview you. Play the roles with a colleague.

Example 1:
What exactly did you see?

Can you describe the scene and the person (or the people)?

How did he/she look like? How did they look like?

What was he/she wearing? What were they wearing?

Example 2:
I saw a woman who was acting strangely. She looked to be impatient. When a man approached her, she gave him a small package. She was taller than you and had black eyes. Her skin was white. She was wearing a brown coat.

Example 3:
I saw two short men. The first one was well-dressed, but the second man was ill-dressed. One of them was wearing…

 ## Exercise 1

Unscramble the words:

| rreinags | otosb | tsanp | irtsk |
| acencekl | ctaorina | T-tirsh | ressd |

 ## Exercise 2

Let's talk about feelings or moods.

How do you feel today?

Now talk about your colleagues' feelings and moods.

He seems to be…
She seems to be…
They seem to be…

VIP PASSENGERS ← UNIT 26

happy – sad – angry – surprised – sleepy – thoughtful – healthy – sick – hungry– thirsty – ashamed – scared – bored – snobbish – discreet – nervous – anxious – patient – impatient – polite – impolite – irritated – calm – annoyed – tired – cheerful – funny – bad – mannered – introverted – extroverted

Describe physical characteristics:

short – tall – fat – obese – slim – thin – brown-haired – dark-haired – blond – brunette.

He had a beard/a moustache.
She wore glasses.

 ## Exercise 3

Why were Alice and Sylvie afraid? What is usually the behavior of VIP passengers?

 ## Exercise 4

If you had seen the scene with the deportee sided by the two federal agents, how would you feel? Discuss with your colleagues.

Unit 27

Consolidation

FOR TEACHERS' USE	GOALS
✦ Vocabulary on diseases	By the end of Unit 27, students must be able to: ✦ Report a medical emergency occurred on board ✦ Report a passenger's health problem

➡ Warm-up and Pre-Listening

Ask students if they can name some diseases.

Listening: Health problems

Appalachian Airlines is operating flight 277 to Paris. Passengers have already boarded and are all accommodated in their seats.

Voice in the loudspeakers: Good evening, ladies and gentlemen! I'm Maria Gonzalez, the chief attendant on this flight. On behalf of Captain Schneider and his crew, I wish to welcome you aboard Appalachian Airlines operating flight 277 with destination to Paris. Now please observe the "Non Smoking" sign and fasten your seat belts. We remind you that by law force, it's prohibited to smoke during all this flight, even in the lavatories. Thank you for your comprehension. (*Speech 1*)

CONSOLIDATION ← UNIT 27

Some minutes after…

Flight attendant: Before takeoff, the cabin crew will show the aircraft's safety features. Besides this, all passengers can find the Emergency Instruction Card in the backrest pocket of each seat. Each and every passenger must make sure to fasten the seat belt every time the sign is on. It is mandatory to have the seat belts fasten during takeoff and landing. The passengers must remain seated as aircraft moves towards the runway, or upon landing, until the aircraft parks at the parking area or terminal. (*Speech 2*)

After the pilot has got clearance to takeoff and the aircraft was taxing…

Flight attendant: Due to the sensitivity of the navigation instruments, we kindly request all

passengers to refrain using any electronic equipment during the takeoff, such as tablets and mobile phones even in airplane mode, until the aircraft reaches cruising altitude. For those passengers who wish to make phone calls during this flight, they will be offered a satellite phone. Payment will be accepted only with credit cards. Thank you. (*Speech 3*)

The estimate flight time is twelve hours as it is a long haul flight, but in the Business Class, between 7 and 8 hours after takeoff, a passenger complains about health problems.

Flight attendant: Yes, sir. Can I help you?

Passenger: My name's Juan Sarmiento and I'm a businessman. I'm not feeling very well… I have been having some health problems lately. So, I have many symptoms at the same time. Maybe with the altitude, my case is getting worse and worse.

Flight attendant: Do you feel any specific pain?

Passenger: That's the problem. I've been diagnosed with kidney stones recently. But I usually suffer with migraine and stomachache too.

Flight attendant: I see… But, what can I do for you to make you feel more comfortable during this flight, sir? I can see that you look pale.

Passenger: I've already taken the prescribed drugs, but they can't make me feel better. Here I have all my doctor's prescriptions.

Flight attendant: Let's wait for some time, until the medicine you've just taken can have its effect in your body. Any other problem, please don't hesitate to call me. My name's Alexandra Carter.

Passenger: Thank you, for now. I'll try to read and get some sleep to relax.

But after one hour and a half, Mr. Juan Sarmiento's pain started getting worse and worse.

Alexandra Carter: For what I can see, sir, you don't feel any better.

Passenger: The last time I had renal colic some weeks ago, the pain was so strong that the doctor had to give me morphine.

Alexandra Carter: I'll talk to Captain Schneider and I'll ask him authorization to give you a shot with one of the sedatives that we have onboard just for pain management.

Passenger: Okay. Thank you.

After fifteen minutes, Mr. Juan Sarmiento was given an injection with sedative, but he still didn't get any better. The poor gentleman cried loudly as he couldn't stand the pain anymore. So, the captain decided to ask for clearance to land to the Tower in Lisbon, the nearest city. He asked for medical assistance and an ambulance at the arrival.

Captain: Ladies and gentlemen, here is Captain Schneider speaking. We have a passenger with a very serious disease here and we don't seem to have all the means to treat him onboard. Then, I apologize but we must have a stopover in Lisbon. The flight will proceed to its destination, Paris, after we have this medical emergency solved. Thank you for your cooperation. (*Speech 4*)

GENERAL ENGLISH → FOR AVIATION

 Time to Practice 1

Divide the class in four groups. Choose a narrator among the students at random and two other people to roleplay Mr. Juan Sarmiento and the flight Attendant, Miss Alexandra Carter.

The narrator will start by saying:

Appalachian Airlines is operating flight 277 to Paris. Passengers have already boarded and are all accommodated in their seats.

Then the first group will read *Speech 1* in unison, and so on.

Roleplay the whole recording, paying close attention to the vocabulary, pronunciation and entonation.

 Time to Practice 2

1) The lady is having hemorrhage. (an abortion/is delivering a baby)
2) The young man has tonsillitis.
3) The baby has a fever.
4) My heart is beating faster and faster.
5) I can't breathe well.
6) I'm short of breath.
7) The passenger has undergone a coronary bypass surgery.
8) The passenger is on drugs and behaving strangely.
9) The passenger is drunk and behaving aggressively.

DRILL EXERCISE 1

1) The passenger has got angina.
2) The lady has got asth ma. (bronchitis/pneumonia)
3) The baby seems to be suffocating.
4) He's got a coronary disease.
5) She's got a stomachache. (headache/back pain/chest pain)
6) The baby's got an earache. (a belly pain)
7) The child's got diarrhea. (a sore throat)
8) The gentleman is having seizures.
9) I have labyrinthitis.

DRILL EXERCISE 2

What medicines/drugs do we have onboard for each disease? Match column 1 to column 2:

Column 1	Column 2
1) Fever	a) aspirins
2) heartburn	b) antidiarrheals
3) headache	c) painkillers
4) diarrhea	d) antihistamines
5) migraine	e) antiacids

We have _____ onboard for _____ .

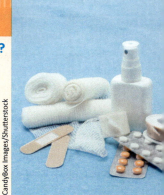

UNIT 28

Baggage claim service

FOR TEACHERS' USE
+ Past Perfect

GOALS
By the end of Unit 28, students must be able to:
+ Know what to do in case of delayed, lost or damaged baggage

 Warm-up and Pre-Listening

Ask students what they would do if they had their baggage delayed, lost or damaged.

TRACK 26

 Listening: Baggage claim procedures

The Taylors and the Parks are back from China, but John and Sarah Park's baggage is delayed. Sarah is calling the airlines Baggage Claim Service. Listen:

Claire: Appalachian Airlines, Baggage Claim Service, good afternoon. Claire speaking.

Sarah Parks: Good afternoon, Claire. My husband and I have just arrived from China, but one of our pieces of baggage didn't come off the conveyor belt.

Claire: Did you communicate that there was a missing piece of baggage to one of our airport agents before leaving the airport?

Sarah: Yes, we did. After we didn't see our piece of baggage on the airlines carousel, we immediately went to the Baggage Claim Area. As my broken leg is still in plaster and I was on a wheelchair, my husband arrived first at the Baggage Claim Area and had already talked to one of the airport agents when I got there.

Claire: I see…

Sarah: My husband had not only talked to the airport agents, but had also shown him the baggage tag.

Claire: Just a few more questions, madame. Did you get a file reference number with our airport agent?

Sarah: Exactly. His name was Paul Williams and he told us that as the first piece of baggage had arrived, probably, the other was only delayed.

Claire: Good! Are you online?

Sarah: No, not yet. Just a moment, please, while I connect to Internet.

Claire: Sure.

Sarah: Okay, now I'm online.

Claire: So, now please access Appalachian Airlines website and click on the link 'Baggage Claim'.

Sarah: Done.

Claire: Then, complete the form with the reference number. Your file reference number is the 8 or 10-digit alphanumeric code located on the front of baggage information folder given to you by Paul Williams when you first reported your baggage delay.

Sarah: Mine is a 10-digit alphanumeric code.

Claire: Now, after the insertion of this code, a report will be filed and we will investigate why your baggage did not arrive. I kindly ask you to provide an accurate description of your baggage and of its content, when you fill out the form. After you fill out the form, you'll be able to verify the progress of your baggage tracking using the same code on our website.

Sarah: But how will the airline be tracking my baggage?

Claire: We search for your baggage using a computerized tracking system. Once your bag has been located and sent to us, we will contact you as soon as possible and, then, arrange delivery. So, don't forget to fill in the form with your address (including the zip code and mailbox) and telephone number. Please fill in the form with your mobile number too.

Sarah: And what will I have to do after this?

Claire: Please print the filled form and retain your e-ticket documents and your baggage receipts, including the baggage tag. If your baggage isn't located within 12 hours, you'll receive a US$ 25-dollar rebate as a previous compensation. Most delayed baggage is located and returned to passengers within 48 hours.

Sarah: Thank you for your explanations.

Claire: You're welcome.

After 48 hours, the Parks received their baggage, but it was damaged. Sarah Park called the Appalachian Airlines again.

Austin: Appalachian Airlines, Baggage Claim Service, good morning. Austin speaking.

Sarah: Good morning, Austin. I'm calling Appalachian Airlines to express my disappointment at the baggage handling.

Austin: What's your full name ma'am?

Sarah: Here is Mrs. Sarah Park speaking.

BAGGAGE CLAIM SERVICE ← UNIT 28

Austin: On behalf of Appalachian Airlines, I would like to apologize for this inconvenient. You probably received your delayed or missing baggage at home and it had been damaged.

Sarah: Exactly, Austin.

Austin: We have a procedure ma'am to repair your damaged baggage. You'll have to fill out a form on our website using the same code of the baggage tracking and mention what kind of damage you have verified after receiving it. Then, the damages will be evaluated by the baggage service personnel. Please attach pictures to the form. Not all damage will be eligible for repair. Appalachian Airlines won't consider a damaged baggage in case of broken wheels or feet or minor cuts and scratches.

Sarah: Thank you! I'll think of what I'm going to do. As the damage is near the wheels and feet, I guess the repair won't be possible. So, I'll write a complaint letter to be compensated with a new piece of baggage.

Austin: As you wish, ma'am. Have a nice day! Goodbye.

Sarah: Bye.

 Time to Practice 1

Read and memorize.

1) My husband and I have just arrived from China.
2) One of our pieces of baggage didn't come off the conveyor belt.
3) Communicate the missing baggage to the airlines representative before leaving the airport.
4) My husband had already printed the claim tag when I saw him./got to him.
5) My husband had already got home when I arrived.
6) I had already bought gifts and souvenirs at the duty-free shop when my husband reached me.

 Time to Practice 2

Read and memorize.

1) Mr. John Park had already talked to the airport agent when Mrs. Park arrived.
2) Did you get a file reference number with our airport agent?
3) You'll need a file reference number to start the baggage claim process.
4) Your file reference number is the 8 or 10-digit alphanumeric code located on the front of baggage information folder.
5) Not all damage will be eligible for repair.

 Exercise 1

Unscramble the words to form sentences:

1) filled Please print the and e-ticket retain your form documents and receipts baggage your.
2) carousel the Baggage didn't After Claim we immediately see our piece Area of on the airlines, we went to baggage.
3) file Did reference you get a airport agent number with our?
4) Appalachian link So, click website now please access Airlines and on the 'Baggage Claim'.

GENERAL ENGLISH → FOR AVIATION

Exercise 2

Which word is out of each category?

1) pink, red, blue, print, yellow, gray
2) coat, dress, raincoat, filled, necklace, boots
3) baby, lady, form, child, gentleman, family

Now form a sentence with the words that were out of each category.

_____ the _____ _____ .

Exercise 3

Complete the sentences with the correct word, according to the recording:

1) Your file reference number is the 8 or 10-digit _____ code (alphanumeric – password – log-in).
2) But how will the airline be _____ my baggage? (looking for – tracking – observing).
3) Retain your e-ticket documents and your baggage _____ , including the claim tag your husband had printed. (badge – documents – receipts)

Exercise 4

1) How will the airline be tracking Mrs. Park baggage?
2) What will happen if the baggage isn't located within 12 hours?
3) What is the procedure to repair damaged baggage?

Roleplay

Roleplay the two situations with your colleagues. Try to memorize some sentences instead of reading them.

UNIT 29

Consolidation

FOR TEACHERS' USE
+ This Unit wil prepare students to talk about incidents between aircraft and birds

GOALS
By the end of Unit 29, students must be able to:
+ Understand the danger of birds around aircraft and in the airport area

 Reading: Preventive measures to avoid bird strike

Instructions:

1) First, read these introductory paragraphs. Then, take a look at the real data compiled by the Bird Strike Committee USA. Choose one of the cases to talk about to your colleague. Pretend that you're both at an ICAO exam, as one of you will be the interviewer and the other the interviewee. After finishing the activity, change roles.

2) What preventive actions could be taken to avoid bird strike? Give examples. Pretend again that you and your colleague are at an ICAO exam, and one of you will be the interviewer and the other the interviewee. After finishing the activity, change roles.

A bird strike, sometimes called bird hit, or BASH (for Bird Aircraft Strike Hazard) is quite common in aviation. (Note that the term avian ingestion is used only if there is ingestion of the bird into an engine). Though the majority of bird strikes (65%) cause little damage to the aircraft, repairs are generally costly to airlines worldwide.

As the airport administrators can't eliminate at once all the birds in a flock, in a V-formation or at rotation, in order to reduce birdstrikes on takeoff and landing, airports prepare strategies and create procedures to bird management. This might include also working with specialized institutes to identify the species (such as hawks, eagles, flocks of starlings, Canadian geese, gulls, geese in V-formation, crows, vultures, mourning doves, horned larks, double-crusted cormorants, lesser scaup, among others) and study their adaptability to the habitat surrounding the airport area, as some control methods have proven not to remain effective for a long time.

The main strategy to reduce the presence of birds is changing the habitat near the airport, by removing vegetation which produces seeds to avoid bird species in general and grasses which are so attractive to geese, for instance. As flocking birds seek roosts at night, trees should be removed and tall structures, if possible, should be modified to discourage birds to use them.

Some airports have bird control vehicles equipped with sounds, lights, laser to try to scare the birds away. The use of dogs, pyrotechinics, radio-controlled airplanes and trained falcons are not uncommon as well.

The following registers were compiled by the Bird Strike Committee USA.

7th February 2000. An American-owned cargo company's DC-10-30 departing Subic Bay, Philippines ingested a fruit bat into 1 engine at 250 feet AGL. Aircraft returned to airport. Five damaged fan blades had to be replaced. Time out of service was 3 days. Total repair and related costs exceeded $ 3 million.

21th January 2001. The #3 engine on an MD-11 departing Portland International Airport (OR) ingested a herring gull during take-off run. The bird ingestion resulted in a fractured fan blade. Damage from the fan blade fracture resulted in the liberation of the forward section of the inlet cowl. Portions of the inlet cowl were ingested back into the engine and shredded. The pilot aborted takeoff during which two tires failed. The 217 passengers were safely deplaned and rerouted to other flights. Bird ID by Smithsonian, Division of Birds.

9th March 2002. A Canadair RJ 200 at Dulles International Airport (VA) struck 2 wild turkeys during the takeoff roll. One shattered the windshield spraying the cockpit with glass fragments and remains. Another hit the fuselage and was ingested. There was a 14- by 4-inch section of fuselage skin damaged below the windshield seal on the flight officer's side. Cost of repairs estimated at $ 200,000. Time out of service was at least 2 weeks.

19th October 2002. A Boeing 767 departing Logan International Airport (MA) encountered a flock of over 20 double-crested cormorants. At least 1 cormorant was ingested into #2 engine. There were immediate indications of engine surging followed by compression stall and smoke from engine. The engine was shutdown. Overweight landing with 1 engine was made without incident. Nose cowl was dented and punctured. There was significant fan blade damage with abnormal engine vibration. One fan blade was found on the runway. Aircraft was towed to the ramp. Hydraulic lines were leaking and several bolts were sheared off inside engine. Many pieces fell out when the cowling was opened. Aircraft was out of service for 3 days. Cost of repairs was $ 1.7 million.

CONSOLIDATION ← UNIT 29

8th January 2003. A Bombardier de Havilland Dash 8 collided with a flock of lesser scaup at 1,300 feet AGL on approach to Rogue Valley International Airport (OR). At least 1 bird penetrated the cabin and hit the pilot who turned control over to the first officer for landing. Emergency power switched on when the birds penetrated the radome and damaged the DC power system and instruments systems. The pilot was treated for cuts and released from the hospital.

4th September 2003. A Fokker 100 struck a flock of at least 5 Canada geese over runway shortly after takeoff at LaGuardia Airport (NY), ingesting 1 or 2 geese into #2 engine. Engine vibration occurred. Pilot was unable to shut engine down with the fuel cutoff lever so fire handle was pulled and engine finally shut down, but vibration continued. The flight was diverted to nearby JFK International Airport where a landing was made.
The NTSB found a 20- by 36-inch wide depression on right side of nose behind radome. Maximum depth was 4 inches. Impact marks on right wing. A fan blade separated from the disk and penetrated the fuselage. Several fan blades were deformed. Holes were found in the engine cowling. Remains were recovered and identified by Wildlife Services.

17th February 2004. A Boeing 757 during takeoff run from Portland International Airport (OR) hit 5 mallards and returned with 1 engine out. At least 1 bird was ingested and parts of 5 birds were collected from the runway. Engine damage was not repairable and engine had to be replaced. Cost was $ 2.5 million and time out of service was 3 days.

15th April 2004. An Airbus 319 climbing out of Portland International Airport (OR) ingested a great blue heron into the #2 engine, causing extensive damage. Pilot shut the engine down as a precaution and made an emergency landing. Runway was closed 38 minutes for cleaning. Flight was cancelled. Engine and nose cowl were replaced.

Time out of service was 72 hours. Damage totaled $ 388,000.

14th June 2004. A Boeing 737 struck a great horned owl during a nighttime landing roll at Greater Pittsburgh International Airport (PA). The bird severed a cable in front main gear. The steering failed, the aircraft ran off the runway and became stuck in mud. Passengers were bused to the terminal. They replaced 2 nose wheels, 2 main wheels and brakes. Aircraft out of service was 24 hours. Cost estimated at $ 20,000.

16th September 2004. A MD 80 departing Chicago O'Hare (IL) hit several double-crested cormorants at 3,000 feet AGL and 4 miles from airport. The #1 engine caught fire and failed, sending metal debris to the ground in a Chicago neighborhood. The aircraft made an emergency landing back at O'Hare with no injuries to the 107 passengers.

24th October 2004. A Boeing 767 departing Chicago O'Hare (IL) hit a flock of birds during takeoff run. A compressor stall caused the engine to flame out. A fire department got calls from local residents who reported seeing flames coming from the plane. Pilot dumped approximately 11,000 gallons of fuel over Lake Michigan before returning to land. Feathers found in engine were sent to the Smithsonian, Division of Birds for identification.

30th March 2005. A SA 227, landing at Dade-Collier Training and Transportation Airport (FL), hit the last deer in a group of 8 crossing the runway, causing a prop to detach and puncture the fuselage. Also damaged was the nose wheel steering and right engine nacelle. Aircraft was a write-off due to cost of repairs $ 580,000 being close to the plane's value of $ 650,000.

1st September 2005. A Falcon 20 departing Lorain County (OH) Airport hit a flock of mourning doves at rotation, causing the #1 engine to flame out. As the gear was retracted, the aircraft hit another flock which caused the #2 engine RPM to roll-back. The pilot was not able to sustain airspeed or altitude and crash-landed, sliding through a ditch and

GENERAL ENGLISH → FOR AVIATION

airport perimeter fence, crossing a highway and ending in a corn field. Aircraft sustained major structural damage beyond economical repairs. Both pilots were taken to hospital. Costs totaled $ 1.4 million.

16th October 2005. A BE-1900 departing Ogdensburg International (NY) struck a coyote during take-off run. The nose gear collapsed causing the plane to skid to a stop on the runway. Propeller blades went through the skin of the aircraft. Engine #1 and #2, propellers, landing gear, nose, fuselage had major damage. Insurance declared aircraft a total loss. Cost of repairs would have been $ 1.5 million.

30th December 2005. A Bell 206 helicopter Pilot flying a Bell 206 helicopter at 500 feet AGL near Washington, LA looked up from instruments to see a large vulture crashing into the windshield. He was temporarily blinded by blood and wind. After regaining control, the pilot tried to land in a bean field nearby but blood was hampering his vision and the left skid hit the ground first causing the aircraft to tip on its side. Pilot was taken to the hospital and had several surgeries to repair his face, teeth and eye. Aircraft was damaged beyond repair. Cost of repairs would have been $ 1.5 million.

1st January 2006. A B-757 ingested a great blue heron into an engine during take-off at Portland International (OR). Engine was shut down and a one-engine landing was made. Fan section of the engine was replaced. Time out of service was 15 hours. Cost was $ 244,000.

3rd August 2006. A Cessna Citation 560 departing a General Aviation airport in Indiana hit Canada geese on the take-off run. Left engine ingested birds causing an uncontained failure. Aircraft went off the runway during the aborted takeoff. Top cowling and fan were replaced. ID by the Smithsonian, Division of Birds. Aircraft was out of service for 13 days and costs were estimated at $ 750,000.

18th August 2006. A CL-RJ 200 departing Salt Lake City International Airport flew through a flock of northern pintails (ducks) at 500 feet AGL. Pilot saw 2 birds and felt them hit the engines. Engines began to vibrate. Aircraft landed without incident and was towed to the hanger. ID by the Smithsonian, Division of Birds. Time out of service was over 24 hours and costs to repair engines totaled $ 811,825.

8th December 2006. The Captain of a B-767 departing JFK International Airport saw 2 birds during initial climb. After bird was ingested into #2 engine, pilot returned aircraft to JFK on Alert 3-3. One badly damaged great blue heron was recovered from the runway. Carcass appeared to have gone through the #2 engine. The engine was replaced and passengers were put on a replacement aircraft.

15th March 2007. A B-767 departing Chicago O'Hare encountered a flock of birds at <500 feet AGL. People on ground reported flames shooting out of the #1 engine. The aircraft returned to land without incident and was towed to the terminal. Birds were ingested in both engines, but only 1 engine was damaged. Remains of nine male canvasback ducks were found near the departure end of runway 9R. ID by the Smithsonian, Division of Birds. Time out of service was 12 days. Estimated cost for repairs is $ 1.8 million. Cost for aircraft's time out of service was $ 309,000.

7th July 2007. A U.S. carrier B-767 flew through a large flock of yellow-legged gulls at 20 feet AGL during departure at Fiumcino International Airport (Rome, Italy). The pilot dumped fuel before returning to land on one engine. Besides birds being ingested into both engines, birds hit the cockpit window, right engine nose cowl, wing, and right main undercarriage. The main gear struts were deflated. Some of the fan blades had large chunks taken out. The left engine had many fan blades damaged midway along the blade leading edge. Both engines were replaced. The replacement engines had to be flown to Rome from the USA. ID by ornithologist, a member of Bird Strike Committee Italy. Time out of service 1 week.

25th August 2007. Pilot of B-737 departing Texas El Paso Airport reported loud bang in cockpit at 14,000 feet AGL during climb. Loud rushing air noise, cabin started to depressurize. Cabin alt horn went off, oxygen masks were donned. Pilot descended to 10,000 feet, notified flight attendants of situation, and then landed at El Paso. Found large hole under captain's left foot side. Also, hole in left horizontal stabilizer the size of a football. First officer's side of cockpit had a dent. Blood and feathers were found. No birds were seen in flight. Ground crew said "turkey buzzards" were in area. Bird was identified as marbled godwit by Smithsonian, Division of Birds. Cost of repairs was $ 144,064. Time out of service was 3 days.

28th August 2007. The pilot of a CRJ-700 declared an emergency after a black vulture smashed in the front fuselage between the radome and the windshield at 2,300 feet AGL on approach to the Louisville, KY International Airport. The strike ripped the skin, broke the avionics door, broke a stringer in half and bent 2 bulkheads. Maintenance made temporary repairs, then aircraft was ferried out for permanent repairs. ID by Smithsonian, Division of Birds. Cost of repairs was $ 200,000. Time out of service was 2 weeks.

11st October 2007. A CRJ-700 departing Denver International struck a flock of sandhill cranes at 1,500 feet AGL. The captain said several "geese" came at them, and they heard 3-4 thuds. The right engine immediately began to run roughly and the VIB gauge was fluctuating rapidly from one extreme to the other. Captain declared an emergency and said he didn't think he was going to make it back to DEN. The aircraft landed safely. The engine fan was damaged and there were dents along the left wing leading edge slat. ID by Smithsonian, Division of Birds. NTSB investigated.

23rd October 2007. A Piper 44 flying at 3,400 feet AGL disappeared during a night training flight from Minneapolis, MN to Grand Forks, ND. The instructor and student pilot did not report any difficulties or anomalies prior to the accident. Wreckage was found 36 hours later, partially submerged upside down in a bog. The NTSB sent part of a wing with suspected bird remains inside to the Smithsonian. Remains identified as Canada goose. The damage that crippled the aircraft was to the left horizontal stabilator. NTSB investigated. Two fatalities.

22nd November 2007. Pilot of a B-767 (U.S. carrier) at Nice Cote d'Azur (France) noticed a flock of gulls on runway during take off. As the aircraft rotated, the flock lifted off the runway. Shortly after that the crew felt multiple strikes and vibrations and returned to land. The #2 engine had fan blade damage. One piece of a fan blade broke off and exited out the front and the core nozzle fell off. The engine was replaced. Birds ID'd as yellow-legged gulls by Smithsonian, Division of Birds. Time out of service was 12 days. Cost of repairs was $ 8,925,000 and other cost was $ 196,000.

27th November 2007. A CRJ-200 descending into Memphis International Airport (TN) encountered a flock of large birds, sustaining ingestion into both engines, a cracked nose panel, damage to the right wing root and left horizontal stabilizer, and left engine anti-ice cowling. Bird remains were subsequently identified as snow geese. Maintenance made temporary repairs before aircraft could be flown for more permanent repairs.

29th January 2008. Flight crew of B-747 reported minor noise and vibration shortly after lift-off from Louisville International Airport. Noise and vibrations later subsided. Upon landing at destination, damage was found to 3 fan blades on the #2 engine. A piece of a liberated fan blade penetrated the cowl. Six fan blade pairs, the fan case outer-front acoustic panel and inlet cowl were replaced. ID by Smithsonian, Division of Birds.

8th April 2008. Shortly after departure, a Challenger 600 suffered multiple, large bird strikes (American white pelicans) at 3,000 feet AGL. One bird penetrated the nose area just below the windshield and continued through the forward cockpit bulkhead. Bird remains were sprayed throughout the cockpit. No injuries reported. Both engines ingested at least 1 bird. The #1 engine had fan damage: the #2 engine lost power and had a dented inlet lip. ID by Smithsonian, Division of Birds. NTSB investigated. Cost exceeded $ 2 million.

20th June 2008. During takeoff run at Chicago O'Hare, a B-747 bound for China ingested a red-tailed hawk. The flight continued takeoff and climbed to 11,000 feet to dump fuel and then returned to the airport with one engine out. Several blades had significant damage. Both the #1 and #2 engines had vibrations but the #2 engine was not damaged. Aircraft taken out of service for repairs; passengers had to be boarded onto another aircraft.

For more relevant information, a comprehensive report with data from 1990 until 2012 is available for consultation on the website: http://www.faa.gov/airports/airport_safety/wildlife/resources/media/StrikeReport1990-2012.pdf

DOLBEER, R. A., WRIGHT, S., WELLER, J., and BEIGER, M. J. 2013. Wildlife strikes to civil aircraft in the United States, 1990-2012. U.S. Department of Transportation, Federal Aviation Administration, Office of Airport Safety and Standards, Serial Report No. 19, Washington, DC., USA. 96 pages. Retrieved on: Feb. 5th 2014.

→ The main parts of aircraft affected by bird strike

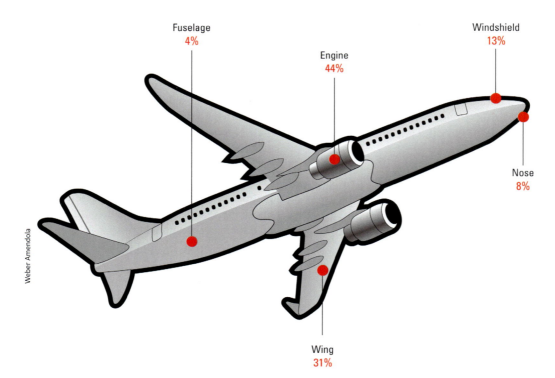

Source: Adapted from Bird Strike Committee USA. Available on: <http://www.birdstrike.org/commlink/signif.htm>. Retrieved on: Apr. 30th 2013.

CONSOLIDATION ← UNIT 29

Exercise 1

Look at the picture below and memorize the airplane parts and their functions.

Horizontal stabilizer: controls pitch.
Vertical stabilizer: controls yaw.
Rudder: changes yaw.
Elevator: changes pitch.
Winglet: decreases drag.
Wing: generates lift.
Flaps: increase lift and drag.
Slats: increases lift.

Spoiler: changes lift, drag and roll.
Turbine engine: generate thrust.
Aileron: changes roll.
Cockpit: command and control.
Fuselage: holds things together.

Work with a partner and ask him/her:
Example:
What is the horizontal stabilizer for?

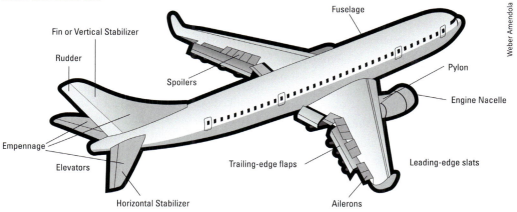

Source: Adapted from Bird Strike Committee USA. Available on: <http://www.birdstrike.org/commlink/signif.htm>. Retrieved on: Apr. 30th 2013.

Exercise 2

Now, identify each part of the aircraft below:

ailerons
elevator
flaps
horizontal stabilizer
main landing gear
nose landing gear
vertical stabilizer
wing

door
empennage
fuselage
leading-edge slats
nose
rudder
wingtip

UNIT 30

A funny story in aviation

This funny real story happened some minutes before the landing procedures in a developing country on an international flight. The airplane was fully booked.

As there had been some delay because of weather conditions, everybody was eager to arrive and get off the plane. A couple of hours before, there had been a strong turbulence, but all passengers seemed to be fine.

The captain started his speech talking about the local weather conditions and at what time we were supposed to land. It wasn't raining and from the aircraft windows, we could see the first light beams of the sunrise.

After breakfast, the flight attendants quickly started to clean up and the fasten seat belt sign was on. The passengers who were standing started to go back to their seats, except one lady who rushed to the lavatory, ignoring the instructions of a steward who warned her, in French, that the landing procedures would start.

Immediately, the flight attendants started to check if all passengers had their seat belts fastened and were prepared for the landing procedures. All of a sudden, one of the flight attendants observed that there was a vacant seat. She started to look for the missing passenger diligently. After a quick check, the last places to be checked were the lavatories. The competent flight attendant finally got to find out that one of the lavatories door was closed.

At first, she saw the sign 'occupied' was on and refrained herself from knocking on the door. Then, she looked at her wrist watch and waited for some seconds. When she heard the captain's announcement that the aircraft would land in some minutes, the flight attendant started knocking violently on the door. As the lady who was in the lavatory didn't answer, she said in a very loud voice that if the lady didn't open the door, she would have to knock it down. The flight attendant seemed to be so angry that the lady had to open the door and didn't say a word. The lady went back to her seat as some passengers looked puzzled at the scene. Other passengers started to complain about the flight attendant's behavior, while she followed the lady closely until the passenger reached her seat. The poor lady seemed to feel humiliated as the flight attendant shouted at her, in French, three or four times that she should hurry up, go back to her seat and fasten the seat belt.

The lady sat down but, apparently, she couldn't understand that she had to fasten her seat belt. Then, a polite man, who was sitting beside the lady, tried to help and repeated the flight attendant's instructions in Portuguese. It seemed to be a communication problem, as the lady didn't act and seemed to be confused. Talking to the lady, the gentleman found out that she spoke only Portuguese and couldn't understand a word of what the flight attendant had said.

Finally, after the translation, the passenger could fasten her seat belt and the flight attendant said, in French: security first!

Now it's your turn!

Do you know any funny story in aviation? Tell it to your colleagues.

APPENDIX 1

Countries, capitals, nationalities and currencies

Country	Capital	Adjective/Nationality	Person	Currency
Afghanistan	Kabul	Afghan	an Afghan	afghani
Albania	Tirana	Albanian	an Albanian	lek
Algeria	Algiers	Algerian	an Algerian	dinar
Andorra	Andorra la Vella	Andorran	an Andorran	euro
Angola	Luanda	Angolan	an Angolan	kwanza
Argentina	Buenos Aires	Argentinian	an Argentinian	Argentinian peso
Armenia	Yerevan	Armenian	an Armenian	dram
Australia	Camberra	Australian	an Australian	Australian dollar
Austria	Vienna	Austrian	an Austrian	euro
Azerbaijan	Baku	Azerbaijani	an Azerbaijani	manat
Bahamas	Nassau	Bahamian	a Bahamian	Bahamian dollar
Bahrain	Manama	Bahraini	a Bahraini	dinar
Bangladesh	Dacca	Bangladeshi	a Bangladeshi	taka
Barbados	Bridgetown	Barbadian	a Barbadian	Barbadian dollars
Belarus	Minsk	Belarusian or Belarusan	a Belarusian or a Belarusan	Belarusian ruble
Belgium	Brussels	Belgian	a Belgian	euro
Belize	Belmopan	Belizean	a Belizean	Belize dollar
Benin	Porto-Novo, but the seat of government is Cotonou	Beninese	a Beninese	CFA franc
Bhutan	Thimphu	Bhutanese	a Bhutanese	ngultrum
Bolivia	La Paz	Bolivian	a Bolivian	boliviano
Bosnia-Herzegovina	Sarajevo	Bosnian	a Bosnian	convertible mark

GENERAL ENGLISH → FOR AVIATION

Country	Capital	Adjective/Nationality	Person	Currency
Botswana	Gaborone	Botswanan	a Batswana	pula
Brazil	Brasilia	Brazilian	a Brazilian	real
Britain	London	British	a Briton	pound
Brunei	Bandar Seri Begawan	Bruneian	a Bruneian	Bruneian dollar
Bulgaria	Sofia	Bulgarian	a Bulgarian	lev
Burkina-Faso	Ouagadougou	Burkinese	a Burkinese	CFA franc
Burma (official name Myanmar)	Naypyitaw	Burmese	a Burmese	kyat
Burundi	Bujumbara	Burundian	a Burundian	Burundian franc
Cambodia	Phnom Penh	Cambodian	a Cambodian	riel
Cameroon	Yaounde	Cameroonian	a Cameroonian	CFA franc
Canada	Ottawa	Canadian	a Canadian	Canadian dollar
Cape Verde Islands	Praia	Cape Verdean	a Cape Verdean	escudo
Chad	N'Djamena (formely, Fort-Lamy)	Chadian	a Chadian	CFA franc
Chile	Santiago	Chilean	a Chilean	Chilean peso
China	Beijing	Chinese	a Chinese	yuan
Colombia	Bogotá	Colombian	a Colombian	Colombian peso
Costa Rica	San José	Costa Rican	a Costa Rican	colon
Croatia	Zagreb	Croat or Croatian	a Croat *or* a Croatian	kuna
Cuba	Havana	Cuban	a Cuban	Cuban peso
Cyprus	Nicosia	Cypriot	a Cypriot	euro
Czech Republic	Prague	Czech	a Czech	koruna
Denmark	Copenhagen	Danish	a Dane	krone
Djibouti	Djibouti City	Djiboutian	a Djiboutian	Djiboutian franc
Dominican Republic	Santo Domingo	Dominican	a Dominican	Dominican peso
Ecuador	Quito	Ecuadorean	an Ecuadorean	Ecuadorean peso
Egypt	Cairo	Egyptian	an Egyptian	Egyptian pound

COUNTRIES, CAPITALS, NATIONALITIES AND CURRENCIES ← APPENDIX 1

Country	Capital	Adjective/Nationality	Person	Currency
El Salvador	San Salvador	Salvadorean	a Salvadorean	Salvadorean colon
England	London	English	an Englishman, an Englishwoman	pound
Eritrea	Asmara	Eritrean	an Eritrean	nakfa
Estonia	Tallinn	Estonian	an Estonian	euro
Ethiopia	Addis Ababa	Ethiopian	an Ethiopian	birr
Fiji	Suva	Fijian	a Fijian	Fijian dollar
Finland	Helsinki	Finnish	a Finn	euro
France	Paris	French	a Frenchman, a Frenchwoman	euro
Gabon	Libreville	Gabonese	a Gabonese	CFA franc
Gambia, the	Banjul	Gambian	a Gambian	dalasi
Georgia	Tbilisi	Georgian	a Georgian	lari
Germany	Berlin	German	a German	euro
Ghana	Accra	Ghanaian	a Ghanaian	Ghana cedi
Greece	Athens	Greek	a Greek	euro
Guatemala	Guatemala City	Guatemalan	a Guatemalan	quetzal
Guinea or French Guyana	Cayenne	Guinean	a Guinean	franc
Guyana	Georgetown	Guyanese	a Guyanese	Guyanese dollar
Haiti	Port-au-Prince	Haitian	a Haitian	gourde
Holland (also Netherlands)	Amsterdam	Dutch	a Dutchman, a Dutchwoman	euro
Honduras	Tegucigalpa	Honduran	a Honduran	lempira
Hungary	Budapest	Hungarian	a Hungarian	forint
Iceland	Reykjavik	Icelandic	an Icelander	krona
India	New Delhi	Indian	an Indian	rupee
Indonesia	Jakarta	Indonesian	an Indonesian	Indonesian rupiah
Iran	Tehran	Iranian	an Iranian	rial
Iraq	Baghdad	Iraqi	an Iraqi	dinar
Ireland, Republic of	Dublin	Irish	an Irishman, an Irishwoman	euro

Country	Capital	Adjective/Nationality	Person	Currency
Italy	Rome	Italian	an Italian	euro
Jamaica	Kingston	Jamaican	a Jamaican	Jamaican dollar
Japan	Tokyo	Japanese	a Japanese	yen
Jordan	Amman	Jordanian	a Jordanian	Jordanian dinar
Kazakhstan	Astana	Kazakh	a Kazakh	tenge
Kenya	Nairobi	Kenyan	a Kenyan	Kenyan shilling
Kuwait	Kuwait City	Kuwaiti	a Kuwaiti	Kuwaiti dinar
Laos	Vientiane	Laotian	a Laotian	kip
Latvia	Riga	Latvian	a Latvian	Latvian lats
Lebanon	Beirut	Lebanese	a Lebanese	Lebanese pound
Liberia	Monrovia	Liberian	a Liberian	Liberian dollar
Libya	Tripoli	Libyan	a Libyan	Libyan dinar
Liechtenstein	Vaduz	–	a Liechtensteiner	franc
Lithuania	Vilnius	Lithuanian	a Lithuanian	litas
Luxembourg	Luxembourg City	–	a Luxembourger	euro
Macedonia	Skopje	Macedonian	a Macedonian	Macedonian denar
Madagascar	Antananarivo	Malagasy *or* Madagascan	a Malagasy *or* a Madagascan	ariary
Malawi	Lilongwe	Malawian	a Malawian	kwacha
Malaysia	Kuala Lumpur	Malaysian	a Malaysian	ringgit
Maldives	Malé	Maldivian	a Maldivian	rufiyaa
Mali	Bamako	Malian	a Malian	CFA franc
Malta	Valletta	Maltese	a Maltese	euro
Mauritania	Nouakchott	Mauritanian	a Mauritanian	ouguiya *or* ougiya
Mauritius	Port Louis	Mauritian	a Mauritian	Mauritian rupee
Mexico	Mexico City	Mexican	a Mexican	Mexican peso
Moldova	Chisinau	Moldovan	a Moldovan	leu
Monaco	Monaco City *or* Monaco-Ville. (Its largest quartier is Monte Carlo).	Monégasque *or* Monacan (for naturalized citizens only)	a Monégasque *or* a Monacan (for naturalized citizens only)	euro

COUNTRIES, CAPITALS, NATIONALITIES AND CURRENCIES ← APPENDIX 1

133

Country	Capital	Adjective/Nationality	Person	Currency
Mongolia	Ulan Bator *or* Ulaanbaatar	Mongolian	a Mongolian	tughrik
Morocco	Rabat	Moroccan	a Moroccan	dirham
Mozambique	Maputo	Mozambican	a Mozambican	metical
Myanmar *see* Burma		–	–	–
Namibia	Windhoek	Namibian	a Namibian	Namibian dollar
Nepal	Kathmandu	Nepalese	a Nepalese	Nepalese rupee
Netherlands, the (*see* Holland)	Amsterdam	Dutch	a Dutchman, a Dutchwoman, *or* a Netherlander	euro
New Zealand	Wellington	New Zealand (used attributively only, as in *New Zealand butter* but not He is New Zealand)	a New Zealander	New Zealand dollar
Nicaragua	Managua	Nicaraguan	a Nicaraguan	córdoba
Niger	Niamey	Nigerien	a Nigerien	CFA franc
Nigeria	Abuja	Nigerian	a Nigerian	naira
North Korea	Pyongyang	North Korean	a North Korean	won
Norway	Oslo	Norwegian	a Norwegian	Norwegian krone
Oman	Muscat	Omani	an Omani	Omani rial
Pakistan	Islamabad	Pakistani	a Pakistani	Pakistani rupee
Panama	Panama City	Panamanian	a Panamanian	balboa
Papua New Guinea	Port Moresby	Papua New Guinean *or* Guinean	a Papua New Guinean *or* a Guinean	kina
Paraguay	Asunción	Paraguayan	a Paraguayan	guaraní
Peru	Lima	Peruvian	a Peruvian	sol
the Philippines	Manila	Philippine	a Filipino	Philippine peso
Poland	Warsaw	Polish	a Pole	zloty
Portugal	Lisbon	Portuguese	a Portuguese	euro
Qatar	Doha	Qatari	a Qatari	Qatari riyal
Romania	Bucharest	Romanian	a Romanian	lei
Russia	Moscow	Russian	a Russian	ruble

134 GENERAL ENGLISH → FOR AVIATION

Country	Capital	Adjective/Nationality	Person	Currency
Rwanda	Kigali	Rwandan	a Rwandan	Rwandan franc
Saudi Arabia	Riyadh	Saudi Arabian *or* Saudi	a Saudi Arabian *or* a Saudi	Saudi Arabian Riyal
Scotland	Edinburgh	Scottish	a Scot	British pound
Senegal	Dakar	Senegalese	a Senegalese	CFA franc
Serbia	Belgrade	Serb *or* Serbian	a Serb *or* a Serbian	Serbian dinar
Seychelles, the	Victoria (also Port Victoria)	Seychellois	a Seychellois	Seychellois rupee
Sierra Leone	Freetown	Sierra Leonean	a Sierra Leonean	leone
Singapore	Singapore City	Singaporean	a Singaporean	Singaporean dollar
Slovakia	Bratislava	Slovak	a Slovak	euro
Slovenia	Ljubljana	Slovene *or* Slovenian	a Slovene *or* a Slovenian	euro
Solomon Islands	Honiara	–	a Solomon Islander	Solomon Island dollars
Somalia	Hargeisa	Somali	a Somali	Somali shilling
South Africa	South Africa has no legally defined capital. Pretoria is the administrative capital and the seat of the President of the Cabinet. Cape Town is the seat of Parliament. Bloemfontein serves as the judicial capital, as the seat of the Supreme Court of Appeal. Johannesburg	South African	a South African	rand
South Korea	Seoul	South Korean	a South Korean	South Korean won
Spain	Madrid	Spanish	a Spaniard	euro

COUNTRIES, CAPITALS, NATIONALITIES AND CURRENCIES ← APPENDIX 1

Country	Capital	Adjective/Nationality	Person	Currency
Sri Lanka	Sri Jayawarde-napura-Kotte *or* Kotte	Sri Lankan	a Sri Lankan	Sri Lankan rupee
Sudan	Khartoum	Sudanese	a Sudanese	Sudanese pound
Suriname	Paramaribo	Surinamese	a Surinamer *or* a Surinamese	Surinamese dollar
Swaziland	Lobamba (royal/legislative), Mbabane (administrative)	Swazi	a Swazi	lilangene
Sweden	Stockholm	Swedish	a Swede	Swedish krona
Switzerland	Bern	Swiss	a Swiss	euro
Syria	Damascus	Syrian	a Syrian	Syrian pound
Taiwan	Taipei	Taiwanese	a Taiwanese	Taiwanese dollar
Tajikistan	Dushanbe	Tajik *or* Tadjik	a Tajik *or* a Tadjik	somani
Tanzania	Dodoma	Tanzanian	a Tanzanian	Tanzanian shillings
Thailand	Bangkok	Thai	a Thai	baht
Togo	Lomé	Togolese	a Togolese	CFA franc
Trinidad and Tobago	Port of Spain	Trinidadian Tobagan/Tobagonian	a Trinidadian a Tobagan/Tobagonian	Trinidad and Tobago dollar
Tunisia	Tunis	Tunisian	a Tunisian	Tunisian dinar
Turkey	Ankara	Turkish	a Turk	lira
Turkmenistan	Ashgabat	Turkmen or Turkoman	a Turkmen or a Turkoman	Turkoman manat
Tuvalu	Funafuti	Tuvaluan	a Tuvaluan	Tuvaluan dollar
Uganda	Kampala	Ugandan	a Ugandan	Ugandan shillings
Ukraine	Kiev	Ukrainian	a Ukrainian	grivna or hryvnia
United Arab Emirates (UAE)	Abu Dhabi	UAE or Emirates (used attributively only, as in *UAE buildings*, *Emirates holidays* but not <u>He is UAE, I am Emirates</u>) *or* Emirati	an Emirati	United Arab Emirates dirham

GENERAL ENGLISH → FOR AVIATION

Country	Capital	Adjective/Nationality	Person	Currency
United Kingdom (UK)	London	UK (used attributively only, as in *UK time* but not <u>He is UK</u>) *or* British	a Briton	pound sterling
United States of America (USA)	Washington, D.C	US (used attributively only, as in the *US Forces* but not <u>He is US</u>)	a US citizen, American	American dollar
Uruguay	Montevideo	Uruguayan	a Uruguayan	Uruguayan peso
Uzbekistan	Tashkent	Uzbek	an Uzbek	som
Vanuatu	Port Vila	Vanuatuan	a Vanuatuan	vatu
Venezuela	Caracas	Venezuelan	a Venezuelan	bolivar
Vietnam	Hanoi	Vietnamese	a Vietnamese	dong
Wales	Cardiff	Welsh	a Welshman, a Welshwoman	pound sterling
Yemen	Sana'a	Yemeni	a Yemeni	Yemeni rial
Yugoslavia	A former country of southeastern Europe consisting of Serbia and Montenegro, the last two remaining constituent states after Bosnia and Herzegovina, Croatia, Macedonia, and Slovenia seceded from Yugoslavia in 1991. The name Yugoslavia was officially abandoned in 2003, and Serbia and Montenegro split into two independent republics in 2006. (American Heritage Dictionary)	Yugoslavian	a Yugoslav	Yugoslavian dinar

COUNTRIES, CAPITALS, NATIONALITIES AND CURRENCIES ← APPENDIX 1

Country	Capital	Adjective/Nationality	Person	Currency
Zaire no longer exists. Now this country is called Democratic Republic of Congo.	Kinshasa	Zaïrean	a Zaïrean	New zaire
Zambia	Lusaka	Zambian	a Zambian	Zambian kwacha
Zimbabwe	Harare	Zimbabwean	a Zimbabwean	Zimbabwean dollar

APPENDIX 2

Cities, airports and 3-letter IATA codes

3-letter IATA Code	City/Country	Airport
A		
AAL	Aalborg, Denmark	Aalborg Airport
AES	Aalesund, Norway	Vigra Airport
AAR	Aarhus, Denmark	Aarhus Airport
YXX	Abbotsford, Canada	Abbotsford Intl Airport
ABZ	Aberdeen, Scotland, United Kingdom	Dyce Airport – Aberdeen Dyce Airport
ABR	Aberdeen, SD, USA Aberdeen Airport	Aberdeen Regional Airport
AHB	Abha, Saudi Arabia	Abha Airport
ABJ	Abidjan, Cote D'ivoire	Port Bouet Airport or Abidjan Félix Houphoiiet – Boigny International Airport
ABI	Abilene, TX, USA	Metropolitan Airport
AUH	Abu Dhabi, United Arab Emirates	Abu Dhabi Intl Airport
ABS	Abu Simbel, Egypt	Abu Simbel Airport (regional)
ABV	Abuja, Nigeria	Abuja International Airport
ACA	Acapulco, Guerrero, Mexico	Alvarez International Airport or General Juan N. Alvarez International Airport
ACC	Accra, Ghana	Kotoka International Airport
ADK	Adak Island, Alaska, USA	Adak Island Airport
ADA	Adana, Turkey	Adana Airport or Adana Sakipasa Airport
ADD	Addis Ababa, Ethiopia	Bole International Airport
ADL	Adelaide, South Australia, Australia	Adelaide International Airport
ADE	Aden, Yemen	Aden International Airport
AGA	Agadir, Morocco Inezgane	Agadir Al-Massira Airport
GUM	Agana, Guam	Guam Ab Wonpat Intl Airport
IXA	Agartala, India	Singerbhil Airport
AGF	Agen, France	La Garenne Airport
AGR	Agra, India	Kheria Aiport
AJI	Agri, Turkey	Agri Airport
BQN	Aguadilla, Puerto Rico, Borinquen	Rafael Hernandez Airport
AGU	Aguascalientes, Aguascalientes, Mexico	Jesus Teran Peredo Intl Airport

CITIES, AIRPORTS AND 3-LETTER IATA CODES ← APPENDIX 2

3-letter IATA Code	City/Country	Airport
IKA	Ahmadabad (Tehran), Iran	Imam Khomeini International Airport
AMD	Ahmedabad, India	Sardar Valldabhbhai Patel Intl Airport
AWZ	Ahwaz, Iran	Ahwaz Airport
QXB	Aix-en-Provence	Aix-en-Provence Airport
AJA	Ajaccio, Corsica, France	Ajaccio Napoleon Bonaparte Airport
AXT	Akita, Japan	Akita Airport
CAK	Akron/Canton, OH, USA	AkronCanton Regional Airport
AKU	Aksu, China	Aksu Airport
PVK	Aktion, Greece	Preveza Lefkas Airport
AKV	Akulivik, Canada	Akulivik Airport
AEY	Akureyri, Iceland	Akureyri Airport
KQA	Akutan, Alaska, USA	Akutan Airport
AAN	Al Ain, United Arab Emirates	Al Ain Airport
AAC	Al Arish, Egypt	Al Arish Airport
ABT	Al Baha, Saudi Arabia	Al Baha Al Aqiq Airport
AHU	Al Hoceima, Morocco	Al Hoceima Airport
ALM	Alamogordo, NM, USA	Alamogordo Municipal Airport
ALS	Alamosa, CO, USA	Bergman Field *or* San Louis Valley Regional
ABC	Albacete, Spain	Albacete Airport
ABY	Albany, GA, USA	Dougherty County Aiport
ALB	Albany, NY, USA	Albany County Airport
ALL	Albenga, Italy	Albenga Airport
ABQ	Albuquerque, NM, USA	Albuquerque Intl Airport
ABX	Albury, New South Wales	Australia Albury Airport
ACI	Alderney, Channel Islands, United Kingdom	The Blaye *or* Alderney Airport
WKK	Aleknagik, Alaska, USA	Aleknagik Airport
AED	Aleneva, Alaska, USA	Aleneva Airport
ALP	Aleppo, Syria Nejrab	Aleppo International Aiport
ALY	Alexandria, Egypt	Alexandria International Aiport *or* El Nozha Airport
HBE	Alexandria, Egypt Borg	El Arab Airport
AEX	Alexandria, LA, USA	Alexandria Intl Airport
AXD	Alexandroupolis, Greece	Alexandroupolis Intl Airport
AHO	Alghero, Sardinia, Italy	Fertilia Airport *or* Alghero – Fertilia Airport
ALG	Algiers, Algeria	Houari Boumedienne Intl Airport
ALC	Alicante, Spain	Alicante Airport
ASP	Alice Springs, Northern Territory, Australia	Alice Springs Airport

GENERAL ENGLISH → FOR AVIATION

3-letter IATA Code	City/Country	Airport
IXD	Allahabad, India	Bamrauli Airport
AET	Allakaket, AK, USA	Allakaket Airport
ABE	Allentown, PA, USA	Allentown Bethlehem Easton Airport
AIA	Alliance, NE, USA	Alliance Airport
ALA	Almaty, Kazakhstan	Almaty Airport
LEI	Almeria, Spain	Almeria Airport
IXV	Along, India	Along Airport
AOR	Alor Setar, Malaysia	Sultan Abdul Halim Airport
GUR	Alotau, Papua New Guinea	Gurney Airport
APN	Alpena, MI, USA	Alpena Regional Airport
ALE	Alpine, TX, USA	Alpine Texas Airport
ALF	Alta, Norway	Elvebakken Alta Airport
ATM	Altamira, Brazil	Altamira Airport
LTI	Altai, Govi, Altai, Mongolia	Altai Airport
AAT	Altay, China	Altay Airport
ACH	Altenrhein, Switzerland	Altenrhein Airport
AOO	Altoona / Martinsburg, PA, USA	Altoona – Blair County Airport
ASJ	Amami O Shima, Japan	Amami O Shima Airport
AMA	Amarillo, TX, USA	Amarillo International Airport
ABL	Ambler, AK, USA	Ambler Airport
AMQ	Ambon, Indonesia	Pattimura Airport
ADJ	Amman, Jordan	Amman – Marka Intl Airport
AMM	Amman, Jordan	Queen Alia International
YEY	Amos, Quebec, Canada	Amos – Magny Municipal Airport
ATQ	Amritsar, Punjab, India	Raja Sansi Intl Airport
AMS	Amsterdam, Netherlands	Schiphol Airport
AAQ	Anapa Airport, Russia	Anapa Airport
ANC	Anchorage, AK, USA	Anchorage International
AOI	Ancona, Italy	Ancona Falconara Airport
AZN	Andizhan, Uzbekistan	Andizhan Airport
ASD	Andros Town, Bahamas	Andros Town Airport
ANG	Angouleme, France	Angouleme – Brie – Champniers Airport
AGN	Angoon, Alaska, USA	Angoon Airport
AXA	Anguilla, Anguilla	Anguilla Wallblake Airport
ANI	Aniak, AK, USA	Aniak Airport
AJN	Anjouan, Comoros	Ouani Airport
ESB	Ankara, Turkey	Ankara Esenboga Airport
AAE	Annaba, Algeria	Les Salines Airport

CITIES, AIRPORTS AND 3-LETTER IATA CODES ← APPENDIX 2

141

3-letter IATA Code	City/Country	Airport
NCY	Annecy, France	Annecy Meythe Airport
ANB	Anniston, AL, USA	Anniston Regional Airport
AQG	Anqing, China	Anqing Tianzhushan Airport
AOG	Anshan, Liaoning Province, China	Anshan Teng'ao Aiport
AYT	Antalya, Turkey	Antalya International Airport
TNR	Antananarivo, Madagascar	Ivato International Airport
ANU	Antigua, Saint Johns, Antigua and Barbuda	V. C. Bird International
ANF	Antofagasta, Chile	Cerro Moreno Intl Airport
ANR	Antwerp, Belgium	Antwerp International Airport
ANV	Anvik, AK, USA	Anvik Airport
AOJ	Aomori, Japan	Aomori Airport
APW	Apia, Samoa	Faleolo International Airport
ATW	Appleton, WI, USA	Outagamie County Airport
AQJ	Aqaba, Jordan Aqaba	Agaba King Hussein Intl Airport
AJU	Aracaju, Sergipe, Brazil	Aerporto Internacional de Aracaju
AUX	Araguaina, Brazil	Araguaina Airport
RAE	Arar, Saudi Arabia	Arar Airport
AUC	Arauca, Colombia	Santiago Pérez Quiroz Airport
AAX	Araxá, Brazil	Araxá Airport
AMH	Arba Mintch, Ethiopia	Arba Mintch Airport
ACV	Arcata, CA, USA Arcata	Eureka Airport
AQP	Arequipa, Peru	Rodriguez Ballon Intl Airport
ARI	Arica, Chile	Chacalluta International Airport
ARH	Arkhangelsk, Russia	Arkhangelsk Airport
AXM	Armenia, Colombia	El Eden Airport
ARM	Armidale, New South Wales, Australia	Armidale Airport
ATC	Arthur's Town, Bahamas	Arthur's Town Airport
AUA	Aruba, Aruba	Aeropuerto Intl Reina Beatrix
AVK	Arvaikheer, Ovorhkangai, Mongolia	Arvaikheer Airport
YEK	Arviat, Canada	Arviat Airport
AJR	Arvidsjaur, Sweden	Arvidsjaur Airport
AKJ	Asahikawa, Japan	Asahikawa Airport
AVL	Asheville/Hendersonville, NC, USA	Asheville Regional Airport
ASB	Ashgabat, Turkmenistan	Ashgabad Airport
ASM	Asmara, Eritrea Asmara	Asmara International Airport
ASO	Asosa, Ethiopia	Asosa Airport
ASE	Aspen, CO, USA	Pitkin County Airport Sardy Field
ATZ	Assiut, Egypt	Assiut Airport
TSE	Astana, Kazakhstan	Astana Airport

GENERAL ENGLISH → FOR AVIATION

3-letter IATA Code	City/Country	Airport
ASF	Astrakhan, Russia	Astrakhan Airport
OVD	Asturias, Spain	Asturias Airport
JTY	Astypalea Island, Greece	Astypalea Airport
ASU	Asuncion, Paraguay	Silvio Pettirossi Airport
ASW	Aswan, Egypt	Daraw Airport
AHN	Athens, GA, USA	Athens – Ben Epps Airport
ATH	Athens, Greece	Athens International Airport
YIB	Atikokan, Ontario, Canada	Atikokan Municipal Airport
ATL	Atlanta, GA, USA	Hartsfield-Jackson Atlanta International Airport
ACY	Atlantic City/Atlantic Cty, NJ, USA	Atlantic City Intl Airport
AIY	Atlantic City, NJ, USA	Bader Field
YAT	Attawapiskat, Canada,	Attawapiskat Airport
AOU	Attopeu, Laos	Attopeu Airport
MER	Atwater/Merced, California, USA	Castle Airport
AKL	Auckland, New Zealand	Auckland International Airport
AGB	Augsburg, Germany	Augsburg Muehlhausen Airport
AGS	Augusta, GA, USA	Bush Field Airport
AUG	Augusta, ME, USA	Augusta State Airport
YPJ	Aupaluk, Canada	Aupaluk Airport
IXU	Aurangabad, India	Chikkalthana Airport *or* Aurangabad Airport
AUS	Austin, TX, USA	Austin Bergstrom International Airport (ABIA)
AVV	Avalon, Australia	Avalon Airport
AVN	Avignon, France	Avignon – Caumont Airport
AYQ	Ayers Rock, Northern Territory, Australia	Connellan Airport

B		
BCD	Bacolod, Philippines	Bacolod – Silay Airport
IXB	Bagdogra, India	Bagdogra Airport
YBG	Bagotville, Canada	Bagotville Airport
BJR	Bahar Dar, Ethiopia	Bahar Dar Airport
BHV	Bahawalpur, Pakistan	Bahawalpur Airport
BHI	Bahia Blanca, Buenos Aires, Argentina	Aeropuerto Comandante Espora
BAH	Bahrain, Bahrain	Bahrain International Bahrain
BAY	Baia Mare, Romania	Baia Mare Airport
YBC	Baie Comeau, Quebec, Canada	Baie Comeau Airport
BKM	Bakalalan, Malaysia	Bakalalan Airport
BFL	Bakersfield, CA, USA	Meadows Field Airport
GYD	Baku, Azerbaijan	Geydar Aliyev Airport

CITIES, AIRPORTS AND 3-LETTER IATA CODES ← APPENDIX 2

3-letter IATA Code	City/Country	Airport
DPS	Bali (Denpasar), Indonesia	Ngurah Rai Intl Airport
BPN	Balikpapan, Indonesia	Balikpapan
BNK	Ballina, Australia	Ballina Airport
BBA	Balmaceda, Chile	Balmaceda
BWI	Baltimore, MD, USA	Baltimore Washington Intl
ABM	Bamaga, Queensland, Australia	Bamaga Injinoo Airport
BKO	Bamako, Mali Senou	Bamako – Senou Intl Airport
HOE	Ban Hat Tai, Laos	Ban Huoeisay Airport (Ban Houei Sai / Ban Houay Xay)
OUI	Ban Hat Tai, Laos	Ban Huoeisay Airport (Ban Houei Sai / Ban Houay Xay)
BMV	Ban Me Thuot, Vietnam	Ban Me Thuot Airport
BND	Bandar Abbas, Iran	Bandar Abbas Airport
BWN	Bandar Seri Begawan, Brunei	Darussalam Brunei International
BDO	Bandung, Indonesia	Husein Sastranegara International Airport
YBA	Banff, Alberta, Canada	Banff Airport
BLR	Bangalore (Bengalooru), India	Kempegowda Intl Aiport
BPX	Bangda, China	Bangda Airport
BKK	Bangkok, Thailand	Bangkok International Airport
BGR	Bangor, ME, USA	Bangor International Airport
BGF	Bangui, Central African Republic	Bangui M'Poko International Airport
BNX	Banja Luka, Bosnia and Herzegovina	Banja Luka Airport
BDJ	Banjarmasin, Indonesia	Syamsudin Noor Airport
BJL	Banjul, Gambia	Yundum International Airport
BAV	Baotou, China	Baotou
BHB	Bar Harbor, ME, USA	Hancock County – Bar Harbor Aiport
BGI	Barbados (Bridgetown, Barbados)	Grantley Adams International
BCI	Barcaldine, Australia	Barcaldine Airport
BCN	Barcelona, Spain	Barcelona – El Prat Airport
BLA	Barcelona, Venezuela	General Jose Antonio Anzoategui Intl Airport
BDU	Bardufoss, Norway	Bardufoss Airport
BRI	Bari, Italy	Palese Airport
BNS	Barinas, Venezuela	Barinas Airport
BBN	Bario, Malaysia	Bario Airport
BAX	Barnaul, Russia	Barnaul Airport
BRM	Barquisimeto, Venezuela	Barquisimeto Airport
BRR	Barra/Hebrides Islands, Scotland, United Kingdom	North Bay *or* Barra Airport
EJA	Barrancabermeja, Colombia	Variguies Airport

GENERAL ENGLISH → FOR AVIATION

3-letter IATA Code	City/Country	Airport
BAQ	Barranquilla, Colombia	Ernesto Cortissoz Intl Airport
BRW	Barrow, Alaska, USA	Barrow Airport
BTI	Barter Island, Alaska, USA	Barter Island Airport [LRRS]
UUN	Baruun	Urt, Sukhbaatar, Mongolia
BSL	Basel, Switzerland	Basel Euro Airport
BIA	Bastia, Corsica, France	Poretta
BTH	Batam, Indonesia	Hang Nadim Airport
ZBF	Bathurst, New Brunswick, Canada	Bathurst Airport
BHS	Bathurst, New South Wales, Australia	Raglan Airport
BRT	Bathurst Island, Northern Territory, Australia	Bathurst Island Airport
BTR	Baton Rouge, LA, USA	Baton Rouge Metropolitan Airport
BAU	Bauru, Brazil	Bauru Airport
MBS	Bay City/Midland/Saginaw, MI, USA	TriCity Airport
BYN	Bayankhongor, Bayankhongor, Mongolia	Bayankhongor Airport
BYU	Bayreuth, Germany	Bindlacher Berg Airport
BPT	Beaumont, TX, USA	Jefferson County Airport
BVA	Beauvais, France	Tillé Airport
BKW	Beckley, WV, USA	Beckley Airport
BED	Bedford, MA, USA	Bedford Airport
YBW	Bedwell Harbor, Canada	Bedwell Harbor Airport
EIS	Beef Island, British Virgin Islands, Tortola/Beef Island	Beef Island Airport
BEI	Beica, Ethiopia	Beica Airport
BHY	Beihai, China	Beihai Fucheng Airport
NAY	Beijing, China	Beijing International
PEK	Beijing, China	Peking Capital Airport
LAQ	Beida, Libya	La Braq Airport
BEW	Beira, Mozambique	Beira Airport
BEY	Beirut, Lebanon	Beirut Rafc Hariri Intl Airport
BEL	Belém, Pará, Brazil	Val de Cans Airport
BHD	Belfast, Northern Ireland, United Kingdom	Belfast Harbor Airport
BFS	Belfast, Northern Ireland, United Kingdom	Belfast International
IXG	Belgaum, India	Sambre Airport
EGO	Belgorod, Russia	Belgorod Airport
BEG	Belgrade, Yugoslavia	Belgrad Nikola Tesla Airport
BZE	Belize City, Belize	Belize International Airport
TZA	Belize City, Belize	Belize Municipal Airport
XVV	Belleville, Ontario, Canada	Belleville/Via Rail Service
BLI	Bellingham, WA, USA	Bellingham Intl Airport

CITIES, AIRPORTS AND 3-LETTER IATA CODES ← APPENDIX 2

3-letter IATA Code	City/Country	Airport
CNF	Belo Horizonte, Minas Gerais, Brazil	Aeroporto Internacional Tancredo Neves
PLU	Belo Horizonte, Minas Gerais, Brazil	Confins/Pampulha
BJI	Bemidji, MN, USA	Bemidji Municipal Airport
BEB	Benbecula, United Kingdom	Benbecula Airport
RDM	Bend, OR, USA	Roberts Field, Redmond Municipal Airport
BEN	Benghazi, Libya	Benina International Airport
BEH	Benton Harbor, MI, USA	Ross Field, Southwest Michigan Regional Airport
BGO	Bergen, Norway	Bergen Airport/Flesland Aiport
EGC	Bergerac, France	Aeroport de Bergerac Perigord Dordogne
BVG	Berlevag, Norway	Berlevag Airport
BER	Berlin, Germany	Berlin Brandenburg Airport
SXF	Berlin, Germany	Berlin Schoenefeld Airport
TXL	Berlin, Germany	Berlin – Tegel Intl Airport
THF	Berlin, Germany	Berlin – Tempelhof Airport
BDA	Bermuda/Hamilton, Bermuda	Kindley Airfield/Civil Air Terminal
BRN	Berne, Switzerland	Berne Airport
BET	Bethel, AK, USA	Bethel Airport
BZR	Beziers, France	Beziers Cap d'Agde Airport
BWA	Bhairawa, Nepal	Bhairawa Airport
BHU	Bhavnagar, India	Bhavnagar Airport
BHO	Bhopal, India	Bhopal Airport
BBI	Bhubaneswar, India	Bhubaneswar Airport
BIK	Biak, Indonesia	Mokmer Airport
BIQ	Biarritz, France	Biarritz Parme Airport
BGK	Big Creek, Belize	Big Creek Airport
BIO	Bilbao, Spain	Bilbao Airport
BIL	Billings, MT, USA	Billings Logan Intnl Airport
BLL	Billund, Denmark	Billund Airport
BIM	Bimini, Bahamas	Bimini Island International
NSB	Bimini, Bahamas	North Seaplane Base
BGM	Binghamton/Endicott/Johnson City, NY, USA	Edwin Alink Field
BTU	Bintulu, Sarawak, Malaysia	Bintulu Airport
BVI	Birdsville, Queensland, Australia	Birdsville Airport
BHM	Birmingham, AL, USA	Birmingham – Shuttesworth International Airport
BHX	Birmingham, England	United Kingdom International

GENERAL ENGLISH → FOR AVIATION

3-letter IATA Code	City/Country	Airport
BHH	Bisha, Saudi Arabia	Bisha Airport
FRU	Bishkek, Kyrgyzstan	Bishkek Airport
BSK	Biskra, Algeria	Biskra Airport
BIS	Bismarck, ND, USA	Bismarck Municipal Airport
OXB	Bissau, Guinea Bissau	Aeroporto Internacional Osvaldo Vieira
BKQ	Blackall, Australia	Blackall Airport
BLK	Blackpool, England, United Kingdom	Blackpool International Airport
BLT	Blackwater, Australia	Blackwater Airport
YBX	Blanc Sablon, Quebec, Canada	Blanc Sablon Airport
BLZ	Blantyre, Malawi	Chileka International Airport
BHE	Blenheim, New Zealand	Woodbourne Airport
BFN	Bloemfontein, South Africa	Bloemfontein Intl Airport
BMI	Bloomington, IL, USA	Bloomington – Normal Airport
BMG	Bloomington, IN, USA	Monroe County Airport
BLF	Bluefield, WV, USA	Mercer Country Airport
BYH	Blytheville, Arkansas, USA	Arkansas International Airport
BVB	Boa Vista, Roraima, Brazil	Aeroporto Internacional de Boa Vista
BOO	Bodo, Norway	Bodo Airport
BXN	Bodrum, Turkey	Imsik Airport
BFI	Boeing Field/Seattle, Seattle WA, USA	Kings County International
BOG	Bogota, Colombia	Aeropuerto Internacional Eldorado
BOI	Boise, ID, USA	Boise Municipal Aiport (Gowen Field)
BLQ	Bologna, Italy	Guglielmo Marconi Airport
BZO	Bolzano, Italy	Bolzano Airport
BOM	Bombay, India	Mumbai
BON	Bonaire, Netherlands	Antilles Flamingo Field
BOB	Bora Bora, French Polynesia	Motu Mute Airport
BOD	Bordeaux, France Merignac	Bordeaux – Marignac Airport
HBE	Borg El Arab/Alexandria, Egypt	Borg El Arab Airport
BLE	Borlange, Sweden	Dala Airport
RNN	Bornholm, Denmark	Arnager Airport
BOS	Boston, MA, USA	Logan International Airport
WBU	Boulder, CO, USA	Boulder Municipal Airport
BOJ	Bourgas, Bulgaria	Bourgas Airport
BZN	Bozeman, MT, USA	Bozeman Yellowstone International Airport
BFD	Bradford, PA, USA	Bradford Regional Airport

CITIES, AIRPORTS AND 3-LETTER IATA CODES ← APPENDIX 2

3-letter IATA Code	City/Country	Airport
BRD	Brainerd, MN, USA	Brainerd Lakes Regional Airport
BMP	Brampton Island, Australia	Brampton Island Airport
YBR	Brandon, Manitoba, Canada	Brandon Municipal Airport
BSB	Brasília, Distrito Federal, Brazil	Aeroporto Internacional de Brasília
BTS	Bratislava, Slovakia	Ivanka Airport
BZV	Brazzaville, Congo	Maya Maya Airport
QKB	Breckenridge, CO, USA	Breckenridge Airport
BRE	Bremen, Germany	Bremen City Airport
PWT	Bremerton, WA, USA	Port of Bremerton National Airport
VBS	Brescia, Italy	Brescia Airport
BES	Brest, France	Guipavas Airport *or* Brest Bretagne Airport
BDR	Bridgeport, CT, USA	Sikorsky Memorial Airport
BGI	Bridgetown, Barbados	Grantley Adams Intl Airport
BDS	Brindisi, Italy	Brindisi Airport
BNE	Brisbane, Queensland, Australia	Brisbane Intl Airport
BRS	Bristol, England, United Kingdom	Bristol International Airport
TRI	Bristol/Johnson City/Kingsport, TN, USA	Municipal TriCity Airport
BVE	Brive La Gaillarde, France	Laroche Airport
BRQ	Brno, Czech Republic	Turany Airport
XBR	Brockville, Ontario, Canada	Brockville Airport
BHQ	Broken Hill, New South Wales, Australia	Broken Hill Airport
BNN	Bronnoysund, Norway	Bronnoy Airport
BKX	Brookings, SD, USA	Brookings Municipal Airport
BME	Broome, Australia	Broome Airport
YVM	Broughton Island, Canada	Broughton Island Airport
BRO	Brownsville, TX, USA	Brownsville South Padre Island International
BWD	Brownwood, Texas, USA	Brownwood Airport
OST	Bruges, Belgium	Ostend/Bruges Intl Airport
BWN	Brunei/Bandar Seri Begawan, Brunei Darussalam	Brunei International
BQK	Brunswick, GA, USA	Glynco Jetport
BRU	Brussels, Belgium National	Brussels Airport
BGA	Bucaramanga, Colombia	Aeropuerto Internacional de Palonegro
BBU	Bucharest, Romania	Bucharest Baneasa Intl Airport
OTP	Bucharest, Romania	Otopeni Intl Airport
BUD	Budapest, Hungary	Liszt Ferenc Intl Airport
EZE	Buenos Aires, Buenos Aires, Argentina	Ezeiza Ministro Pistarini International Airport

148 GENERAL ENGLISH → FOR AVIATION

3-letter IATA Code	City/Country	Airport
AEP	Buenos Aires, Buenos Aires, Argentina	Jorge Newberry
BUF	Buffalo, NY, USA	Buffalo Niagara International Airport (formerly Greater Buffalo Intl Airport)
BJM	Bujumbura, Burundi	Bujumbura Airport
BHK	Bukhara, Uzbekistan	Bukhara Inernational Airport
BUQ	Bulawayo, Zimbabwe	Bulawayo Airport
UGA	Bulgan, Bulgan, Mongolia	Bulgan Airport
IFP	Bullhead City, AZ, USA	Bullhead International Airport
BDB	Bundaberg, Australia	Bundaberg Airport
BUX	Bunia, Democratic Republic of the Congo (Zaire)	Bunia Airport
BUR	Burbank, CA, USA	Burbank Glendale Pasadena Airport
BRL	Burlington, IA, USA	Burlington Municipal Airport
BTV	Burlington, VT, USA	Burlington International Airport
BWT	Burnie, Australia	Burnie Airport
YPZ	Burns Lake, British Columbia, Canada	Burns Lake Airport
BTM	Butte, MT, USA	Butte Airport
YKZ	Buttonville, Canada	Buttonville Municipal Airport
BXU	Butuan, Philippines	Butuan Airport
BZG	Bydgoszcz, Poland	Bydgoszcz Ignacy Jan Paderewski Airport

	C	
CFR	Caen, France	Caen – Carpiquet Airport
CGY	Cagayan De Oro, Philippines	Lumbia Airport
CAG	Cagliari, Sardinia, Italy	Cagliani Elmas Airport
PLS	Caicos, Turks and Caicos Islands	Providenciales
CNS	Cairns, Queensland, Australia	Cairns International Airport
CAI	Cairo, Egypt	Cairo International Airport
CJA	Cajamarca, Peru	Cjamarca Airport
CJC	Calama, Chile	El Loa Airport
CCU	Calcutta (Kolkata), India	Calcutta International Airport
CDW	Caldwell, New Jersey, USA	Caldwell Airport
YYC	Calgary, Alberta, Canada	Calgary Intl Airport
CLO	Cali, Colombia	Alfonso Bonilla Aragon International Airport
CCJ	Calicut, India	Calicut International Airport
CLY	Calvi, Corsica, France	Calvi – Sainte Catherine Airport
XAZ	Cambellton, New Brunswick, Canada	Campbellton Airport
CBG	Cambridge, England, United Kingdom	Cambridge Airport

CITIES, AIRPORTS AND 3-LETTER IATA CODES ← APPENDIX 2

3-letter IATA Code	City/Country	Airport
YCB	Cambridge Bay, Canada	Cambridge Bay Airport
CDH	Camden, AR, USA	
YBL	Campbell River British Columbia, Canada	Campbell River Airport Metropolitan Area
YHH	Campbell River Harbor, Canada	Campbell River Harbor
CAL	Campbeltown, United Kindgom	Campbeltown Airport
CPE	Campeche, Mexico	Campeche Airport
CPV	Campina Grande, Brazil	Campina Grande Airport
CPQ	Campinas, São Paulo, Brazil	Aeroporto Internacional de Viracopos
CGR	Campo Grande, Mato Grosso do Sul, Brazil	Aeroporto Internacional de Campor Grande
CAJ	Canaima, Venezuela	Canaima Airport
LPA	Canary Islands, Gran Canaria, Canary Islands, Spain	Aeropuerto De Gran Canaria
CBR	Canberra, Australian Capital Territory, Australia	Canberra Intl Airport
CUN	Cancun, Mexico	Cancun Intl Airport
JCA	Cannes, France	Croisette Heliport
YTE	Cape Dorset, Canada	Cape Dorset Airport
CIW	Canouan Island, St Vincent and the Grenadines	Canouan Island Airport
CNY	Canyonlands, UT, USA	Canyonlands
CGI	Cape Girardeau, MO, USA	Cape Girardeau Municipal Airport
EHM	Cape Newenham, Alaska, USA	Cape Newenham Airport
CPT	Cape Town, South Africa	Cape Town Intl Airport
PRJ	Capri, Italy	Capri Airport
CCS	Caracas, Venezuela	Simon Bolivar International
CKS	Carajás, Pará, Brazil	Aeroporto de Carajás – Parauapebas
MDH	Carbondale, IL, USA	Southern Illinois Airport
CCF	Carcassonne, France	Carcassonne Airport
CWL	Cardiff, Wales, United Kingdom	Cardiff Airport
CLD	Carlsbad, CA, USA	McClellan – Palomar Airport
CNM	Carlsbad, NM, USA	Carlsbad Airport/Cavern City Terminal
CRU	Carriacou Island, Grenada	Carriacou Island Airport
CTG	Cartagena, Colombia	Rafael Nunez Intl Airport
CUP	Carupano, Venezuela	Carupano Airport
LRM	Casa De Campo, Dominican Republic	La Romana Intl Airport
CAS	Casablanca, Morocco	Casablanca – Anfa Airport
CMN	Casablanca, Morocco	Mohamed V Intl Airport
CAC	Cascavel, Brazil	Cascavel Airport
CPR	Casper, WY, USA	Natrona County Intl Airport

GENERAL ENGLISH → FOR AVIATION

3-letter IATA Code	City/Country	Airport
YCG	Castlegar, British Columbia, Canada	West Kootenay Regional Airport
CTA	Catania, Sicily, Italy	Fontanarossa Airport
SDQ	Causedo/Santo Domingo, Dominican Republic	Las Americas International Airport
CXJ	Caxias do Sul, Brazil	Caxias do Sul Airport
CAY	Cayenne, French Guiana	Cayenne – Félix Eboué Airport
CYB	Cayman Brac Island, Cayman Islands	Captain Charles Kirkconnell Intl Airport
GCM	Cayman Islands, Grand Cayman Island	Owen Roberts Intl Airport
CEB	Cebu, Philippines	Mactan Cebu Intl Airport
CDC	Cedar City, UT, USA	Cedar City Regional Airport
CED	Ceduna, Australia	Ceduna Airport
SFB	Cantral Florida, Orlando, FL, USA	Sanford Central Florida Regional Airport
CDR	Chadron, NE, USA	Chadron Municipal Airport
CMF	Chambery, France	Chambéry – Savoie Airport
CMI	Champaign, IL, USA	Univ of Illinois Willard Airport
IXC	Chandigarh, India	Chandigarh Airport
CGQ	Changchun, China	Changchun Longjia Intl Airport
CGD	Changde, China	Changde Taohuayuan Airport
CSX	Changsha, China	Changsha Huanghua Intl Airport
CIH	Changzhi, China	Changzhi Wangcun Airport
CZX	Changzhu, China	Changzhou Benniu Airport
CHQ	Chania, Crete Island, Greece	Chania Intl Airport
LEC	Chapada Diamantina, Brazil	Chapada Diamantina Airport
XAP	Chapecó, Brazil	Chapecó Airport
CPC	San Martin de Los Andes, Neuquen, Argentina	Aeropuerto Chapelco
YLD	Chapleau, Ontario, Canada	Chapleau Airport
CHS	Charleston, SC, USA	Charleston International Airport
CRW	Charleston, WV, USA	Yeager Airport
CTL	Charleville, Queensland, Australia	Charleville Airport
CLT	Charlotte, NC, USA	Charlotte/Douglas Intl Airport
STT	Charlotte, St Thomas Island, VI, USA	Cyril E King Airport
CHO	Charlottesville, VA, USA	Charlottesville/Albemarle Airport
YYG	Charlottetown, Prince Edward Island, Canada	Charlottetown Airport
XCM	Chatham, Ontario, Canada	Chatham Airport
CHA	Chattanooga, TN, USA	Lovell Field Airport
CYF	Chefornak, Alaska, USA	Chefornak Airport
CJU	Cheju, South Korea	Cheju Intl Airport

CITIES, AIRPORTS AND 3-LETTER IATA CODES ← APPENDIX 2

3-letter IATA Code	City/Country	Airport
CEK	Chelyabinsk, Russia	Chelyabinsk Airport
CTU	Chengdu, China	Chengdu Shuangliu Intl Airport
MAA	Chennai (Madras), India	Chennai International Airport
STT	Charlotte, St Thomas Island, VI, USA	Cyril E King Arpt
CEK	Chelyabinsk, Russia	Chelyabinsk Airport
CJJ	Cheong Ju City, Republic of Korea	Cheong Ju City Airport
CER	Cherbourg, France	Maupertus Airport
CTM	Chetumal, Mexico	Chetumal Airport
VAK	Chevak, Alaska	Chevak Airport
YHR	Chevery, Canada	Chevery Airport
CYS	Cheyenne, WY, USA	Cheyenne Municipal Airport
CNX	Chiang Mai, Thailand	Chiang Mai Airport
CEI	Chiang Rai, Thailand	Chiang Rai Airport
CYI	Chiayi, Taiwan	Chiayi Airport
YMT	Chibougamau, Quebec, Canada	Chibougamau Chapais Airport
CGX	Chicago, IL, USA	Merrill C. Meigs Field
CHI	Chicago, IL, USA	Chicago FSS
DPA	Chicago, IL, USA	Dupage County
GYY	Chicago, IN, USA	Gary Airport
MDW	Chicago, IL, USA	Midway
NOH	Chicago, IL, USA	Chicago NAS
ORD	Chicago, IL, USA	O'hare International Airport
PWK	Chicago, IL, USA Pal	Waukee Airport
RFD	Chicago/Rockford, IL, USA	Chicago Rockford International Airport
CIX	Chiclayo, Peru	Cornel Ruiz Airport
CIC	Chico, CA, USA	Chico Municipal Air Terminal
KCG	Chignik, AK, USA	Chignik Fisheries Airport
KCL	Chignik, AK, USA	Chignik Lagoon Airport
KCQ	Chignik Lake, Alaska, USA	Chignik Lake Airport
CUU	Chihuahua, Chihuahua, Mexico	Genvillalobos Airport
YAI	Chillan, Chile	Chillan Airport
HIN	Chinju, Republic of Korea	Chinju Airport
JKH	Chios, Greece	Chios Airport
YKU	Chisasibi, Canada	Chisasibi Airport
KIV	Chisinau (Kishinev), Moldova	Chisinau (Kishinev)
CJL	Chitral, Pakistan	Chitral Airport
CGP	Chittagong, Bangladesh	Patenga Airport
COQ	Choibalsan, Dornod, Mongolia	Choibalsan Airport
CKG	Chongqing, China	Chongqing Jiangbei Airport

GENERAL ENGLISH → FOR AVIATION

3-letter IATA Code	City/Country	Airport
CHC	Christchurch, New Zealand	Christchurch Intl Airport
STX	Christiansted, St Croix Island, VI, USA	Alexander Hamilton Airport
CXI	Christmas Island, Australia	Cassidy Airport
YYQ	Churchill, Manitoba, Canada	Churchill Airport
CIA	Ciampino, Rome, Italy	Ciampino Airport
CVG	Cincinnati, OH, USA	Greater Cincinnati Intl Airport
LUK	Cincinnati, Ohio, USA	Lunken Field Airport
CBL	Ciudad Bolivar, Venezuela	Tomás de Heres Airport
CME	Ciudad Del Carmen, Campeche, Mexico	
CJS	Ciudad Juarez, Chihuahua, Mexico	International Abraham Gonzalez
CEN	Ciudad Obregon, Sonora, Mexico	Ciudad Obregon Airport
CVM	Ciudad Victoria, Mexico	Ciudad Victoria Airport
CKB	Clarksburg, WV, USA Clarksburg	Benedum Airport
CFE	Clermont-ferrand, France	Clermont-ferrand Auvergne Airport
CLE	Cleveland, OH, USA	Hopkins International Airport
BKL	Cleveland Lakefront, OH, USA	Burke Lakefront Airport
CNJ	Cloncurry, Australia	Cloncurry Airport
CVN	Clovis, NM, USA	Clovis Municipal Airport
CLJ	Cluj, Romania	Cluj-Napoca International Airport
YCY	Clyde River, Canada	Clyde River Airport
XGJ	Cobourg, Ontario, Canada	Cobourg/Via Rial Service
CBB	Cochabamba, Bolivia	Jorge Wilstermann International Airport (formerly San Jose de La Banda)
COK	Cochin, India	Naval Air Station
COD	Cody, Wyoming, USA	Yellowstone Regional Airport
CFA	Coffee Point, Alaska, USA	Coffee Point Airport
CFS	Coffs Harbour, Australia	Coffs Harbour Airport
CJB	Coimbatore, India	Coimbatore International Airport
CDB	Cold Bay, Alaska, USA	Cold Bay Airport
CLQ	Colima, Colima, Mexico	Colima Airport
CGN	Cologne/Bonn, Germany	Koeln/Bonn Airport
CMB	Colombo, Sri Lanka	Katunayake International
CYR	Colonia, Uruguay	Colonia Airport
COS	Colorado Springs, CO, USA	Colorado Springs Municipal
COU	Columbia, MO, USA	Columbia Regional
CAE	Columbia, SC, USA	Columbia Metropolitan Airport

CITIES, AIRPORTS AND 3-LETTER IATA CODES ← APPENDIX 2

3-letter IATA Code	City/Country	Airport
CSG	Columbus, GA, USA	Columbus Metropolitan / Fort Benning
GTR	Columbus, MS, USA	Golden Airport
CMH	Columbus, OH, USA	Port Columbus Intl Airport
CJT	Comitan, Mexico	Comitan Airport
CRD	Comodoro Rivadavia, Chubut, Argentina	Comodoro Rivadavia
YQQ	Comox, British Columbia, Canada	Comox Civil Air Terminal
CKY	Conakry, Guinea	Conakry International Airport
CCP	Concepcion, Chile	Carriel Sur
NOC	Connaught, Rep of Ireland	Ireland West Airport Knock
CND	Constanta, Romania	Kogalniceanu Airport
CZL	Constantine, Algeria	Ain El Bey Airport
CPD	Coober Pedy, Australia	Coober Pedy Airport
OOM	Cooma, New South Wales, Australia	Cooma – Snowy Mountains Airport
CPH	Copenhagen, Denmark	Copenhagen Airport
CPO	Copiapo, Chile	Chamonate Airport
YCO	Coppermine, Northwest Territories, Canada	Coppermine Airport
COR	Cordoba, Cordoba, Argentina	Pajas Blancas
CDV	Cordova, AK, USA	Merle K (Mudhole) Smith Airport
CFU	Corfu (Kerkyra), Greece	Kerkyra
ORK	Cork, Ireland Cork	Cork Airport
YCC	Cornwall, Ontario, Canada	Cornwall Regional Airport
CZE	Coro, Venezuela	Coro Airport
CRP	Corpus Christi, TX, USA	Corpus Christi International Airport
CNQ	Corrientes, Argentina	Corrientes Airport
CEZ	Cortez, CO, USA	Montezuma County Airport
CMG	Corumbá, Mato Grosso do Sul, Brazil	Aeroporto Interncional de Corumbá
OLB	Costa Smeralda	Olbia, Italy
CBO	Cotabato, Philippines	Cotabato Airport
XGK	Coteau, Quebec, Canada	Coteau/Via Rail Service
COO	Cotonou, Benin	Cotonou Airport
YCA	Courtenay, British Columbia, Canada	Courtenay Aripark
CWT	Cowra, New South Wales, Australia	Cowra Airport
GXQ	Coyhaique, Chile	Teniente Vidal Coihaique Airport
CZM	Cozumel, Quintana Roo, Mexico	Aeropuerto Intl de Cozumel
YXC	Cranbrook, British Columbia, Canada	Cranbrook

GENERAL ENGLISH → FOR AVIATION

3-letter IATA Code	City/Country	Airport
CEC	Crescent City, CA, USA	Crescent City Municipal Airport
CRI	Crooked Island, Bahamas	Colonel Hill Airport
CRV	Crotone, Italy	Crotone Airport
CZS	Cruzeiro do Sul, Brazil	Cruzeiro do Sul
CUC	Cucuta, Colombia	Camilo Daza International Airport
CUE	Cuenca, Ecuador	Mariscal Lamar Airport
CVJ	Cuernavaca, Mexico	Cuernavaca Airport
CGB	Cuiabá, Mato Grosso, Brazil	Cuiabá
AGT	Cuidad Del Este, Paraguay	Cuidad Del Este Airport
CPX	Culebra, Puerto Rico	Culebra Airport
CUL	Culiacan, Sinaloa, Mexico	Aeropuerto Internacional de Culiacan
CUM	Cumana, Venezuela	Antonio Jose de Sucre Airport
CBE	Cumberland, MD, USA	Cumberland Regional Airport
CWB	Curitiba, Paraná, Brazil	Aeroporto Internacional Afonso Pena
CUZ	Cuzco, Peru	Velazco Astete International Airport

	D	
DAD	Da Nang, Vietnam	Da Nang International Airport
DKR	Dakar, Senegal	Yoff-Léopold Sédar Senghor International Airport
VIL	Dakhla, Morocco	Dakla Airport
DLM	Dalaman, Turkey	Dalaman Airport
DLZ	Dalanzadgad, Omnogovi, Mongolia	Dalanzadgad Airport
DLI	Dalat, Vietnam	Dalat Airport
DLU	Dali City, China	Dali City
DLC	Dalian, China	Dalian Zhoushuizi International Airport
DAL	Dallas, TX, USA	Dallas Love Field
DFW	Dallas/Ft Worth, TX, USA	Dallas Ft Worth International
DAM	Damascus, Syria	Damascus Intl
DMM	Damman, Saudi Arabia	King Fahad Airport
DDG	Dandong, China	Dandong
DGA	Dangriga, Belize	Dangriga Airport
DNV	Danville, IL, USA	Vermilion County Airport
DAR	Dar Es Salaam, Tanzania International	Dar Es Salaam International Airport
DRW	Darwin, Northern Territory, Australia	Darwin International Airport
YDN	Dauphin, Manitoba, Canada	Dauphin Airport

CITIES, AIRPORTS AND 3-LETTER IATA CODES ← APPENDIX 2

3-letter IATA Code	City/Country	Airport
DVO	Davao, Philippines Mati	Francisco Bangoy Intl Airport
YDI	Davis Inlet, Canada	Davis Inlet Airport
DWD	Dawadmi, Saudi Arabia	Dawadmi Airport
YDQ	Dawson Creek, British Columbia, Canada	Dawson Creek Airport
DYG	Dayong, China	Dayong Airport
DAY	Dayton, OH, USA	James M Cox Dayton International Airport
DAB	Daytona Beach, FL, USA	Daytona Beach Intl Airport
LGI	Deadman's Cay / Long Island, Bahamas	Deadman's Cay Airport
DOL	Deauville, France	Deauville – Saint Gatien Airport
DBM	Debre Marcos, Ethiopia	Debre Marcos Airport
DEB	Debrechen, Hungary	Debrechen Airport
DEC	Decatur, IL, USA	Decatur Airport
YDF	Deer Lake, Newfoundland, Canada Deer Lake	Deer Lake Airport
YVZ	Deer Lake, Ontario, Canada	Deer Lake Regional Airport
DRT	Del Rio, TX, USA	Del Rio Intl Airport
DEL	Delhi, India	Indira Gandhi International Airport
DEM	Dembidollo, Ethiopia	Dembidollo Airport
DNM	Denham, Western Australia	Denham Airport
DNZ	Denizli, Turkey	Denizli Airport
DPS	Denpasar Bali, Indonesia	Ngurah Rai Intl Airport
DEN	Denver, CO, USA	Denver International Airport
DEA	Dera Ghazi Khan, Pakistan	Dera Ghazi Khan Airport
DSK	Dera Ismail Khan, Pakistan	Dera Ismail Khan Airport
DNF	Derna, Libya	Martuba Airport
DSM	Des Moines, IA, USA	Des Moines Intl Airport
YDS	Desolation Sound, Canada	Desolation Sound Airport
DSE	Dessie, Ethiopia	Dessie Airport
DSI	Destin, FL, USA	Fort Walton Beach Aiport
DTW	Detroit, MI, USA Detroit	Detroit Metropolitan Wayne County Airport
YIP	Detroit, MI, USA	Willow Run Airport, Ypsilanti
DVL	Devils Lake, North Dakota, USA	Devils Lake Airport
DPO	Devonport, Tasmania, Australia	Devonport Airport
DHA	Dhahran, Saudi Arabia	Dhahran Intl Aiport
DAC	Dhaka, Bangladesh	Dhaka/Hazrat Shahjalal International Airport
DHM	Dharamsala/Kangra, Himachal Pradesh, India	Kangra Gaggal Dharamsala Airport
DIB	Dibrugarh, India Chabua	Dibrugarh Airport

GENERAL ENGLISH → FOR AVIATION

3-letter IATA Code	City/Country	Airport
DIJ	Dijon, France Longvic	Dijon Airport
DIK	Dickinson, North Dakota, USA	Dickinson Airport
DIN	Dien Bien Phu, Vietnam	Dien Bien Phy Airport
DIL	Dili, East Timor	Timor
DLG	Dillingham, Alaska, USA	Dillingham Airport
DPL	Dipolog, Philippines	Dipolog Airport
DIG	Diqing, China	Diqing Airport
DIR	Dire Dawa, Ethiopia	Dire Dawa Airport
DIU	Diu, India	Diu Airort
DIY	Diyarbakir, Turkey	Diyarbakir Airport
DJE	Djerba, Tunisia	Melita Airport
JIB	Djibouti, Djibouti-Ambouli	Djibouti-Ambouli Intl Airport
DNK	Dnepropetrovsk, Ukraine	Dnepropetrovsk Airport
DDC	Dodge City, KS, USA	Dodge City Regional Airport
DOH	Doha, Qatar	Doha Intl Airport
DCF	Dominica, Dominica	Cane Field
DOM	Dominica, Dominica	Melville Halll Airport
DSA	Doncaster, Sheffield, UK	Robin Hood Airport
DOK	Donetsk, Ukraine	Sergey Prokofiev Intl Airport
DTM	Dortmund, Germany Wickede	Dortmund Airport
DHN	Dothan, AL, USA	Dothan Regional Airport
DLA	Douala, Cameroon	Douala Intl Airport
DRS	Dresden, Germany	Dresden Airport
XDM	Drummondville, Quebec, Canada	Drummondville Airport
YHD	Dryden, Ontario, Canada	Dryden Regional Airport
DUJ	Du Bois, PA, USA	Jefferson County Airport
DXB	Dubai, United Arab Emirates	Dubai International Airport
DBO	Dubbo, New South Wales, Australia	Dubbo City Regional Airport
DUB	Dublin, Ireland	Dublin Airport
DBV	Dubrovnik, Croatia	Dubrovnik Airport
DBQ	Dubuque, IA, USA	Dubuque Regional Airport
DLH	Duluth, MN, USA	Duluth International Airport
DGT	Dumaguete, Philippines	Dumaguete Airport
DUQ	Duncan/Quam, British Columbia, Canada	Duncan – Quam Airport
DND	Dundee, Scotland, United Kingdom	Dundee Airport
DUD	Dunedin, New Zealand	Dunedin Intl Airport
DNH	Dunhuang, China	Dunhuang Airport
DRO	Durango, CO, USA	Durango La Plata County Airport

CITIES, AIRPORTS AND 3-LETTER IATA CODES ← APPENDIX 2

157

3-letter IATA Code	City/Country	Airport
DGO	Durango, Durango, Mexico	General Guadalupe Victoria Intl Airport
DUR	Durban/La Mercy, South Africa	King Shaka International Airport (La Mercy Airport, Replaced Louis Botha airport)
DUS	Dusseldorf, Germany	Dusseldorf Airport
DUT	Dutch Harbor, AK, USA	Dutch Harbor Aiport
E		
ELS	East London, South Africa	East London Airport
EMA	East Midlands, England, United Kingdom	East Midlands Intl Airport
IPC	Easter Island, Chile	Mataveri Intl Airport
ESD	Eastsound, WA, USA	Orcas Island Airport
EAU	Eau Claire, WI, USA	Eau Claire Airport
ECH	Echuca, Australia	Echuca Airport
EDI	Edinburgh, Scotland, United Kingdom	Edinburgh Airport
YEG	Edmonton, Alberta, Canada	Edmonton International Airport
YXD	Edmonton, Alberta, Canada	Edmonton City Center Airport
EDR	Edward River, Queensland, Australia	Edward River Airport
EIN	Eindhoven, Netherlands	Eindhoven Airport
SVX	Ekaterinburg, Russia	Sheremtyevo Airport
BCQ	El Beida, Libya	Brala *or* Brack Airport
FTE	El Calafate, Argentina	El Calafate Airport
AZS	El Catey, Dominican Republic	Samana El Catey International Airport
ELP	El Paso, TX, USA	El Paso International Airport
ESR	El Salvador, Chile	Ricardo García Posada Airport
ETH	Elat, Israel Elat	Eilat Airport
EBA	Elba Island, Italy	Marina Di Campo – Elba Airport
EKO	Elko, NV, USA	Elko Regional Airport
YEL	Elliot Lake, Ontario, Canada	Elliot Lake Airport
ELM	Elmira/Corning, NY, USA	Elmira Corning Regional Airport
ELY	Ely, NV, USA	Ely Municipal Airport
EMD	Emerald, Queensland, Australia	Emerald Airport
WDG	Enid, OK, USA	Enid Woodring Municipal Airport
ENS	Enschede, Netherlands	Enschede Airport Twente
EBB	Entebbe/Kampala, Uganda	Entebbe Intl Airport
ERF	Erfurt, Germany	Erfurt Airport
ERI	Erie, PA, USA	Erie International Airport
ERZ	Erzurum, Turkey	Erzurum Airport

GENERAL ENGLISH → FOR AVIATION

3-letter IATA Code	City/Country	Airport
EBJ	Esbjerg, Denmark	Esbjerg Airport
ESC	Escanaba, MI, USA	Delta County Airport
EQS	Esquel, Argentina	Esquel Airport
EPR	Esperance, Western Australia, Australia	Esperance Airport
YPF	Esquimalt, British Columbia, Canada	Esquimalt Airport
EUG	Eugene, OR, USA	Eugene Airport
EVV	Evansville, IN, USA	Evansville Regional Airport
EVE	Evenes, Norway	Harstad/Narvik Airport
EXT	Exeter, England, United Kingdom	Exeter Intl Airport

	F	
FAI	Fairbanks, AK, USA	Fairbanks International Airport
FRM	Fairmont, MN, USA	Fairmont Municipal Airport
LYP	Faisalabad, Pakistan	Faisalabad Intl Airport
FAR	Fargo, ND, USA	Hector International Airport
FRG	Farmingdale, Long Island, NY, USA	Republic Airport
FMN	Farmington, NM, USA	Four Corners Regional Airport
FAO	Faro, Portugal	Aeroporto de Faro
FAE	Faroe Islands, Faroe Islands	Vagar Airport
FYV	Fayetteville, AR, USA	Fayetteville Executive Airport (Drake Field)
XNA	Fayetteville, AR, USA	Northwest Arkansas Regional
FAY	Fayetteville, NC, USA	Fayetteville Regional Airport
FFM	Fergus Falls, MN, USA	Fergus Falls Municipal Airport
FEN	Fernando de Noronha, Brazil	Fernando de Noronha Airport
FEZ	Fez, Morocco	Fez – Sais Airport
FLG	Flagstaff, AZ, USA	Flagstaff Pulliam Airport
YFO	Flin Flon, Canada	Flin Flon Airport
FNT	Flint, MI, USA	Bishop Intl Airport
FLR	Florence, Italy	Florence Airport
FLO	Florence, SC, USA	Florence Regional Airport
FRS	Flores, Guatemala	Flores Intl Airport *or* Aeropuerto Internacional Mundo Maya
FLN	Florianópolis, Santa Catarina, Brazil	Hercilio Luz Airport
FRO	Floro, Norway	Floro Airport
FDE	Forde, Norway	Forde Airport
FMA	Formosa, Formosa, Argentina	Formosa Airport
YFA	Fort Albany, Canada	Fort Albany Airport
YVP	Fort Chimo (Kuujjuaq), Quebec, Canada	Fort Chimo Airport
FNL	Fort Collins/Loveland, CO, USA	Fort Collins/Loveland Airport

CITIES, AIRPORTS AND 3-LETTER IATA CODES ← APPENDIX 2

3-letter IATA Code	City/Country	Airport
FDF	Fort ee France, Martinique	Fort de France – Martinique Aimé Césaire Intl Airport
FOD	Fort Dodge, IA, USA	Fort Dodge Regional Airport
FHU	Fort Huachuca/Sierra Vista, AZ, USA	Sierra Vista Municipal Airport
FLL	Fort Lauderdale, FL, USA	Ft Lauderdale / Hollywood Intl Airport
TBN	Fort Leonard Wood, MO, USA	Waynesville – St. Robert Regional Airport
YMM	Fort Mcmurray, Alberta, Canada	Fort Mcmurray Airport
RSW	Fort Myers, FL, USA	Florida Intl Airport
YYE	Fort Nelson, Canada	Fort Nelson Airport
YXJ	Fort Saint John, British Columbia, Canada	North Peace Regional Airport
YFS	Fort Simpson, Northwest Territories, Canada	Fort Simpson Airport
FSM	Fort Smith, AR, USA	Fort Smith Regional Airport
YSM	Fort Smith, Northwest Territories, Canada	Fort Smith Airport
FWA	Fort Wayne, IN, USA	Fort Wayne Intl Airport
FOR	Fortaleza, Ceara, Brazil Fortaleza	Pinto Martins Airport
FRA	Frankfurt, Germany	Frankfurt International
HHN	Frankfurt, Germany	Frankfurt-Hahn Airport
FKL	Franklin, PA, USA Chess Lamberton	Venango Regional Airport
YXX	Fraser Valley/Abbotsford, Canada	Abbotsford Airport
EZF	Fredericksburg, Virginia, USA	Shannon Airport
YFC	Fredericton, New Brunswick, Canada	Fredericton Municipal Airport
FPO	Freeport, Bahamas	Freeport Intl Airport/Grand Bahamas Intl Airport
FAT	Fresno, CA, USA	Fresno Yosemite Intl Airport
FRD	Friday Harbor, WA, USA	Friday Harbor Airport
FDH	Friedrichshafen, Germany	Friedrichshafen Airport
YFA	Ft Albany, Canada	Fort Albany Airport
YVP	Ft Chimo (Kuujjuaq), Quebec, Canada	Fort Chimo Airport
FUE	Fuerteventura/Puerto Del Rosario, Canary Islands	Puerto del Rosario Airport
FUK	Fukuoka, Japan	Fukuoka Airport
FUN	Funafuti, Funafuti Atol	Tuvalu International Airport
FNC	Funchal, Madeira Islands, Portugal	Aeroporto de Madeira
FUG	Fuyang, China	Fuyang Airport
FOC	Fuzhou, China	Fuzhou Airport

	G	
GBE	Gaborone, Botswana	Sii Seretse Khrama Intl Airport
GNV	Gainesville, FL, USA	Gainesville Regional Airport

GENERAL ENGLISH → FOR AVIATION

3-letter IATA Code	City/Country	Airport
GPS	Galapagos Islands, Ecuador	Baltra Airport *or* Seymon Airport
GAL	Galena, AK, USA	Galena Aiport
GBG	Galesburg, IL, USA	Galesburg Airport
GUP	Gallup, NM, USA	Gallup Municipal Airport
GLS	Galveston, TX, USA	Scholes Intl Airport
GWY	Galway, Ireland	Galway Airport
YQX	Gander, Newfoundland, Canada	Gander Intl Airport
YGG	Ganges Harbor, Canada	Ganges Harbor Airport
KOW	Ganzhou, China	Ganzhou
GCK	Garden City, KS, USA	Garden City Municipal Airport
GYY	Gary, IN, USA	Gary Regional
YGP	Gaspe, Quebec, Canada	Michel – Pouliot Gaspé Airport
ELQ	Gassim, Saudi Arabia	Gassim Airport
YND	Gatineau, Quebec, Canada	Gatineau – Ottawa Executive Airport
GAU	Gauhati, India	Borjhar Airport
GDN	Gdansk, Poland	Rebiechowo Airport
GVA	Geneva, Switzerland	Geneva Airport
GOA	Genova, Italy	Christoforo Colombo Airport
GGT	George Town, Bahamas	Exuma International Airport
GRJ	George, South Africa	George Airport
GEO	Georgetown, Guyana	Timehri Cheddi Jogan Intl Airport
GRO	Gerona, Spain	Costa Brava Airport
GHT	Ghat, Libya	Ghat Airport
GIB	Gibraltar	Gibraltar International Airport
GIL	Gilgit, Pakistan	Gilgit Airport
GCC	Gillette, WY, USA	Campbell County Airport
YGB	Gillies Bay, British Columbia, Canada	Gillies Bay Airport
GIZ	Gizan (Jizan), Jizan province, Saudi Arabia	Gizan Airport
YHK	Gjoa Haven, Canada	Gjoa Haven Airport
GLT	Gladstone, Australia	Gladstone Airport
GGW	Glasgow, MT, USA	Wokad Field
GLA	Glasgow, Scotland, United Kingdom	Glasgow Airport
PIK	Glasgow, Scotland, United Kingdom	Glasgow Prestwick Airport
GDV	Glendive, MT, USA	Dawson Community Airport
GOI	Goa, India	Dabolim Airport
YGO	Gods Narrows, Canada	Gods Narrows Airport
ZGI	Gods River, Manitoba, Canada	Gods River Airport
GYN	Goiânia, Brazil	Aeroporto de Goiânia

CITIES, AIRPORTS AND 3-LETTER IATA CODES ← APPENDIX 2

3-letter IATA Code	City/Country	Airport
OOL	Gold Coast, Queensland, Australia	Gold Coast Airport
GLF	Golfito, Costa Rica	Golfito Airport
GLV	Golovin, AK, USA	Golovin Airport
GLD	Goodland, KS, USA Renner Field	Goodland Municipal Airport
YYR	Goose Bay, Newfoundland, Canada	Goose Bay Municipal Airport
GKA	Goroka, Papua New Guinea	Goroka Airport
GTO	Gorontalo, Indonesia	Tolotio Airport
GOT	Gothenburg, Sweden	Gothenburg – Landvetter Airport
GOV	Gove, Northern Territory, Australia	Gove Airport
GHB	Governor's Harbour, Bahamas	Governor's Harbour Airport
LPA	Gran Canaria, Canary Islands, Spain	Aeropuerto De Gran Canaria
GRX	Granada, Spain	Federico Garcia Lorca/ Granada-Jaén Airport
GCN	Grand Canyon, AZ, USA	Grand Canyon National Park Airport
GCM	Grand Cayman Island, Cayman Islands	Owen Roberts Intl Airport
GFK	Grand Forks, ND, USA	Grand Forks International Airport
GRI	Grand Island, NE, USA	Central Nebraska Regional Airport
GJT	Grand Junction, CO, USA	Walker Field Grand Junction Regional Airport
GRR	Grand Rapids, MI, USA	Gerald R. Ford Intl Airport
GDT	Grand Turk Is, Turks and Caicos Islands	Grand Turk Island Airport
YQU	Grande Prairie, Alberta, Canada	Grande Prairie Airport
GRZ	Graz, Austria	Graz Airport
GBD	Great Bend, Kansas, USA	Great Bend Municipal Airport
GTF	Great Falls, MT, USA	Great Falls International
GRB	Green Bay, WI, USA	Austin Straubel International Airport (Austin/Straybel Field)
LWB	Greenbrier, WV, USA	Greenbrier Valley Airport
GSO	Greensboro / High Point, NC, USA	Piedmont Triad Intl Airport
GRE	Greenville, IL, USA	Municipal
PGV	Greenville, NC, USA	Pitt
GLH	Greenville, MS, USA	Greenville
GDC	Greenville, SC, USA	Donaldson Center
GMU	Greenville, SC, USA	Downtown
GSP	Greenville, SC, USA	Greenville
GCY	Greenville, TN, USA	Municipal
GVT	Greenville, TX, USA	Majors Field
YGN	Greenway Sound, Canada	Greenway Sound Airport

GENERAL ENGLISH → FOR AVIATION

3-letter IATA Code	City/Country	Airport
GNB	Grenoble, France	Grenoble – Isère Airport
GFF	Griffith, Australia	Griffith Airport
GRQ	Groningen, Netherlands	Groningen Airport Elde
GON	Groton/New London, CT, USA	Groton-New London Airport
GDL	Guadalajara, Jalisco, Mexico	Dom Miguel Hidalgo y Castilla Intl Airport
GUM	Guam, Guam	Ab Wonpat Intl Airport
CAN	Guangzhou, China	Baiyun Airport
GUA	Guatemala City, Guatemala	La Aurora Intl Airport
GYE	Guayaquil, Ecuador	Simon Bolivar Intl Airport
GYA	Guayaramerin, Bolivia	Buayaramerin Airport
GYM	Guaymas, Sonora, Mexico	General Jose M. Yanez Airport
GCI	Guernsey, Channel Islands, United Kingdom	Guernsey Airport
GUB	Guerrero Negro, Baja California Sur, Mexico	Guerrero Negro Airport
KWL	Guilin, China	Giulin Liangjiang Intl Airport
KWE	Guiyang, China	Guiyang
GPT	Gulfport, MS, USA	Gulfport/Biloxi Intl Airport
GUC	Gunnison, CO, USA	Gunnison County Airport
URY	Gurayat, Saudi Arabia	Gurayat Airport
GST	Gustavus, Alaska, USA	Gustavus Airport
GWD	Gwadar, Pakistan	Gwadar Intl Airport

	H	
HPA	Ha'Apai, Tonga	Ha'Apai Airport
HBT	Hafr Albatin, Saudi Arabia	Hafr Albatin Airport
HGR	Hagerstown, MD, USA	Hagerstown Regional Airport
HFA	Haifa, Israel	Haifa Airport
HAK	Haikou, China	Haikou Airport
HAS	Hail, Saudi Arabia	Hail Airport
HLD	Hailar, China	Hailar
HNS	Haines, AK, USA	Haines Airport
HPH	Haiphong, Vietnam	Haiphong Airport
HAC	Hachijo Jima, Japan	Hachijo Jima Airport
HKD	Hakodate, Japan	Hakodate Airport
YHZ	Halifax, Nova Scotia, Canada	Halifax International
YUX	Hall Beach, Canada	Hall Beach Airport
HAD	Halmstad, Sweden	Halmstad City Airport
HAM	Hamburg, Germany	Hamburg Airport
HTI	Hamilton Island, Queensland, Australia	Hamilton Island Airport
HLZ	Hamilton, New Zealand	Hamilton Intl Airport

CITIES, AIRPORTS AND 3-LETTER IATA CODES ← APPENDIX 2

3-letter IATA Code	City/Country	Airport
YHM	Hamilton, Ontario, Canada	John C. Munro Hamilton Intl Airport
HFT	Hammerfest, Norway	Hammerfest Airport
HNM	Hana, Hawaii, USA	Hana Airport
CMX	Hancock, MI, USA	Houghton County/Memorial
HGH	Hangzhou, China	Hangzhou Xiaoxan Intl Airport
HAN	Hanoi, Vietnam	Noibai Airport
HAJ	Hanover, Germany Langenhagen	Hanover Airport
HRE	Harare, Zimbabwe	Harare Intl Airport
ZNA	Harbour/Nanaimo, British Columbia, Canada	Harbor Airport
HRB	Harbin, China	Harbin Taiping Intl Airport
HGA	Hargeisa, Somalia	Hargeisa Airport
HRL	Harlingen, TX, USA	Valley Intl Airport
MDT	Harrisburg, PA, USA	Harrisburg International Airport
HRO	Harrison, AR, USA	Boone County Regional Airport
BDL	Hartford, CT, USA	Bradley International Airport
HSI	Hastings, NE, USA	Hastings Airport
HDY	Hat Yai, Thailand	Hat Yai Intl Airport
HAU	Haugesund, Norway	Haugesund Airport
HAV	Havana, Cuba	Jose Marti Intl Airport
HVR	Havre, MT, USA	Havre City County Airport
YHY	Hay River, Northwest Territories, Canada	Hay River Airport
HDN	Hayden, CO, USA	Yampa Valley Regional Airport
HIS	Hayman Island, Queensland, Australia	Hayman Island Airport
HYS	Hays, KS, USA	Hays Regional Airport
HFE	Hefei, China	Hefei Xinqiao Airport
HEH	Heho, Myanmar (Burma)	Heho Airport
HDB	Heidelberg, Germany	Heidelberg Airport
HLN	Helena, MT, USA	Helena Regional Airport
AGH	Helsingborg, Sweden	Angelholm/Helsingborg Airport
JHE	Helsingborg, Sweden	Helsingborg Heliport
HEL	Helsinki, Finland	Helsinki Airport
HER	Heraklion, Crete Island, Greece	Heraklion Airport
HEA	Herat, Afghanistan	Herat Intl Airport
HDF	Heringsdorf, Germany	Heringsdorf Airport
HMO	Hermosillo, Sonora, Mexico	General Ignacio Pesqueira Garcia Intl Airport
HVB	Hervey Bay, Queensland, Australia	Hervey Bay Airport

GENERAL ENGLISH → FOR AVIATION

3-letter IATA Code	City/Country	Airport
HIB	Hibbing/Chisholm, MN, USA	Hibbing Chisholm Airport
HKY	Hickory, NC, USA	Hickory Regional Airport
YOJ	High Level, Alberta, Canada	Footner Lake Airport
ITO	Hilo, HI, USA	Hilo Intl Airport
HHH	Hilton Head, SC, USA	Hilton Head Airport
HIJ	Hiroshima, Japan	Hiroshima Airport
SGN	Ho Chi Minh City, Vietnam	Tan Son Nhat Intl Airport
HBA	Hobart, Tasmania, Australia	Hobart Cambridge Airport
HOB	Hobbs, NM, USA	Lea County Regional Airport
HDS	Hoedspruit, South Africa	Hoedspruit Airport
HOQ	Hof, Germany	Hof Airport
HOF	Hofuf, Saudi Arabia	Hofuf Airport
HET	Hohhot, China	Hohhot Baita Intl Airport
HKK	Hokitika, New Zealand	Hokitika Airport
YHI	Holman Island, Northwest Territories, Canada	Holman Airport
HOM	Homer, AK, USA	Homer Airport
HKG	Hong Kong	Honh Kong Intl Airport
HIR	Honiara/Guadalcanal, Solomon Islands	Henderson International Airport
HVG	Honningsvag, Norway	Honningsvag Airport
HNL	Honolulu, HI, USA	Honolulu International Airport
MKK	Hoolehua, HI, USA	Molokai Airport
HNH	Hoonah, AK, USA	Hoonah Airport
HPB	Hooper Bay, AK, USA	Hooper Bay Airport
HID	Horn Island, Australia	Horn Island Airport
YHN	Hornepayne, Ontario, Canada	Hornepayne Municipal Airport
HSM	Horsham, Australia	Horsham Airport
HOR	Horta, Portugal	Horta Airport
HKN	Hoskins, Papua New Guinea	Hoskins Airport
HOT	Hot Springs, AR, USA	Hot Springs National Park Arkansas – Memorial Field Airport
HTN	Hotan, China	Hotan Airport
HUM	Houma, LA, USA	Houma – Terrebonne Airport
HUQ	Houn, Libya	Houn Airport
IAH	Houston, TX, USA	George Bush Intercontinental Houston Airport
EFD	Houston, TX, USA	Ellington Field
HOU	Houston, TX, USA	William P. Hobby Airport
HUH	Huahine, French Polynesia	Huahine Airport
HUN	Hualien, Taiwan	Hualien Airport
HYN	Huangyan, China	Huangyan Luqiao Airport

CITIES, AIRPORTS AND 3-LETTER IATA CODES ← APPENDIX 2

3-letter IATA Code	City/Country	Airport
HUX	Huatulco, Oaxaca, Mexico	Bahías de Huatulco Intl Airport
YHB	Hudson Bay, Saskatchewan, Canada	Hudson Bay Airport
HUI	Hue, Vietnam	Hue Airport / Phu Bai Airport
HUY	Humberside, England, United Kingdom	Humberside Airport
HTS	Huntington/Ashland, WV, USA	Huntington TriState Airport
HSV	Huntsville/Decatur, AL, USA	Huntsville Intl Airport
HRG	Hurghada, Egypt	Hurghada Intl Airport
HON	Huron, SD, USA	Huron Regional Airport
HWN	Hwange National Park, Zimbabwe	Hwange National Park Airport
HYA	Hyannis, MA, USA	Barnstable Municipal Airport
HYG	Hydaburg, AK, USA	Hydaburg Airport
HYD	Hyderabad, India	Ragiv Gandhi Intl Airport

I

3-letter IATA Code	City/Country	Airport
IAS	Iasi, Romania	Iasi Airport
IBZ	Ibiza, Spain	Ibiza Airport
IDA	Idaho Falls, ID, USA	Idaho Falls Regional Airport
IGG	Igiugig, Alaska, USA	Iguigig Airport
YGT	Igloolik, Northwest Territories, Canada	Igloolik Airport
IGU	Foz do Iguaçu, Paraná, Brazil	Aeroporto Internacional de Foz do Iguaçu
IGR	Iguazu, Misiones, Argentina	Cataratas del Iaguazú Intl Airport
JIK	Ikaria Island, Greece	Ikaria Airport
YGR	Iles De La Madeleine, Quebec, Canada	Iles De La Madeleine Airport
ILF	Ilford, Manitoba, Canada	Ilford Airport
IOS	Ilheus, Bahia, Brazil	Jorge Amado Airport
ILI	Iliamna, AK, USA	Iliamna Airport
ILO	Iloilo, Philippines	Iloilo Airport
JAV	Ilulissat, Greenland	Ilulissat Airport
IMP	Imperatriz, Maranhao, Brazil	Aeroporto de Imperatriz – Prefeito Renato Moreira
IMF	Imphal, India	Imphal Municipal Airport
IGA	Inagua, Bahamas	Inagua Airport
ICN	Incheon [Seoul], South Korea	Incheon International Airport
SHC	Indaselassie, Ethiopia	Indaselassie Airport
IND	Indianapolis, IN, USA	Indianapolis International Airport
IDR	Indore, India	Indore Airport
INN	Innsbruck, Austria	Innsbruck Airport
INL	International Falls, MN, USA	Falls International Airport

GENERAL ENGLISH → FOR AVIATION

3-letter IATA Code	City/Country	Airport
YPH	Inukjuak, Canada	Inukjuak Airport
YEV	Inuvik, Northwest Territories, Canada	Inuvik International Airport
IVC	Invercargill, New Zealand	Invercargill Airport
INV	Inverness, Scotland, United Kingdom	Inverness Airport
IYK	Inyokern, CA, USA	Inyokern Airport
IOA	Ioannina, Greece	Ioannina Intl Airport
IPI	Ipiales, Colombia	San Luis Ipiales Airport
IPH	Ipoh, Malaysia	Ipoh Airport
YFB	Iqaluit, Northwest Territories, Canada	Iqaluit Airport
IQQ	Iquique, Chile	Iquique – Diego Aracena Intl Airport
IQT	Iquitos, Peru	C.F. Secada Airport
IKT	Irkutsk, Russia	Irkutsk Airport
IMT	Iron Mountain, MI, USA	Ford Airport
IWD	Ironwood, MI, USA	Gogebic County Airport
ISH	Ischia, Italy	Ischia Airport
IFN	Isfahan, Iran	Isfahan Airport
ISG	Ishigaki, Japan	Ishigaki Airport
ISB	Islamabad, Pakistan	Islamabad Intl Airport
ILY	Islay, Scotland, United Kingdom	Islay Airport
IOM	Isle of Man, Isle of Man, United Kingdom	Ronaldsway Airport
ISC	Isles of Scilly, Isles of Scilly, United Kingdom	Saint Mary's Airport
ISP	Islip, NY, USA Long Island	MacArthur Airport
IST	Istanbul, Turkey	Ataturk Intl Airport
QIE	Istres, France	Le Tube airport
ITB	Itaituba, Brazil	Itaituba Airport
ITH	Ithaca, NY, USA	Tompkins County Airport
IVL	Ivalo, Finland	Ivalo Airport
IFO	Ivano	Frankovsk, Ukraine
YIK	Ivujivik, Canada	Ivujivik Airport
IWJ	Iwami, Japan	Iwami Airport
ZIH	Ixtapa/Zihuatanejo, Guerrero, Mexico	Ixtapa/Zihuatanejo Intl Airport
IJK	Izhevsk, Russia	Izhevsk Airport
ADB	Izmir, Turkey	Adnan Menderes Airport
IZO	Izumo, Japan	Izumo Airport

J		
JAG	Jacobabad, Pakistan	Jacobabad Airport
JAT	Jabat, Marshall Islands	Jabar Airport

CITIES, AIRPORTS AND 3-LETTER IATA CODES ← APPENDIX 2

3-letter IATA Code	City/Country	Airport
JAC	Jackson Hole, WY, USA	Jackson Hole Airport
JAN	Jackson, MS, USA	Jackson – Medgar Wiley Evens Intl Airport
MKL	Jackson, TN, USA	Mc Kellar – Sipes Regional Airport
JAX	Jacksonville, FL, USA	Jacksonville International Airport
CRG	Jacksonville, Florida, USA	Craig Municipal Airport
OAJ	Jacksonville, NC, USA	Albert J. Ellis Airport
JAI	Jaipur, India Sanganeer	Jaipur Intl Airport
HLP	Jakarta, Indonesia	Halim Perdana kusama Airport
CGK	Jakarta, Indonesia	Soekarno Hatta International
JAL	Jalapa, Mexico	Jalapa Airport
JMS	Jamestown, ND, USA	Jamestown Municipal Airport
JHW	Jamestown, NY, USA	Chautauqua County Airport
IXJ	Jammu, India Satwari	Jammu Airport
JGA	Jamnagar, India	Govardhanpur Jamnagar Airport
IXW	Jamshedpur, India	Sonari Airport
YJA	Jasper, Alberta, Canada	Jasper Airport
DJJ	Jayapura, Indonesia	Sentani Airport
JED	Jeddah, Saudi Arabia	Jeddah King Abdulaziz Intl Airport
XRY	Jerez De La Frontera, Spain	Jerez Airport
JER	Jersey, Channel Islands, United Kingdom States	Jersey Airport
JIJ	Jijiga, Ethiopia	Jijiga Airport
JIL	Jilin, China	Jilin Ertaizi Airport
JIM	Jimma, Ethiopia	Jimma Airport
TNA	Jinan, China	Jinan Yaqiang Intl Airport
JHG	Jinghong, China	Jinghong Airport
JJN	Jinjiang, China	Jinjiang Airport
GIZ	Jizan (Gizan), Jizan province, Saudi Arabia	Jizan Regional Airport
JPA	João Pessoa, Brazil	Aeroporto Presidente Castro Pinto
JDH	Jodhpur, India	Jodhpur Airport
JOE	Joensuu, Finland	Joensuu Airport
JNB	Johannesburg, South Africa	O R Tambo International Airport (formerly Jan Smuts)
JON	Johnston Island, US	Johnston Island Airport
JST	Johnstown, PA, USA	Johnstown Cambria County Airport
JHB	Johor Bahru, Malaysia	Sultan Ismail Intl Airport

GENERAL ENGLISH → FOR AVIATION

3-letter IATA Code	City/Country	Airport
JOI	Joinville, Santa Catarina, Brazil	Aeroporto de Joinville – Lauro Carneiro de Loyola
XJL	Joliette, Quebec, Canada	Joliette / Via Rail Service
JMO	Jomsom, Nepal	Jomsom Airport
JBR	Jonesboro, AR, USA	Jonesboro Municipal Airport
JKG	Jonkoping, Sweden	Jonkoping Airport
XJQ	Jonquiere, Quebec, Canada	Jonquiere / Via Rail Service
JLN	Joplin, MO, USA	Joplin Airport
JRH	Jorhat, India	Jorhat Airport
JOS	Jos, Nigeria	Jos Airport
AJF	Jouf, Saudi Arabia	Jouf Airport
JDO	Juazeiro do Norte, Brazil	Juazeiro do Norte Airport
JUJ	Jujuy, Provincia Jujuy, Argentina	El Cadillal Airport
JUL	Juliaca, Peru	Juliaca Airport
JNU	Juneau, AK, USA	Juneau Airport
JYV	Jyvaskyla, Finland	Jyvaskyla Airport

	K	
ABK	Kabri Dar, Ethiopia	Kabri Dar Airport
KBL	Kabul, Afghanistan	Khwaja Rawash
DNA	Kadena AFB, Okinawa, Japan	Kadena Air Force Base
KOJ	Kagoshima, Japan	Kagoshima Airport
OGG	Kahului, HI, USA	Kahului Airport
IXH	Kailashahar, India	Kailashahar Airport
KAT	Kaitaia, New Zealand	Kaitaia Airport
KAJ	Kajaani, Finland	Kajaani Airport
KAE	Kake, AK, USA	Kake Airport (Sea Plane Bay)
AZO	Kalamazoo, MI, USA	Kalamazoo / Battle Creek Intl Airport
LUP	Kalaupapa, Hawaii, USA	Kalaupapa Airport
KGI	Kalgoorlie, Australia	Kalgoorlie Airport
KLO	Kalibo, Philippines	Kalibo Intl Airport
KGD	Kaliningrad, Russia	Kaliningrad Airport
GPI	Kalispell, MT, USA	Glacier Park International
KLR	Kalmar, Sweden	Kalmar Airport
KAL	Kaltag, AK, USA	Kaltag Airport
IXQ	Kamalpur, India	Kamalpur Airport
YKA	Kamloops, British Columbia, Canada	Kamloops Airport
MUE	Kamuela, Hawaii, USA	Waimea – Kohala Airport
KDH	Kandahar, Afghanistan	Kandahar Intl Airport

CITIES, AIRPORTS AND 3-LETTER IATA CODES ← APPENDIX 2

3-letter IATA Code	City/Country	Airport
IXY	Kandla, India	Kandla Airport
SFJ	Kangerlussuaq, Greenland	Kangerlussuaq Airport
XGR	Kangiqsualujjuaq, Canada, Georges River	Kangiqsualujjuaq Airport
YWB	Kangiqsujuaq, Canada, Wakeham Bay	Kangiqsujuaq Airport
YKG	Kangirsuk, Canada	Kangirsuk Airport
KAG	Kangnung, Republic of Korea	Kangnung Airport
DHM	Kangra, Himachal Pradesh, India	Kangra Gaggal Dharamsala Airport
KAN	Kano, Nigeria	Aminu Kano International Airport
MKC	Kansas City, MO, USA	Charles B. Wheeler Downtown Airport
MCI	Kansas City, MO, USA	Kansas City International Airport
KHH	Kaohsiung, Taiwan	Kaohsiung Intl Airport
JHM	Kapalua, HI, USA	Kapalua Airport
YYU	Kapuskasing, Ontario, Canada	Kapuskasing Airport
KHI	Karachi, Pakistan	Quaid – E – Azam Intl Airport
KAB	Kariba, Zimbabwe	Kariba Airport
KLV	Karlovy Vary, Czech Republic	Karlovy Vary Airport
FKB	Karlsruhe/Baden, Germany	Karlsruhe
KSD	Karlstad, Sweden	Karlstad Airport
AOK	Karpathos, Greece	Karpathos Island National Airport
KTA	Karratha, Australia	Karratha Airport
KSY	Kars, Turkey	Kars Airport
KSQ	Karshi, Uzbekistan	Karshi Airport
KRP	Karup, Denmark	Karup Airport
BBK	Kasane, Botswana	Kasane Airport
ZKE	Kaschechewan, Canada	Kaschechewan Airport
KHG	Kashi, China	Kashi
KSJ	Kasos Island, Greece	Kasos Island Airport
KSF	Kassel, Germany	Kassel Airport
KZS	Kastelorizo Island, Greece	Kastelorizo Airport
KSO	Kastoria,Greece	Kastoria Airport
KTR	Katherine, Northern Territory, Australia	Tindal Airport
KTM	Kathmandu, Nepal	Tribhuvan Intl Airport
KTW	Katowice, Poland	Katowice Airport
LIH	Lihue, Kauai Island, HI, USA	Lihue Municipal Airport
HPV	Kauai Island, HI, USA	Princeville Airport
KUN	Kaunas, Lithuania	Kaunas Intl Airport

GENERAL ENGLISH → FOR AVIATION

3-letter IATA Code	City/Country	Airport
KVA	Kavala, Greece	Kavala Intl Airport
MKK	Kaunakakai/Hoolehua, HI, USA	Molokai Municipal Airport
ASR	Kayseri, Turkey	Kayseri Airport
KZN	Kazan, Russia	Kazan Intl Airport
EAR	Kearney, NE, USA	Kearney Regional Airport
EEN	Keene / Brattleboro, NH, USA	Keene – Dillant Hopkins Airport
EFL	Kefallinia Island, Greece	Kefallinia Airport
YLW	Kelowna, British Columbia, Canada	Ellison Field Airport
KEJ	Kemerovo, Russia	Kemerovo Intl Airport
KEM	Kemi/Tornio, Finland	Kemi/Tornio Airport
KPS	Kempsey, Australia	Kempsey Airport
ENA	Kenai, AK, USA	Kenai Municipal Airport
KEH	Kenmore Air Harbor, WA, USA	Kenmore Air Harbor Airport
YQK	Kenora, Ontario, Canada	Kenora Airport
KMA	Kerema, Papua New Guinea	Kerema Airport
CFU	Kerkyra, Greece	Corfu Intl Airport
KER	Kerman, Iran	Kerman Airport
KSH	Kermanshah, Iran	Shahid Ashrafi Esfahani Airport
KKE	Kerikeri, New Zealand	Kerikeri Airport
KIR	Kerry County, Ireland	Kerry County Airport
IXK	Keshod, India	Keshod Airport
KTN	Ketchikan, AK, USA	Ketchikan International Airport
EYW	Key West, FL, USA	Key West Intl Airport
KHV	Khabarovsk, Russia	Khabarovsk Novy Airport
HJR	Khajuraho, India	Khajuraho Airport
KHR	Kharkhorin, Ovorkhangai, Mongolia	Kharkhorin Airport
HRK	Kharkov, Ukraine	International Airport Kharku
KRT	Khartoum, Sudan	Khartoum Intl Airport
QKO	Khoms (Al Khums), Libya	Airport of Khoms (Al Khums)
KKC	Khon Kaen, Thailand	Khon Kaen Airport
KOG	Khong Island, Laos	Khong Island Airport
HVD	Khovd, Khovd, Mongolia	Khovd Airport
IXN	Khowai, India	Khowai Airport
HJT	Khujirt, Ovorkhangai, Mongolia	Khujirt Airport
KEL	Kiel, Germany	Holtenau Airport
KBP	Kiev, Ukraine	Kiev/Kyiv Borispol Intl Airport
IEV	Kiev, Ukraine	Zhulhany Intl Airport
KGL	Kigali, Rwanda	Kigali Intl Airport

CITIES, AIRPORTS AND 3-LETTER IATA CODES ← APPENDIX 2

3-letter IATA Code	City/Country	Airport
TKQ	Kigoma, Tanzania	Kigoma Airport
JRO	Kilimanjaro, Tanzania	Kilimanjaro Intl Airport
ILE	Killeen, TX, USA	Killeen Municipal Airport
KIM	Kimberley, South Africa	Kimberley Airport
KVC	King Cove, Alaska, USA	King Cove Airport
KNS	King Island, Tasmania, Australia	King Island Airport
AKN	King Salmon, Alaska, USA	King Salmon Airport
IGM	Kingman, AZ, USA	Kingman Airport
KGC	Kingscote, South Australia, Australia	Kingscote Airport
KIN	Kingston, Jamaica	Norman Manley Intl Airport
YGK	Kingston, Ontario, Canada	Kingston Airport
KNH	Kinmen, Taiwan	Kinmen Island Airport
FIH	Kinshasa, Zaire	N'Djili Airport
ISO	Kinston, NC, USA	Kinston Regional Jetport at Stallings Field
KPN	Kipnuk, AK, USA	Kipnuk Airport
KKN	Kirkenes, Norway Hoeyburtmoen	Hoeyburtmoen Airport
IRK	Kirksville, Missouri, USA	Kirksville Airport
KOI	Kirkwall / Orkney Island, Scotland, United Kingdom	Kirkwall Airport
KRN	Kiruna, Sweden	Kiruna Airport
KIV	Kishinev, Moldova	Chisinau Intl Airport
KKJ	Kitakyushu, Japan	Kitakyushu Airport
YKF	Kitchener, Ontario, Canada	Kitchener Airport
KIT	Kithira Island, Greece	Kithira Airport
KTT	Kittila, Finland	Kittila Airport
KVL	Kivalina, Alaska, USA	Kivalina Airport
KLU	Klagenfurt, Austria	Klagenfurt Airport
LMT	Klamath Falls, OR, USA	Kingsley Field Airport
KLW	Klawock, AK, USA	Klawock Airport
TYS	Knoxville, TN, USA	Knoxville Mcghee Tyson Airport
KCZ	Kochi, Japan	Kochi Airport
ADQ	Kodiak, AK, USA	Kodiak Airport
USM	Koh Samui, Thailand	Koh Samui Airport
KOK	Kokkola/Pietarsaari, Finland	Kruunupyy, Kokkola/ Pietarsaari Airport
KLH	Kolhapur (Ujlaiwadi), Maharashtra, India	Kolhapur Airport
KGK	Koliganek, Alaska, USA	Koliganek Airport
CCU	Kolkata (Calcutta), India	Calcutta International Airport
KMQ	Komatsu, Japan	Komatsu Airport
KOA	Kona, HI, USA	Keahole Airport

172

GENERAL ENGLISH → FOR AVIATION

3-letter IATA Code	City/Country	Airport
KKH	Kongiganak, Alaska, USA	Kongiganak Airport
KYA	Konya, Turkey	Konya Airport
KRL	Korla, China	Korla
ROR	Koror, Palau Airai	Koror Airport
KGS	Kos Island, Greece	Kos Airport
KSC	Kosice, Slovakia	Kosice Intl Airport
KSA	Kosrae, Caroline Islands, Micronesia	Kosrae Intl Airport
OSZ	Koszalin, Poland	Koszalin Airport
KBR	Kota Bharu, Malaysia	Sultan Ismail Petra Airport
BKI	Kota Kinabalu, Sabah, Malaysia	Kota Kinabalu Airport
OTZ	Kotzebue, AK, USA	Kotzebue Airport
KZI	Kozani, Macedonia, Greece	Kozani Airport
KBV	Krabi, Thailand	Krabi Airport
KRK	Krakow, Poland	John Paul II Intl Airport Krakow – Balice
KRF	Kramfors, Sweden	Kramfors Airport
KRR	Krasnodar, Russia	Krasnodar Intl Airport
KJA	Krasnojarsk, Russia	Yemelyanovo Intl Airport
KRS	Kristiansand, Norway, Kjevik	Kristiansand Airport
KID	Kristianstad, Sweden	Kristianstad Osterlen Airport
KSU	Kristiansund, Norway, Kvernberget	Kristiansund Airport
HLA	Krugersdorp, South Africa	Lanseria International Airport
KUL	Kuala Lumpur, Malaysia	KLIA Kuala Lumpur International
SZB	Kuala Lumpur, Subang, Malaysia	Sultan Abdul Aziz Shah Airport
TGG	Kuala Terengganu, Malaysia	Sultan Mahmood Airport
KUA	Kuantan, Malaysia	Kuantan Airport / Sultan Ahmad Shah Airport
KCH	Kuching, Sarawak, Malaysia	Kuching Intl Airport
KUD	Kudat, Malaysia	Kudat Airport
AKF	Kufrah, Libya	Kufrah Airport
KUS	Kulusuk, Greenland Metropolitan Area	Kulusuk Airport Metropolitan Area
KMJ	Kumamoto, Japan	Kumamoto Airport
UEO	Kume Jima, Japan	Kume Jima Airport
KMG	Kunming, China	Kunming Changshui Intl Airport
KUV	Kunsan, South Korea	Kunsan (or Gunsan) Airport
KNX	Kununurra, Australia	Kununurra Airport
KUO	Kuopio, Finland	Kuopio Airport
KCA	Kuqa, China	Kuqa Airport

CITIES, AIRPORTS AND 3-LETTER IATA CODES ← APPENDIX 2

3-letter IATA Code	City/Country	Airport
KUH	Kushiro, Japan	Kushiro Airport
YVP	Kuujjuaq, Quebec, Canada	Kuujjuaq Airport
YGW	Kuujjuarapik, Quebec, Canada	Kuujjuarapik Airport
KAO	Kuusamo, Finland	Kuusamo Airport
KWI	Kuwait, Kuwait	Kuwait International Airport
KWA	Kwajalein, Marshall Islands	Kwajalein Airport
KWJ	Kwangju, Republic of Korea	Kwangju Airport

	L	
LCE	La Ceiba, Honduras International	Golosón Intl Airport
LCG	La Coruna, Spain	La Coruña Airport
LSE	La Crosse, WI, USA	La Crosse Regional Airport
YGL	La Grande, Canada	La Grande Airport
LAP	La Paz, Baja California Sur, Mexico	Aeropuerto General Marquez De Leon
LPB	La Paz, Bolivia	El Alto Intl Airport
IRJ	La Rioja, Argentina	La Rioja Airport
LRH	La Rochelle, France	La Rochelle – Ile de Ré Airport
LRM	La Romana, Dominican Republic	La Romana
YVC	La Ronge, Saskatchewan, Canada	La Ronge (Barber Field) Airport
SSQ	La Sarre, Quebec, Canada	La Sarre Airport
LSC	La Serena, Chile	La Florida Airport
YLQ	La Tuque, Quebec, Canada	La Tuque Airport
EUN	Laayoune, Morocco	Laayoune Hassan I Morocco
LBS	Labasa, Fiji	Labasa Airport
LBU	Labuan, Sabah, Malaysia	Labuan Airport
XEE	Lac Edouard, Quebec, Canada	Lac Edouard / Via Rail Service
LAE	Lae, Papua New Guinea	Lae Nadzab Airport
LFT	Lafayette/New Iberia, LA, USA	Lafayette Regional Airport
LAF	Lafayette, IN, USA	Purdue University Airport
LOS	Lagos, Nigeria	Murtala Muhammed Airport
LDU	Lahad Datu, Sabah, Malaysia	Lahad Datu Airport
LHE	Lahore, Pakistan	Lahore Airport
LCH	Lake Charles, LA, USA	Lake Charles Regional Airport
YLC	Lake Harbour, Canada	Lake Harbour Airport
HII	Lake Havasu City, AZ, USA	Lake Havasu City Municipal Airport
LKE	Seattle, WA, USA	Lake Union Sea Plane Base
LKL	Lakselv, Norway	Banak Airport

GENERAL ENGLISH → FOR AVIATION

3-letter IATA Code	City/Country	Airport
LLI	Lalibela, Ethiopia	Lalibela Airport
SUF	Lamezia	Terme, Italy
LPT	Lampang, Thailand	Lampang Airport
LMP	Lampedusa Island, Italy	Lampedusa Airport
LNY	Lanai City, HI, USA	Lanai Airport
LNS	Lancaster, PA, USA	Lancaster Airport
LGK	Langkawi, Malaysia	Langkawi Intl Airport
LAI	Lannion, France	Lannion Airport
LAN	Lansing, MI, USA	Capital City Airport
ACE	Lanzarote, Canary Islands, Spain	Lanzarote Airport
LHW	Lanzhou, China	Lanzhou City Airport
ZGC	Lanzhou, China	Lanzhou Zhongchuan Airport
LAO	Laoag, Philippines	Laoag Airport
LPP	Lappeenranta, Finland	Lappeenranta Airport
LAR	Laramie, WY, USA	Laramie Regional Airport
LRD	Laredo, TX, USA	Laredo Intl Airport
LCA	Larnaca, Cyprus	Larnaca Intl Airport
LRU	Las Cruces, NM, USA	Las Cruces Airport
LSP	Las Piedras, Venezuela	Josefa Camejo Intl Airport
LAS	Las Vegas, NV, USA	Mc Carran International Airport
VGT	Las Vegas, NV, USA	Las Vegas Airport
LBE	Latrobe, PA, USA	Westmoreland County Airport
LST	Launceston, Tasmania, Australia	Launceston Airport
PIB	Laurel, MS, USA	Laurel-Hattiesburg Regional Airport
NAN	Lautoka/Nadi, Fiji	Nadi Intl Airport
LWY	Lawas, Sarawak, Malaysia Lawas	Lawas Airport
LAW	Lawton, OK, USA	Lawton – Fort Sill Regional Airport
LZC	Lazaro Cardenas, Michoacan, Mexico	Lázaro Cardenas Airport
LEH	Le Havre, France	Le Havre Octeville Airport
LEA	Learmonth, Western Australia, Australia	Learmonth Airport
LEB	Lebanon/Hanover/White River, NH, USA	Lebanon Regional Airport
LBA	Leeds/Bradford, England, United Kingdom	Leeds Bradford Intl Airport
PVK	Lefkas, Greece	Preveza Airport
LGP	Legaspi, Philippines	Legaspi Airport
IXL	Leh, India	Leh Airport
LEJ	Leipzig, Germany	Leipzig Halle Airport
LKN	Leknes, Norway	Leknes Airport
LEN	Leon, Spain	Leon Airport

CITIES, AIRPORTS AND 3-LETTER IATA CODES ← APPENDIX 2

3-letter IATA Code	City/Country	Airport
BJX	Leon/Guanajuato, Guanajuato, Mexico	Del Bajio Intl Airport
LRS	Leros, Greece	Leros Island National Airport
YQL	Lethbridge, Alberta, Canada	Lethbridge Airport
LET	Leticia, Colombia	General Alfredo Vásquez Cobo Airport / Leticia Airport
KLL	Levelock, Alaska, USA	Levelock Airport
LWB	Lewisburg, WV, USA	Lewisburg
LWS	Lewiston, ID, USA	Lewiston Nez-Perce Airport
LWT	Lewistown, MT, USA	Lewistown Municipal Airport
LEX	Lexington, KY, USA	Blue Grass Airport
LXA	Lhasa, Tibet Autonomous Region, China	Lhasa Airport
LYG	Lianyungang, China	Lianyungang Airport
LBL	Liberal, KS, USA	Liberal Mid-America Regional Airport
LIR	Liberia, Costa Rica	Liberia Airport (Daniel Oduber Queiros Intl Airport)
LBV	Libreville, Gabon	Libreville Intl Airport
LGG	Liege, Belgium	Bierset Airport
LIF	Lifou Island, New Caledonia	Lifou Airport
LJG	Lijiang, China	Lijiang City Airport
IXI	Lilabari, India	Lilabari Airport
LIL	Lille, France Lille	Lesquin Airport
LLW	Lilongwe, Malawi	Lilongwe Intl Airport
LIM	Lima, Peru	Aeropuerto Internacional Jorge Chávez
LMN	Limbang, Sarawak, Malaysia	Limbang Airport
LIG	Limoges, France	Limoges – Bellegarde Airport
LNJ	Lincang, China	Lincang Airport
LNK	Lincoln, NE, USA	Lincoln Municipal Airport
LPI	Linkoping, Sweden	Linkoping City Airport
LNZ	Linz, Austria	Linz Airport
LIS	Lisbon, Portugal	Lisboa Airport
LSY	Lismore, New South Wales, Australia	Lismore Airport
LIT	Little Rock, AR, USA	Little Rock National Airport
LZH	Liuzhou, China	Liuzhou Bailian Airport
LPL	Liverpool, England, United Kingdom	John Lennon Airport
LVI	Livingstone, Zambia	Livingstone Airport
LJU	Ljubljana, Slovenia, Brnik	Brnik Ljubljana Airport
LFW	Lome, Togo	Lome – Tokoin Airport
LNV	Londolovit, Papua New Guinea	Lihir Island Airport
LGW	London, England, United Kingdom	Gatwick Airport

GENERAL ENGLISH → FOR AVIATION

3-letter IATA Code	City/Country	Airport
LHR	London, England, United Kingdom	Heathrow Airport
LCY	London, England, United Kingdom	London City Airport
LTN	London, England, United Kingdom	London Luton International
STN	London, England, United Kingdom	London Stansted Airport
YXU	London, Ontario, Canada	London Municipal
LDB	Londrina, Paraná, Brazil	Aeroporto Governador José Richa or Londrina Airport
LGB	Long Beach, CA, USA	Long Beach Municipal Airport
LRE	Longreach, Australia	Longreach Airport
GGG	Longview/Gladewater/Kilgore, TX, USA	Gregg County Airport
LYR	Longyearbyen, Norway	Svalbard Airport
LDH	Lord Howe Island, Australia	Lord Howe Island Airport
LTO	Loreto, Baja California Sur, Mexico	Loreto Intl Airport
LRT	Lorient, France	Lorient South Brittany Airport
LAX	Los Angeles, CA, USA	Los Angeles Intl Airport
LSQ	Los Angeles, Chile	Maria Dolores Airport
LMM	Los Mochis, Sinaloa, Mexico	Los Mochis Intl Airport
SDF	Louisville, KY, USA	Louisville Intl Airport
LDE	Lourdes/Tarbes, France	Tarbes – Lourdes Pyrenees Airport
LAD	Luanda, Angola	Aeroporto Quatro de Fevereiro
LBB	Lubbock, TX, USA	Lubbock International Airport
LKO	Lucknow, India	Lucknow Airport
LUD	Luderitz, Namibia	Luderitz Airport
LUG	Lugano, Switzerland	Lugano – Agno Airport
VSG	Lugansk, Ukraine	Lugansk Intl Airport
LUA	Lukla, Nepal	Lukla Airport
LLA	Lulea, Sweden	Lulea Airport
LYA	Luoyang, China	Luoyang Beijiao Airport
LUN	Lusaka, Zambia	Lusaka Airport
LUX	Luxembourg, Luxembourg	Luxembourg Airport
LUM	Luxi, China	Dehong Mangahi Airport
LXR	Luxor, Egypt	Luxor Airport
LZO	Luzhou, China	Luzhou Lantian Airport
CRK	Pampanga, Philippines	Clark Int Airport
LWO	Lvov, Ukraine	Snilow Airport
LYB	Little Cayman, Cayman Islands	Little Cayman Airport
LCJ	Lodz, Poland	Lodz Airport
RJL	Logrono, Spain	Logrono Airport
LDY	Londonderry, Northern Ireland, United Kingdom	Londonderry Airport

CITIES, AIRPORTS AND 3-LETTER IATA CODES ← APPENDIX 2

3-letter IATA Code	City/Country	Airport
LKH	Long Akah, Malaysia	Long Akah Airport
LBP	Long Banga, Malaysia	Long Banga Airport
LGL	Long Lellang, Malaysia	Long Lellang Airport
ODN	Long Seridan, Malaysia	Long Seridan Airport
LPS	Lopez Island, Washington, USA	Lopez Island Airport
SJD	Los Cabos, San Jose Del Cabo, Baja California Sur, Mexico	Los Cabos Intl Airport
LXG	Luang Namtha, Laos	Luang Namtha Airport
LPQ	Luang Prabang, Laos	Luang Prabang International Airport
LXR	Luxor, Egypt	Luxor
LYC	Lycksele, Sweden	Lycksele Airport
LYH	Lynchburg, VA, USA	Lynchburg Regional Airport
LYS	Lyon, France	Lyon Saint Exupery Intl Airport

M		
MST	Maastricht, Netherlands	Maastricht – Aachen Airport
MCP	Macapá, Amapá, Brazil	Aeroporto Internacional de Macapá
MFM	Macau, China	Macau Intl Airport
MCZ	Maceió, Brazil	Aeroporto Internacional Zumbi dos Palmares
MKY	Mackay, Queensland, Australia	Mackay Airport
MCN	Macon, GA, USA	Lewis B. Wilson Airport
MAG	Madang, Papua New Guinea	Madang Airport
MED	Madinah, Saudi Arabia	Prince Mohammad Bin Abdulaziz
MSN	Madison, WI, USA	Dane County Regional Airport
MAA	Madras (Chennai), India	Chennai Airport
MAD	Madrid, Spain	Aeropuerto de Barajas
IXM	Madurai, India	Madurai Airport
HGN	Mae Hong Son, Thailand	Mae Hong Son Airport
GDX	Magadan, Russia	Magadan Airport
SEZ	Mahe Island, Seychelles	Seychelles Intl Airport
MMO	Maio, Cape Verde	Maio Airport
MAJ	Majuro, Marshall Islands International	Majuro, Marshall Islands International Airport
MQX	Makale, Ethiopia	Makale Airport
MZG	Makung, Taiwan	Makung (or Magong) Airport
AAM	Kruger Park, South Africa	Mala Mala Aerodrome or Malamala Aerodrome
SSG	Malabo, Equatorial Guinea	Santa Isabel Airport or Malabo Airport

GENERAL ENGLISH → FOR AVIATION

3-letter IATA Code	City/Country	Airport
AGP	Malaga, Spain	Malaga Airport
MLG	Malang, Indonesia	Malang Airport
MLX	Malatya, Turkey	Malatya Airport
MLE	Male, Maldives	Male International Airport *or* Ibrahim Nasir Intl Airport
MMX	Malmö, Sweden	Malmö – Sturup Airport
PTF	Malololailai, Fiji	Malololailai Airport
MLA	Malta, Malta Luqa	Malta Luqa International Airport
MMH	Mammoth Lakes, CA, USA	Mammoth Lakes Airport
MNF	Mana Island, Fiji	Mana Airport
MDC	Manado, Indonesia	Samratulang International Airport
MGA	Managua, Nicaragua	Aeropuerto Internacional Augusto César Sandino
MAO	Manaus, Amazonas, Brazil	Aeroporto Internacional Eduardo Gomes
MAN	Manchester, England, United Kingdom	Manchester Airport
MHT	Manchester, NH, USA	Manchester – Boston Regional Airport
MDL	Mandalay, Myanmar (Burma)	Annisaton Airport
MXW	Mandalgovi, Dundgovi, Mongolia	Mandalgovi Airport
IXE	Mangalore, India	Bajpe Airport
MAY	Mangrove Cay, Bahamas	Mangrove Cay Airport
MHK	Manhattan, KS, USA	Manhattan Regional Airport
MNL	Manila, Philippines	Ninoy Aquino International Airport
MBL	Manistee, MI, USA	Manistee County – Blacker Airport
YTH	Manitoba, Manitoba, Canada	Thompson Airport
MZL	Manizales, Colombia	Santagueda La Nubia Airport
MHG	Mannheim, Germany	Mannheim Airport
KMO	Manokotak, Alaska, USA	Manokotak Airport
MKW	Manokwari, Indonesia	Rendani Airport
MSE	Manston, Kent, United Kingdom	Kent International Airport
ZLO	Manzanillo, Colima, Mexico	Aeropuerto International Manzanillo
MTS	Manzini, Swaziland	Manzini Airport
MXS	Maotoa, (Western) Samoa	Savaii Airport
MPM	Maputo, Mozambique	Maputo International Airport
MDQ	Mar Del Plata, Buenos Aires, Argentina	Mar Del Plata Airport (Aeropuerto Internacional Ástor Piazzolla)

CITIES, AIRPORTS AND 3-LETTER IATA CODES ← APPENDIX 2

3-letter IATA Code	City/Country	Airport
MAB	Marabá, Brazil	Marabá Airport
MAR	Maracaibo, Venezuela	La Chinita Intl Airport
MTH	Marathon, FL, USA	Florida Keys Marathon Airport
YSP	Marathon, Ontario, Canada	Marathon Airport
MRK	Marco Island, FL, USA	Marco Island Executive Airport
MQM	Mardin, Turkey	Mardin Airport
MGH	Margate, South Africa	Margate Airport
MBX	Maribor Airport	Orehova Vas/Slivnica, Slovenia
MHQ	Mariehamn, Aland Island, Finland	Mariehamn Airport
MGF	Maringá, Brazil	Aeroporto Regional de Maringá
MWA	Marion, IL, USA	Williamson County Regional Airport
MQT	Marquette, MI, USA	Marquette County Airport
RAK	Marrakech, Morocco	Menara Airport
MRS	Marseille, France	Marseille Provence Airport
MHH	Marsh Harbour, Bahamas	Marsh Harbour Intl Airport
RMF	Marsa Alam, Egypt	Marsa Alam Airport
LMQ	Marsa Brega, Libya	Marsa Brega Airport
MVY	Martha's Vineyard, MA, USA	Martha's Vineyard Airport
MUR	Marudi, Malaysia	Marudi Airport
MSU	Maseru, Lesotho	Maseru Airport
MHD	Mashad, Iran	Mashad Airport
MCW	Mason City, IA, USA	Mason City Municipal Airport
MSS	Massena, NY, USA	Massena Intl Airport
MAM	Matamoros, Tamaulipas, Mexico	Servando Canales Int Airport
AMI	Mataram, Indonesia	Selaparang Airport
MMJ	Matsumoto, Japan	Matsumoto Airport
MYJ	Matsuyama, Japan	Matsuyama Airport
MUN	Maturin, Venezuela	Maturin Airport
MUB	Maun, Botswana	Maun Airport
MRU	Mauritius	Plaisance International Airport
XID	Maxville, Ontario, Canada	Maxville / Via Rail Service
MYG	Mayaguana, Bahamas	Mayaguana Airport
MAZ	Mayaguez, PR, USA	El Maui Airport
MZT	Mazatlan, Sinaloa, Mexico	General Rafael Buelma Intl Airport
MFE	McAllen/Mission, TX, USA	McAllen Intl Airport
MCK	McCook, NE, USA	McCook Regional Airport
MCG	McGrath, AK, USA	McGrath Airport
MES	Medan, Indonesia	Polonia Airport
EOH	Medellin, Colombia	Enrique Olaya Herrera

GENERAL ENGLISH → FOR AVIATION

3-letter IATA Code	City/Country	Airport
MDE	Medellin, Colombia	Jose Maria Cordova/ Metropolitan Area
MFR	Medford, OR, USA	Medford/Jackson County Airport
YXH	Medicine Hat, Alberta, Canada	Medicine Hat Airport
MED	Medinah, Saudi Arabia	Madinah Prince Mohammad Bin Abdulaziz
MEY	Meghauli, Nepal	Meghauli Airport
MEH	Mehamn, Norway	Mehamn Airport
MXZ	Meixian, China	Meixian
MKS	Mekane Selam, Ethiopia	Mekane Selam Airport
MYU	Mekoryuk, Alaska, USA	Mekoryuk Airport
MLB	Melbourne, FL, USA	Melbourne International Airport
MEL	Melbourne, Victoria, Australia	Tullamarine
MLN	Melilla, Spain	Melilla Airport
XEK	Melville, Saskatchewan, Canada	Melville / Via Rail Service
MMB	Memanbetsu, Japan	Memanbetsu Airport
MEM	Memphis, TN, USA	Memphis International Airport
MDZ	Mendoza, Mendoza, Argentina	El Plumerillo Airport
MNM	Menominee, MI, USA	Twin County Airport
MAH	Menorca, Spain	Aeropuerto de Menorca
MCE	Merced, California	Merced Airport
MRD	Merida, Venezuela	Alberto Carnevalli
MID	Merida, Yucatan, Mexico	Merida International
MEI	Meridian, MS, USA	Key Field
MIM	Merimbula, Australia	Merimbula Airport
AZA	Mesa, Arizona, USA	Phoenix
ETZ	Metz/Nancy, France	Metz/Nancy – Lorraine Airport
MXL	Mexicali, Baja California, Mexico	General Rodolfo Sanchez Taboada Intl Airport
MEX	Mexico City, Distrito Federal, Mexico	Benito Juarez Intl Airport
MIA	Miami, FL, USA	Miami International Airport
MPB	Miami, FL, USA	Miami Public Seaplane Base
OPF	Miami, FL, USA	Opa Locka Airport
MBS	Midland/Bay City/Saginaw, MI, USA	MBS TriCity Airport
MAF	Midland/Odessa, TX, USA Midland Intl Airport	
MYE	Mikake Jima, Japan	Mikake Jima Airport
JMK	Mikonos, Greece	Mikonos Island National Airport
LIN	Milan, Italy	Linate Airport
MXP	Milan, Italy	Malpensa Airport

CITIES, AIRPORTS AND 3-LETTER IATA CODES ← APPENDIX 2

3-letter IATA Code	City/Country	Airport
BGY	Milan, Italy	Bergamo Orio Al Serio Intl Airport
MQL	Mildura, Victoria, Australia	Mildura Airport
MLS	Miles City, MT, USA	Miles City Municipal Airport
MFN	Milford Sound, New Zealand	Milford Sound Airport
MLT	Millinocket, Maine, USA	Millinocket Airport
MLO	Milos, Greece	Milos Island National Airport
MKE	Milwaukee, WI, USA	General Mitchell Airport
MTT	Minatitlan, Mexico	Minatitlan Airport
MSP	Minneapolis, MN, USA	Minneapolis-St Paul Intl Airport
MOT	Minot, ND, USA	Minot International Airport
MRV	Min Vody, Russia	Min Vody Airport
MSQ	Minsk, Belarus	Minsk Intl Airport
MYY	Miri, Sarawak, Malaysia	Miri Airport
MSJ	Misawa, Japan	Misawa Airport
MCQ	Miskolc, Hungary	Miskolc Airport
MSO	Missoula, MT, USA	Missoula International Airport
MRA	Misurata, Libya	Misurata Airport
KMI	Miyazaki, Japan	Miyazaki Airport
MMY	Miyako Jima, Japan	Miyako Jima Airport
MTF	Mizan Teferi, Ethiopia	Mizan Teferi Airport
MBD	Mmabatho, South Africa	Mmabatho Airport
MQN	Mo I Rana, Norway	Mo I Rana Airport
CNY	Moab, UT, USA	Canyonlands Field Airport
MOB	Mobile, AL, USA	Mobile Regional Airport
MOD	Modesto, CA, USA	Modesto City – County Airport
MGL	Moenchengladbach, Germany	Moenchengladbach Airport
MGQ	Mogadishu, Somalia	Mogadishu Intl Airport
NWA	Moheli, Comoros	Moheli Airport
MJD	Mohenjodaro, Pakistan	Mohenjodaro Airport
MPK	Mokpo, Republic of Korea	Mokpo Airport
MOL	Molde, Norway Aro	Molde Airport
MLI	Moline, IL, USA	Quad City Intl Airport
MBA	Mombasa, Kenya	Moi International Airport
MIR	Monastir, Tunisia	Monastir – Habib Burguiba Intl Airport
MBE	Monbetsu, Japan	Monbetsu Airport
LOV	Monclova, Coahuila, Mexico	Monclova Intl Airport
YQM	Moncton, New Brunswick, Canada	Greater Moncton International Airport

GENERAL ENGLISH → FOR AVIATION

3-letter IATA Code	City/Country	Airport
MLU	Monroe, LA, USA	Monroe Regional Airport
ROB	Monrovia, Liberia	Roberts International Airport
MLW	Monrovia, Liberia	Spriggs Payne Airport
YYY	Mont Joli, Quebec, Canada	Mont Joli Airport
MCM	Monte Carlo, Monaco	Monte Carlo Heliport
MEU	Monte Dourado, Brazil	Monte Dourado Airport
MBJ	Montego Bay, Jamaica	Sangster Intl Airport
MRY	Monterey/Carmel, CA, USA	Monterey Peninsula Airport
MTY	Monterrey, Nuevo Leon, Mexico	Escobedo Airport
MOC	Montes Claros, Brazil	Montes Claros Airport
MVD	Montevideo, Uruguay	Aeropuerto Internacional de Carrasco
MGM	Montgomery, AL, USA	Dannelly Field/Montgomery Regional Airport
MPL	Montpellier, France	Montpellier – Mediterranée Airport
YMQ	Montreal, QC (Quebec), Canada	"metro code", represents all major airports in the metropolitan area of Montreal
YMX	Montreal	Mirabel, Quebec, Canada
YUL	Montreal	Dorval, Quebec, Canada
YHU	Montreal, Canada	St. Hubert Airport
MTJ	Montrose, CO, USA	Montrose County Airport
MNI	Montserrat, Montserrat	Blackburne
MOZ	Moorea Island, French Polynesia	Temae Airport
YMO	Moosonee, Ontario, Canada	Moosonee
MRZ	Moree, Australia	Moree Airport
MLM	Morelia, Michoacan, Mexico	Aeropuerto Internacional Francisco Mujica (Morelia)
MGW	Morgantown, WV, USA	Morgantown Municipal Airport
HNA	Morioka, Japan Hanamaki	Iwate Hanamaki Airport
ONG	Mornington, Queensland, Australia	Mornington Airport
MXV	Moron, Khovsgol, Mongolia	Moron Airport
HAH	Moroni (Hahaya), Comoros	Prince Said Ibrahim Intl Airport
YVA	Moroni (Hahaya/Iconi), Comoros	Moroni/Iconi Airport
MMU	Morristown, NJ, USA	Morristown Municipal Airport
MYA	Moruya, New South Wales, Australia	Moruya Airport
MOW	Moscow, Russia	Moscow Airport
DME	Moscow, Russia	Domodedovo
SVO	Moscow, Russia	Sheremetyevo

CITIES, AIRPORTS AND 3-LETTER IATA CODES ← APPENDIX 2

3-letter IATA Code	City/Country	Airport
VKO	Moscow, Russia	Vnukovo
MWH	Moses Lake, Washington, USA	Grant County Airport
JRO	Moshi, Tanzania	Kilimanjaro Airport
CWA	Mosinee/Wausau, WI, USA	Central Wisconsin Airport
MJF	Mosjoen, Norway	Kjaerstad Airport
MGB	Mount Gambier, Australia	Mt Gambier Airport
HGU	Mount Hagen, Papua New Guinea	Kagamuga Airport
LLY	Mount Holly, NJ, USA	Mount Holly Airport
MHU	Mount Hotham, Australia	Mount Hotham Airport
ISA	Mount Isa, Australia	Mount Isa Airport
MPN	Mount Pleasant, Falkland Islands (Islas Malvinas)	Mount Pleasant Airport
TPR	Mount Tom Price, Australia	Mount Tom Price Airport
MVN	Mount Vernon, IL, USA	Mount Vernon Outland Airport
WMH	Mountain Home, AR, USA	Mountain Home Municipal Airport
MPA	Mpacha, Namibia	Mpacha Airport
ODY	Muang Xay, Laos	Oudomsay Airport
MDG	Mudanjiang, China	Mudanjiang
FMO	Muenster, Germany	Muenster Osnabrück Intl Airport
MKM	Mukah, Sarawak, Malaysia	Mukah Airport
MLH	Mulhouse, France	Euroairport Basel – Mulhouse Freiburg
MUX	Multan, Pakistan	Multan Airport
MZV	Mulu, Malaysia	Mulu Airport
BOM	Mumbai (Bombay), India	Mumbai
MIE	Muncie, IN, USA	Delaware County Airport
MUC	Munich, Germany	Franz Josef Strauss Airport
MIG	Munich, Germany	Neubiberg Air Base Airport
MJV	Murcia, Spain	Murcia – San Javier Airport
MMK	Murmansk, Russia	Murmansk Airport
QMQ	Murzuq (Marzuq), Libya	Murzuq Airport
MSR	Mus, Turkey	Mus Airport
MCT	Muscat, Oman Seeb	Muscat Intl Airport
MSL	Muscle Shoals/Florence/Sheffield, AL, USA	Muscle Shoals
MKG	Muskegon, MI, USA	Muskegon County Intl Airport
MQS	Mustique, Saint Vincent and The Grenadines	Mustique Airport
MWZ	Mwanza, Tanzania	Mwanza Airport
MYR	Myrtle Beach, SC, USA	Myrtle Beach Intl Airport
MJT	Mytilene, Greece Mytilene	Mytilene Intl Airport

GENERAL ENGLISH → FOR AVIATION

3-letter IATA Code	City/Country	Airport
N		
NDJ	N Djamena, Chad	N'Djamena Intl Airport
NAN	Nadi, Fiji	Nadi Intl Airport
NDR	Nador, Morocco	Nador Airport
WNP	Naga, Philippines	Naga Airport
NGS	Nagasaki, Japan	Nagasaki Airport
NGO	Nagoya, Japan	Chubu Centrair International Airport
NKM	Nagoya/Komaki, Japan	Nagoya Airfield
NAG	Nagpur, India	Sonegaon Airport
NAH	Naha, Indonesia	Naha Airport
NBO	Nairobi, Kenya	Jomo Kenyatta International Airport
WIL	Nairobi, Kenya	Wilson Airport
SHB	Nakashibetsu, Japan	Nakashibetsu Airport
NAK	Nakhon Ratchasima, Thailand	Nakhon Ratchasima Airport
NST	Nakhon Si Thammarat, Thailand	Nakhon Si Thammarat Airport
NMA	Namangan, Uzbekistan	Namangan Airport
APL	Nampula, Mozambique	Nampula Airport
ZNA	Nanaimo, British Columbia, Canada	Nanaimo Harbor Water Airport
YCD	Nanaimo, British Columbia, Canada	Cassidy Airport
KHN	Nanchang, China	Nanchang
YSR	Nanisivik, Canada	Nanisivik Airport
NKG	Nanjing, China	Nanjing Lushou Intl Airport
NNY	Nanyang, China	Nanyang Airport
SHM	Nanki Shirahama, Japan	Nanki – Shirahama Airport
NNG	Nanning, China	Nanning Wuxu Intl Airport
NTE	Nantes, France	Nantes Atlantique Airport
NTG	Nantong, China	Nantong Xingdong Airport
ACK	Nantucket, MA, USA	Nantucket Memorial Airport
WNA	Napakiak, AK, USA	Napakiak Airport
NPE	Napier, New Zealand	Hawke's Bay Airport
APF	Naples, FL, USA	Naples Municipal Airport
NAP	Naples, Italy	Capodichino Airport
NAA	Narrabri, Australia	Narrabri Airport
NRA	Narrandera, Australia	Narrandera Airport
UAK	Narsarsuaq, Greenland	Narsarsuaq Airport
JNS	Narsaq, Greenland	Narsaq Heliport
NNM	Naryan, Arkhangelsk Oblast, Russia	Naryan – Mar Airport
BNA	Nashville, TN, USA	Nashville Metropolitan Airport

CITIES, AIRPORTS AND 3-LETTER IATA CODES ← APPENDIX 2

3-letter IATA Code	City/Country	Airport
NAS	Nassau, Bahamas	Nassau International Airport
PID	Nassau, Bahamas	Paradise Island Airport
NAT	Natal, Rio Grande do Norte, Brazil	Aeroporto Internacional Augusto Severo
YNA	Natashquan, Canada	Natashquan Airport
INU	Nauru, Nauru	Nauru Islan Intl Airport
NVT	Navegantes, Santa Catarina, Brazil	Aeroporto Internacional de Navegantes
JNX	Naxos, Cyclades Islands, Greece	Naxos Island National Airport
NLA	Ndola, Zambia	Ndola Airport
NEC	Necochea, Buenos Aires, Argentina	Necochea Airport
EAM	Nejran, Saudi Arabia	Nejran Airport
NSN	Nelson, New Zealand	Nelson Airport
NLG	Nelson Lagoon, Alaska, USA	Nelson Lagoon Airport
NLP	Nelspruit, South Africa	Nelspruit Airport
MQP	Nelspruit, South Africa	Kruger Mpumalanga Airport
NER	Neryungri, Russia	Neryungri Airport
KEP	Nepalganj, Nepal	Nepalganj Airport
NQN	Neuquen, Argentina	Neuquen Airport
NEV	Nevis, Leeward Islands	Saint Kitts and Nevis Airport
EWB	New Bedford/Fall River, MA, USA	New Bedford Regional Airport
EWN	New Bern, NC, USA	Coastal Carolina Regional Airport
XEL	New Carlisle, Quebec, Canada	New Carlisle / Via Rail Service
HVN	New Haven, CT, USA	Tweed New Haven Airport
MSY	New Orleans, LA, USA	Louis Armstrong New Orleans International Airport (Moisant International Airport)
NPL	New Plymouth, New Zealand	New Plymouth Airport
XEM	New Richmond, Quebec, Canada	New Richmond / Via Rail Service
KNW	New Stuyahok, Alaska, USA	New Stuyahok Airport
JRA	New York City, NY, USA	West 34th Street Heliport
TSS	New York, NY, USA	East 34th Street Heliport
JFK	New York, NY, USA	John F Kennedy Intl Airport
LGA	New York, NY, USA	La Guardia Airport
EWR	Newark, NJ, USA	Newark International Airport
SWF	Newburgh/Poughkeepsie, NY, USA	Stweart Intl Airport
NCL	Newcastle, England, United Kingdom	Newcastle Intl Airport
XEY	Newcastle, New Brunswick, Canada	Newcastle / Via Rail Service
BEO	Newcastle, New South Wales, Australia	Belmont Airport

3-letter IATA Code	City/Country	Airport
NTL	Newcastle, New South Wales, Australia	Williamtown Airport
ZNE	Newman, Western Australia, Australia	Newman Airport
PHF	Newport News/Williamsburg/Hampton, VA, USA	Newport News/Williamsburg Intl Airport
NQY	Newquay, England, United Kingdom	Newquay Cornwall Airport
WWT	Newtok, Alaska, USA	Newtok Airport
NHA	Nha Trang, Vietnam	Nha Trang Airport
XLV	Niagara Falls, Ontario, Canada	Rail Station
NIM	Niamey, Niger	Niamey Airport
NCE	Nice, France	Nice – Cote D'azur Airport
NME	Nightmute, Alaska, USA	Nightmute Airport
KIJ	Niigata, Japan	Niigata Airport
IKO	Nikolski, Alaska, USA	Nikolski Airport
FNI	Nimes, France	Nimes Airport
NGB	Ningbo, China	Ningbo Lishe Intl Airport
NIX	Nioro, Mali	Nioro Airport
NFO	Niuafo'Ou, Tonga	Niuafo'Ou (Mata'aho Airport)
NTT	Niuatoputapu, Tonga	Niuatoputapu Airport
IUE	Niue, Island	Niue Airport
NJC	Nizhnevartovsk, Russia	Nizhnevartovsk Airport
GOJ	Nizhniy Novgorod, Russia	Nizhniy Novgorod Airport
OME	Nome, AK, USA	Nome Airport
OFK	Norfolk, NE, USA	Karl Stefan Memorial Airport
ORF	Norfolk, VA, USA	Norfolk International Airport
NLK	Norfolk Island, Australia	Norfolk Island Airport
NSK	Norilsk, Russia	Norilsk Airport
NRK	Norrkoping, Sweden	Kungsangen Airport
YYB	North Bay, Ontario, Canada	North Bay/Jack Garland Airport
OTH	North Bend, OR, USA	North Bend Airport
NCA	North Caicos, Turks and Caicos Islands	North Caicos Airport
ELH	North Eleuthera, Bahamas	North Eleuthera Intl Airport
LBF	North Platte, NE, USA	Lee Bird Field/North Platte Regional Airport
NWI	Norwich, England, United Kingdom	Norwich Intl Airport
OWD	Norwood, MA, USA	Norwood Memorial Airport
NKC	Nouakchott, Mauritania	Nouakchott Intl Airport
GEA	Noumeá, New Caledonia	Noumeá Magenta Airport
NOU	Noumeá, New Caledonia	La Tontouta Intl Airport
OVB	Novosibirsk, Russia	Tolmachevo Airport
NUX	Novy Urengoy, Russia	Novy Urengoy Airport

CITIES, AIRPORTS AND 3-LETTER IATA CODES ← APPENDIX 2

3-letter IATA Code	City/Country	Airport
NLD	Nuevo Laredo, Tamaulipas, Mexico	Quetzalcóatl Intl Airport
TBU	Nuku'alofa/Tongatapu	Fua'amotu Intl Airport
NCU	Nukus, Uzbekistan	Nukus Airport
NUE	Nuremberg, Germany	Nuremberg Airport
GOH	Nuuk, Greenland	Nuuk Airport
NYU	Nyaung U, Myanmar (Burma)	Nyaung Airport

	O	
ODW	Oak Harbor, WA, USA	Oak Harbor Airport
OAK	Oakland, CA, USA	Oakland Intl Airport
XOK	Oakville, Ontario, Canada	Oakville / Via Rail Service
OAX	Oaxaca, Mexico	Xoxocotlán Airport
OBO	Obihiro, Japan	Obihiro Airport
OCJ	Ochos Rios, Jamaica	Ochos Rios Airport
ONJ	Odate Noshiro, Japan	Odate Noshiro Airport
ODE	Odense, Denmark	Odense Airport
ODS	Odessa, Ukraine	Odessa Intl Airport
OGS	Ogdensburg, NY, USA	Ogdensburg Intl Airport
OHD	Ohrid, Macedonia	St. Paul the Apostle Airport
OIT	Oita, Japan	Oita Airport
VPS	Okaloosa County/Valparaiso, FL, USA	Fort Walton Beach/Okaloosa County Regional Airport
OKJ	Okayama, Japan	Okayama AIrport
OKA	Okinawa, Ryukyu Islands, Japan	Naha Airport
OKC	Oklahoma City, OK, USA	Will Rogers World Airport
OLB	Olbia, Italy	Costa Smeralda Airport
ULG	Olgii, Bayan Olgii, Mongolia	Olgii Airport
OLM	Olympia, WA, USA	Olympia Regional Airport
OLP	Olympic Dam, Australia	Olympic Dam Airport
OMA	Omaha, NE, USA	Eppley Airfield
OMS	Omsk, Russia	Omsk Airport
UNR	Ondorkhaan, Khentii, Mongolia	Ondorkhaan Airport
ONT	Ontario, CA, USA	Ontario International Airport
OMR	Oradea, Romania	Oradea Intl Airport
ORN	Oran, Algeria	Es Senia Airport
OAG	Orange, New South Wales, Australia	Springhill Airport or Orange Airport
ORB	Orebro, Sweden	Orebro – Bofors Airport
MBX	Orehova Vas/Slivnica, Slovenia	Maribor Airport
ORL	Orlando, FL, USA Herndon	Orlando Executive Airport

188   GENERAL ENGLISH → FOR AVIATION

3-letter IATA Code	City/Country	Airport
MCO	Orlando, FL, USA	Orlando International Airport
SFB	Orlando, FL, USA	Sanford Central Florida Regional Airport
OER	Ornskoldsvik, Sweden	Ornskoldsvik Airport
ITM	Osaka, Japan	Itami Airport
KIX	Osaka, Japan	Kansai International Airport
OSA	Osaka, Japan	Osaka International Airport
YOO	Oshawa, Ontario, Canada	Oshawa Municipal Airport
OIM	Oshima, Japan	Oshima Airport
OSH	Oshkosh, WI, USA	Wittman Field Airport
OSL	Oslo, Norway	Oslo Gardermoen Airport
ZOS	Osorno, Chile	Osorno Airport
OST	Ostend, Belgium	Ostend/Bruges International Airport
OSD	Ostersund, Sweden	Are Ostersund Airport
OSR	Ostrava, Czech Republic	Ostrava Airport
YOW	Ottawa, Ontario, Canada	Ottawa International Airport
OTM	Ottumwa, IA, USA	Ottumwa Industrial Airport
OUA	Ouagadougou, Burkina Faso	Ouagadougou Airport
OZZ	Ouarzazate, Morocco	Ouarzazate Airport
OUD	Oujda, Morocco	Oujda, Le Angadis Airport
OUL	Oulu, Finland	Oulu Airport
VDA	Ovda, Israel	Ovda Intl Airport
OVD	Oviedo/Asturias, Spain	Asturias Airport
OWB	Owensboro, KY, USA	Owensboro – Davis County Regional Airport
OXR	Oxnard/Ventura, CA, USA	Oxnard Airport

	P	
PDG	Padang, Indonesia	Minangkabau Intl Airport
PAD	Paderborn, Germany	Paderborn Lippstadt Airport
PAH	Paducah, KY, USA	Barkley Regional Airport
PGA	Page, AZ, USA	Page Municipal Airport
PPG	Pago Pago, American Samoa	Pago Pago Intl Airport
PKZ	Pakse, Laos	Pakse International Airport
YIF	Pakuashipi, Canada	Pakuashipi Airport
PLQ	Palanga, Lithuania	Palanga Intl Airport
PLM	Palembang, Indonesia	Sultan Mahmud Badaruddin Ii
PMO	Palermo, Sicily, Italy	Punta Raisi Airport
PBI	Palm Beach/West Palm Beach, FL, USA	Palm Beach International Airport

CITIES, AIRPORTS AND 3-LETTER IATA CODES ← APPENDIX 2

3-letter IATA Code	City/Country	Airport
PSP	Palm Springs, CA, USA	Palm Springs Intl Airport
PMI	Palma de Mallorca, Mallorca Island, Spain	Palma de Mallorca Airport
PMW	Palmas, Brazil	Aeroporto de Palmas
PMD	Palmdale, CA, USA	Palmdale Air Force 42 Base Airport
PMR	Palmerston North, New Zealand	Palmerstown North Airport
PAO	Palo Alto, California, United States	Palo Alto of Santa Clara County Airport
PLW	Palu, Indonesia	Mutiara Airport
PNA	Pamplona, Spain	Pamplona Airport
PLU	Belo Horizonte, Minas Gerais, Brasil	Aeroporto Pampulha – Carlos Drummond de Andrade
PFN	Panama City, FL, USA	Bay County Airport
PAC	Panama City, Panama	Paitilla Airport
PTY	Panama City, Panama	Tocumen International Airport
PAM	Panama City, Florida, USA	Tyndall AFB
YXP	Pangnirtung, Canada	Pangnirtung Airport
PJG	Panjgur, Pakistan	Panjgur Airport
PNL	Pantelleria, Italy	Pantelleria Airport
PPT	Papeete, French Polynesia	Tahiti Faa'a Airport
PFO	Paphos, Cyprus	Paphos Intl Airport
PBO	Paraburdoo, Western Australia, Australia	Paraburdoo Airport
PBM	Paramaribo, Suriname	Zanderij Intl Airport/Johan Adolf Pengel Intl Airport
XFE	Parent, Quebec, Canada	Parent / Via Rail Service
CDG	Paris, France	Charles de Gaulle
JDP	Paris, France	Issy Les Moulineaux (Heliport de Paris)
LBG	Paris, France	Le Bourget Airport
ORY	Paris, France	Paris – Orly Airport
BVA	Paris	Paris – Beauvais Tillé Airport
PKB	Parkersburg / Marietta, WV, USA	Wood County Airport
PKE	Parkes, New South Wales, Australia	Parkes Airport
XPB	Parksville, British Columbia, Canada	Parksville / Via Rail Service
PMF	Parma, Italy	Parma Airport
PAS	Paros, Greece	Paros Airport
PSC	Pasco, Washington, USA	Pasco Airport
IXT	Pasighat, India	Pasighat Airport
PSI	Pasni, Pakistan	Pasni Airport
PFB	Passo Fundo, Brazil	Passo Fundo Airport
PSO	Pasto, Colombia	Cano Airport

GENERAL ENGLISH → FOR AVIATION

3-letter IATA Code	City/Country	Airport
IXP	Pathankot, India	Pathankot Airport
PAT	Patna, India	Patna Airport
PUF	Pau, France Pau	Pau Pyrénées Airport
YPE	Peace River, Alberta, Canada	Peace River Airport
PKU	Pekanbaru, Indonesia	Sultan Syarif Parin II Intl Airport Airport
PLN	Pellston, MI, USA	Pellston Regional Airport
YBB	Pelly Bay, Canada	Townsite Airport
YTA	Pembroke, Ontario, Canada	Pembroke Airport
PEN	Penang, Malaysia	Penang International Airport
YPT	Pender Harbor, Canada	Pender Harbor Airport
PDT	Pendleton, OR, USA	Eastern Oregon Regional Airport
PNS	Pensacola, FL, USA	Pensacola Intl Airport
YYF	Penticton, British Columbia, Canada	Penticton Regional Airport
PZE	Penzance, England, United Kingdom	Penzance Airport
PIA	Peoria, IL, USA	Greater Peoria Regional Airport
XFG	Perce, Quebec, Canada	Perce / Via Rail Service
PEI	Pereira, Colombia	Matecana Intl Airport
PGX	Périgueux, France	Périgueux Bassillac Airport
PEE	Perm, Russia	Perm Airport
KPV	Perryville, Alaska, USA	Perryville Airport
PGF	Perpignan, France	Llabanere Airport
PER	Perth, Western Australia	Perth Airport
PEG	Perugia, Italy	Perugia (San Egidio)Airport
PSR	Pescara, Italy	Liberi Airport
PEW	Peshawar, Pakistan	Bacha Khan Intl Airport (former Peshawar Airport)
PSG	Petersburg, AK, USA Municipal	
PNZ	Petrolina, Brazil	Petrolina International Airport (Aeroporto Senador Lino Coelho)
PKC	Petropavlovsk, Russia	Petropavlovsk Kamchatsky Airport
PES	Petrozavodsk, Russia	Petrozavodsk Kamchatsky Airport
PHW	Phalaborwa, South Africa	Phalaborwa Airport
PHL	Philadelphia, PA, USA	Philadelphia International Airport
PHS	Phitsanulok, Thailand	Phitsanulok Airport
PNH	Phnom Penh, Cambodia	Phnom Penh Intl Airport

CITIES, AIRPORTS AND 3-LETTER IATA CODES ← APPENDIX 2

3-letter IATA Code	City/Country	Airport
PHX	Phoenix, AZ, USA	Phoenix Sky Harbor International Airport
AZA	Phoenix/Messa, Arizona, USA	Phoenix – Mesa Gateway Airport
XKH	Phonsavan, Laos	Xieng Khouang Airport
HKT	Phuket, Thailand	Phuket Intl Airport
PQC	Phuquoc, Vietnam	Phuquoc Airport
PDS	Piedras Negras, Mexico	Piedras Negras Airport
PIR	Pierre, SD, USA	Pierre Regional Airport
PTG	Pietersburg, South Africa	Polokwane Intl Airport
PZB	Pietermaritzburg, South Africa	Pietermaritzburg Airport
PIW	Pikwitonei, Manitoba, Canada	Pikwitonei Airport
PIP	Pilot Point, Alaska, USA	Pilot Point Airport
UGB	Pilot Point, Alaska, USA	Ugashik Bay Airport
PSA	Pisa, Italy	Galileo Galilei Intl Airport
AGC	Pittsburgh/Allegheny County, PA, USA	Allegheny County Airport
PIT	Pittsburgh, PA, USA	Pittsburgh International Airport
THU	Pituffik, Greenland	Thule Air Base Airport
PIU	Piura, Peru	Piura Airport
PTU	Platinum, Alaska, USA	Platinum Airport
PLB	Plattsburgh, NY, USA	Plattsburgh Intl Airport
PXU	Pleiku, Vietnam	Pleiku Airport
PLH	Plymouth, England, United Kingdom	Plymouth City Airport
PIH	Pocatello, ID, USA	Pocatello Regional Airport
TGD	Podgorica, Montenegro	Podgorica Airport
KPO	Pohang, South Korea	Pohang Airport
PNI	Pohnpei, Caroline Islands, Micronesia	Pohnpei International Airport
PHO	Point Hope, AK, USA	Point Hope Airprot
PTP	Pointe à Pitre, Guadeloupe	Pointe-à-Pitre Intl Airport
PNR	Pointe Noire, Congo	Pointe Noire Airport
XPX	PointeAuxTrembles, Quebec, Canada	Pointe Aux Trembles/Via Rail Service
PIS	Poitiers, France	Poitiers – Biard Airport
PKR	Pokhara, Nepal	Pokhara Airport
PNC	Ponca City, OK, USA	Ponca City Regional Airport
PSE	Ponce, PR, USA	Mercedita Intl Airport
YIO	Pond Inlet, Canada	Pond Inlet Airport
PDL	Ponta Delgada, Azores Islands, Portugal	Aeroporto de Ponta Delgada João Paulo II
PNK	Pontianak, Indonesia	Supadio Airport

GENERAL ENGLISH → FOR AVIATION

3-letter IATA Code	City/Country	Airport
PNQ	Poona, India	Lohegaon Poona (*or* Pune) Intl Airport
TAT	Poprad, Slovakia	Tatry/Poprad Airport
PBD	Porbandar, India	Porbandar Airport
POR	Pori, Finland	Pori Airport
PMV	Porlamar, Venezuela	Margarita Airport
CLM	Port Angeles, WA, USA	William R. Airport
PAP	Port-au-Prince, Haiti	Mais Gate Airport
IXZ	Port Blair, India	Port Blair Airport
PLZ	Port Elizabeth, South Africa	Port Elizabeth Airport
BQU	Port Elizabeth, Saint Vincent and The Grenadines	Bequia Airport
POG	Port Gentil, Gabon	Port-Gentil Intl Airport
PHC	Port Harcourt, Nigeria	Port Harcourt Airport
YZT	Port Hardy, British Columbia, Canada	Port Hardy Airport
PHE	Port Hedland, Western Australia, Australia	Pt Hedlan
PTH	Port Heiden, Alaska, USA	Port Heiden Airport
PLO	Port Lincoln, South Australia, Australia	Pt Lincoln
PQQ	Port Macquarie, New South Wales, Australia	Pt Macquarie
YMP	Port Mcneil, Canada	Port Mcneil Airport
PML	Port Moller, Alaska, USA	Port Moller Airport
POM	Port Moresby, Papua New Guinea	Jacksons Intl Airport
POS	Port of Spain, Trinidad, Trinidad and Tobago	Piarco International Airport
VLI	Port Vila, Vanuatu	Bauerfield Airport
PCA	Portage Creek, Alaska, USA	Portage Creek Airport
PTJ	Portland, Australia	Portland Airport
PWM	Portland, ME, USA	Portland International Jetport
PDX	Portland, OR, USA	Portland International Airport
OPO	Porto, Portugal, Porto	Aeroporto Francisco Sá Carneiro
POA	Porto Alegre, Rio Grande do Sul, Brazil	Aeroporto Internacional de Porto Alegre Salgado Filho
PXO	Porto Santo, Madeira Islands, Portugal	Porto Santo Airport
BPS	Porto Seguro, Bahia, Brazil	Aeroporto de Porto Seguro
PVH	Porto Velho, Brazil	Aeroporto Internacional de Porto Velho
PSM	Portsmouth, NH, USA	Pease Intl Tradeport
PSS	Posadas, Argentina	Posadas Airport
POU	Poughkeepsie, NY, USA	Dutchess County Airport
YPX	Povungnituk, Canada	Poungnituk Airport
YPW	Powell River, British Columbia, Canada	Powell River Airport
PAZ	Poza Rica, Veracruz, Mexico	El Tajín National Airport

CITIES, AIRPORTS AND 3-LETTER IATA CODES ← APPENDIX 2

3-letter IATA Code	City/Country	Airport
POZ	Poznan, Poland	Poznan – Lawica Airport
PRG	Prague, Czech Republic	Prague Ruzyne Airport
RAI	Praia, Cape Verde	Mendes Airport
PRI	Praslin Island, Seychelles	Praslin Island Airport
PRC	Prescott, AZ, USA	Prescott Municipal Airport
PQI	Presque Isle, ME, USA	Presque Isle Municipal Airport
PVK	Preveza, Greece	Preveza Airport
YPA	Prince Albert, Canada	Prince Albert Airport
YXS	Prince George, British Columbia, Canada	Prince George Airport
YPR	Prince Rupert/Princ Rupert, British Columbia, Canada	Digby Island Airport
PCT	Princeton, NJ, USA	Princeton Municipal Airport
PRN	Pristina, Kosovo, Serbia	Pristina Airport
ZJJ	Procida Harbour, Italy	Procida Harbour Airport
PPP	Proserpine, Australia	Proserpine Airport
PVD	Providence, RI, USA	Theodore Francis Green Memorial Airport
PLS	Providenciales, Turks and Caicos Islands	Providenciales Intl Airport
PVC	Provincetown, MA, USA	Provincetown Municipal Airport
PVU	Provo, UT, USA	Provo Airport
SCC	Prudhoe Bay, Alaska	Deadhorse Airport
PCL	Pucallpa, Peru	Captain Rolden Airport
PBC	Puebla, Puebla, Mexico	Aeropuerto Internacional de Puebla
PUB	Pueblo, CO, USA	Pueblo Memorial Airport
PUZ	Puerto Cabezas, Nicaragua	Puerto Cabezas Airport
PXM	Puerto Escondido, Oaxaca, Mexico	
PEM	Puerto Maldonado, Peru	Puerto Maldonado Airport
PMC	Puerto Montt, Chile	El Tepual Airport
PZO	Puerto Ordaz, Venezuela	Puerto Ordaz Airport
POP	Puerto Plata, Dominican Republic	Gregorio Luperón Intl Airport
PPS	Puerto Princesa, Philippines	Puerto Princesa Airport
PSZ	Puerto Suarez, Bolivia	Puerto Suarez Airport
PVR	Puerto Vallarta, Jalisco, Mexico	Gustavo Diaz Ordaz Airport
PUY	Pula, Croatia (Hrvatska)	Pula Airport
PUW	Pullman, WA, USA	Pullman – Moscou Regional Airport
PUQ	Punta Arenas, Chile	Aeropuerto Internacional Presidente Carlos Ibañez del Campo
PUJ	Punta Cana, Dominican Republic	Aeropuerto Internacional de Punta Cana

194

GENERAL ENGLISH → FOR AVIATION

3-letter IATA Code	City/Country	Airport
SDQ	Punta Causedo, Santo Domingo, Dominican Republic	Punta Causedo Airport
PDP	Punta del Este, Uruguay	Punta del Este Airport
PUS	Pusan, South Korea	Kimhae (*or* Gimhae) Intl Airport

	Q	
AQI	Qaisumah, Saudi Arabia	Qaisumah Airport
IQM	Qiemo, China	Qiemo
TAO	Qingdao, China	Qingdao Airport
SHP	Qinhuangdao, China	Qinhuangdao
NDG	Qiqihar, China	Qiqihar
XQU	Qualicum, British Columbia, Canada	Qualicum Beach Airport
YQC	Quaqtaq, Quebec, Canada	Quaqtaq Airport
YQB	Quebec, Quebec, Canada	Quebec City Jean Lesage Intl Airport
ZQN	Queenstown, New Zealand Frankton	Queenstown Intl Airport
UEL	Quelimane, Mozambique	Quelimane Airport
XQP	Quepos, Costa Rica	Quepos Monagua Airport
QRO	Queretaro, Queretaro, Mexico	Aeropuerto Intercontinenta de Queretaro
YQZ	Quesnel, British Columbia, Canada	Quesnel Airport
UET	Quetta, Pakistan	Quetta Intl Airport
UIB	Quibdo, Colombia	Aeropuerto El Caraño
UIP	Quimper, France Pluguffan	Aéroport de Quimper – Cornouaille
UIN	Quincy, IL, USA	Baldwin Field
KWN	Quinhagak, Alaska, USA	Quinhagak Airport
UIH	Quinhon, Vietnam	Quinhon Airport
UIO	Quito, Ecuador	Aeropuerto Internacional Mariscal Sucre

	R	
RBA	Rabat, Morocco Sale	Rabat – Salé Airport
RAB	Rabaul, Papua New Guinea Lakunai	Rabaul *or* Tokua Airport
BVC	Rabil, Cape Verde	Rabil Airport
VKG	Rachgia, Vietnam	Rachgia Airport
BEK	Rae Bareli, Uttar Pradesh, India	Raebareli Fursatganj Airfield
RAH	Rafha, Saudi Arabia	Rafha Airport
RYK	Rahim Yar Khan, Pakistan	Rahim Yar Khan Airport
RFP	Raiatea, French Polynesia	Raiatea
YOP	Rainbow Lake, Alberta, Canada	Rainbow Lake Airport

CITIES, AIRPORTS AND 3-LETTER IATA CODES ← APPENDIX 2

3-letter IATA Code	City/Country	Airport
RPR	Raipur, India	Raipur Airport
RAJ	Rajkot, India	Rajkot Airport
RDU	Raleigh/Durham, NC, USA	Raleigh Durham International Airport
IXR	Ranchi, India	Birsa Munda Airport
YRT	Rankin Inlet, Canada	Rankin Inlet Airport
RAP	Rapid City, SD, USA	Rapid City Regional Airport
RAR	Rarotonga, Cook Islands	Rarotonga Intl Airport
RKT	Ras Al Khaimah, United Arab Emirates	Ras Al Khaimah Airport
RAS	Rasht, Iran	Rasht Airport
RDG	Reading, PA, USA	Reading Regional Airport
REC	Recife, Pernambuco, Brazil Guararapes	Aeroporto Internacional do Recife/Guararapes – Gilberto Freire
YRL	Red Lake, Ontario, Canada	Red Lake Airport
RDD	Redding, CA, USA	Redding Municipal Airport
RDM	Redmond/Bend, OR, USA	Roberts Field
REG	Reggio Calabria, Italy	Tito Menniti Airport
YQR	Regina, Saskatchewan, Canada	Regina International Airport
RNS	Rennes, France	Rennes – Saint-Jacques Airport
RNO	Reno/Tahoe, NV, USA	Reno – Tahoe Intl Airport
RES	Resistencia, Chaco, Argentina	Resistencia Intl Airport
YRB	Resolute, Northwest Territories, Canada	Resolute Bay Airport
REU	Reus, Spain	Reus Airport
KEF	Reykjavik, Iceland	Keflavik Intl Airport
REK	Reykjavik, Iceland	Reykjavik Airport – Metropolitan Area
RKV	Reykjavik, Iceland	Reykjavik Domestic Airport
REX	Reynosa, Tamaulipas, Mexico	General Lucio Blanco Airport
RHI	Rhinelander, WI, USA	Rhinelander Oneida County Airport
RHO	Rhodes, Greece	Rhodes Airport
RAO	Ribeirão Preto, Brazil	Aeroporto Leite Lopes (Ribeirão Preto Airport)
RCB	Richards Bay, South Africa	Richards Bay Airport
RIC	Richmond, VA, USA	Richmond International Airport
RIX	Riga, Latvia	Riga Intl Airport
RMI	Rimini, Italy	Rimini Airport
TIA	Rinas (Tirana), Albania	Tirana International Airport Nene Tereza
RBR	Rio Branco, Brazil	Presidente Medici Airport

GENERAL ENGLISH → FOR AVIATION

3-letter IATA Code	City/Country	Airport
RIO or GIG	Rio de Janeiro, Rio de Janeiro, Brazil	Aeroporto Internacional do Rio de Janeiro or Galeão – Antônio Carlos Jobim
SDU	Rio de Janeiro, Rio de Janeiro, Brazil	Aeroporto Santos Dumont
RGL	Rio Gallegos, Santa Cruz, Argentina	Rio Gallegos Internacional
RGA	Rio Grande, Tierra Del Fuego, Argentina	Aeropuerto Ermes Quijada
RIS	Rishiri, Japan	Rishiri Airport
RIW	Riverton, WY, USA	Riverton Regional Airport
XRP	Riviere A Pierre, Quebec, Canada	Riviere A Pierre/Via Rail Service
YRI	Riviere du Loup, Quebec, Canada	Ville de Riviere
RUH	Riyadh, Saudi Arabia	King Khaled Intl Airport
ROA	Roanoke, VA, USA	Roanoke Regional Airport
RTB	Roatan, Honduras	Aeropuerto Internacional Juan Manuel Galvez
YRJ	Roberval, Canada	Roberval Airport
RCE	Roche Harbor, WA, USA	Roche Harbor Airport
RST	Rochester, MN, USA	Rochester Intl Airport
ROC	Rochester, NY, USA	Greater Rochester Intl Airport
RSD	Rock Sound, Bahamas	Rock Sound Airport
RKS	Rock Springs, WY, USA	Rock Springs Sweetwater City Airport
RFD	Rockford, IL, USA	Chicago/Rockford Intl Airport
ROK	Rockhampton, Australia	Rockhampton Airport
RKD	Rockland, ME, USA	Knox County Regional Airport
RWI	Rocky Mount, NC, USA	Rock Mount – Wilson Airport Field
RDZ	Rodez, France	Rodez Airport
RRG	Rodrigues Island, Mauritius	Rodrigues Island Airport
RMA	Roma, Queensland, Australia	Roma Airport
CIA	Rome, Italy	Aeroporto di Roma – Ciampino
ROM or FCO	Rome, Italy	Leonardo da Vinci/Fiumicino
RNN	Ronne/Bornholm, Denmark	Arnager Airport
RNB	Ronneby, Sweden	Vallinge – Ronneby Airport
ROS	Rosario, Santa Fe, Argentina	Fisherton Airport
RPN	Rosh Pina, Israel	Rosh Pina Airport
RLG	Rostock, Germany	Laage Airport
ROV	Rostov, Russia	Rostov – na-Dony Airport
ROW	Roswell, NM, USA	Roswell Intl Airport
ROP	Rota, Northern Mariana Islands	Rota Intl Airport
ROT	Rotorua, New Zealand	Rotorua Airport

CITIES, AIRPORTS AND 3-LETTER IATA CODES ← APPENDIX 2

3-letter IATA Code	City/Country	Airport
RTM	Rotterdam, Netherlands	Rotterdam – The Hague Airport
URO	Rouen, France	Rouen / Boos Airport
YUY	Rouyn Noranda, Canada	Rouyn
RVN	Rovaniemi, Finland	Rovaniemi Airport
RXS	Roxas, Philippines	Roxas Airport
RUI	Ruidoso, NM, USA	Ruidoso Municipal Airport
RUT	Rutland, VT, USA	Rutland Southern Vermont Regional Airport
RZE	Rzeszow, Poland	Rzeszow Airport

	S	
SCN	Saarbruecken, Germany	Saarbruecken Airport
SAB	Saba Island, Netherlands	Juancho E. Yrausquim Airport
SMF	Sacramento, CA, USA	Sacramento Metropolitan Intl Airport
HSG	Saga, Japan	Saga Airport
MBS	Saginaw/Bay City/Midland, MI, USA	TriCity Airport
SPD	Saidpur, Bangladesh	Saidpur Airport
YAY	Saint Anthony, Canada	St Anthony Airport
SBH	Saint Barthelemy, Guadeloupe	Saint Barthelemy – Gustaf III Airport
YCM	Saint Catharines, Ontario, Canada	Saint Catharines Airport
STC	Saint Cloud, MN, USA	Saint Cloud Regional Airport
STX	Saint Croix Island, VI, USA	Henry E. Rohlsen Airport
SSB	Saint Croix Island, VI, USA	Saint Croix – Sea Plane Base
RUN	Saint Denis De La Reunion, Reunion	Roland Garros Airport
SGO	Saint George, Queensland, Australia	St George Airport
SGU	Saint George, UT, USA	St George Municipa Airport
GND	Saint Georges/Grenada	Maurice Bishops Intl Airport
YSJ	Saint John, New Brunswick, Canada	Saint John Airport
YYT	Saint John's, Newfoundland, Canada	St John's International Airport
ANU	Saint Johns/Antigua, Antigua and Barbuda	VC Bird International Airport
XIM	Saint Hyacinthe, Quebec, Canada	Saint Hyacinthe/Via Rail Service
SKB	Saint Kitts, Saint Kitts and Nevis	Golden Rock Airport (Robert Le Bradshau Intl Airport)
YSL	Saint Leonard, New Brunswick, Canada	St Leonard Aerodrome
STL	Saint Louis, MO, USA	Lambert St Louis Intl Airport
UVF	Saint Lucia, Saint Lucia	Hewanorra Intl Airport
SLU	Saint Lucia, Saint Lucia	Vigie Field
SXM	Saint Maarten, Netherlands Antilles	Princess Juliana Intl Airport

GENERAL ENGLISH → FOR AVIATION

3-letter IATA Code	City/Country	Airport
SMS	Saint Marie, Madagascar	Saint Marie Airport
SFG	Saint Martin, Netherlands Antilles	Lo Esperance Airport
XIO	Saint Marys, Ontario, Canada	St Marys / Via Rail Service
STP	Saint Paul, MN, USA	Downtown Airport
SNP	Saint Paul Island, Alaska, USA	St Paul Island Airport
LED	Saint Petersburg, Russia	Pulkovo Airport
PIE	Saint Petersburg/Clearwater, FL, USA	St Petersburg/Clearwater Intl
FSP	Saint Pierre, St. Pierre and Miquelon	Saint Pierre Airport
STT	Saint Thomas Island, VI, USA	Cyril E King Airport
SPB	Saint Thomas Island, VI, USA	Saint Thomas Seaplane Base
SVD	Saint Vincent, St. Vincent and The Grenadines	E. T. Joshua Airport
SPN	Saipan, Northern Mariana Islands	Saipan Intl Northrn Mariana Isles
SNO	Sakon Nakhon, Thailand	Sakon Nakhon Airport Passenger Terminal
SID	Sal, Cape Verde	Aeroporto Internacional Amilcar Cabral
SLL	Salalah, Oman	Salalah International Airport
SLM	Salamanca, Spain	Salamanca Airport
SLN	Salina, KS, USA	Salina Municipal Airport
SCX	Salina Cruz, Mexico	Salina Cruz Airport
SBY	Salisbury, MD, USA	Salisbury Wicomico Regional Airport
YZG	Salluit, Canada	Salluit Airport
YSN	Salmon Arm, British Columbia, Canada	Salmon Arm Airport
SLC	Salt Lake City, UT, USA	Salt Lake City International Airport
SLA	Salta, Argentina	Aeropuerto Internacional Martín Miguel de Guemes
SLW	Saltillo, Coahuila, Mexico	Saltillo Airport
SSA	Salvador, Bahia, Brazil	Aeroporto Internacional de Salvador – Deputado Luís Eduardo Magalhães
SZG	Salzburg, Austria	Salzburg Airport
NEU	Sam Neua, Laos	Sam Neua Airport
AZS	Samana/El Catey, Dominican Republic	Samana El Catey International Airport
KUF	Samara, Russia	Samara Airport
SKD	Samarkand, Uzbekistan	Samarkand Airport
SMI	Samos Island, Greece	Samos Airport
SZF	Samsun, Turkey	Samsun Airport
ADZ	San Andres Island, Colombia	San Andres Island Airport
SAQ	San Andros, Bahamas	San Andros Airport

CITIES, AIRPORTS AND 3-LETTER IATA CODES ← APPENDIX 2

3-letter IATA Code	City/Country	Airport
SJT	San Angelo, TX, USA	San Angelo Airport
SAT	San Antonio, TX, USA	San Antonio International
SVZ	San Antonio, Venezuela	San Antonio Airport
SQL	San Carlos, California, United States	San Carlos Airport
BRC	San Carlos de Bariloche, Rio Negro, Argentina	San Carlos de Bariloche Airport
SZT	San Cristobel de las Casas, Mexico	San Cristobal de las Casas Airport
SAN	San Diego, CA, USA	Lindbergh International Airport
SFO	San Francisco, CA, USA	San Francisco Intl Airport
SJD	San Jose del Cabo, Baja California Sur, Mexico	Los Cabos Intl Airport
SJC	San Jose, CA, USA	San Jose International Airport
SJO	San Jose, Costa Rica	Juan Santamaria International
SJI	San Jose, Philippines	Mcguire Field
SIG	San Juan, Puerto Rico	Isla Grande Airport
SJU	San Juan, PR, USA	Luis Munoz Marin Intl
UAQ	San Juan, San Juan, Argentina	Domingo Faustino Sarniento Airport
LUQ	San Luis, Argentina	San Luis Airport
SBP	San Luis Obispo, CA, USA	San Luis Obispo County Airport
SLP	San Luis Potosi, San Luis Potosi, Mexico	San Luis Potosi Airport
CPC	San Martin de Los Andes, Neuquen, Argentina	Aeropuerto de Chapelco
SAP	San Pedro Sula, Honduras	Aeropuerto Internacional Ramón Villeda Morales
SPR	San Pedro, Belize	San Pedro Airport
AFA	San Rafael, Argentina	San Rafael Airport
ZSA	San Salvador, Bahamas	San Salvador Airport
SAL	San Salvador, El Salvador	El Salvadore Intl Airport
EAS	San Sebastian, Spain	San Sebastián Airport
SOM	San Tome, Venezuela	San Tome Airport
SAH	Sana'a, Yemen	Sana'a Intl Airport
SDP	Sand Point, Alaska, USA	Sand Point Airport
SDK	Sandakan, Sabah, Malaysia	Sandakan Airport
SDN	Sandane, Norway	Sandane Airport
TRF	Sandefjord, Norway	Sandefjord Airport
SSJ	Sandnessjoen, Norway, Stokka	Stokka Sandnessjoen Airport
YZP	Sandspit, Canada	Sandspit Airport
SFB	Sanford/Orlando, FL, USA	Central Florida Regional Airport
YSK	Sanikiluaq, Canada	Sanikiluaq Airport

GENERAL ENGLISH → FOR AVIATION

3-letter IATA Code	City/Country	Airport
SFQ	Sanliurfa, Turkey	Sanliurga Airport
SNA	Santa Ana, CA, USA	John Wayne Airport
SBA	Santa Barbara, CA, USA	Santa Barbara Airport
SNU	Santa Clara, Cuba	Abel Santa Maria Airport
PAO	Santa Clara County, California, United States	Palo Alto of Santa Clara County Airport
SPC	Santa Cruz La Palma, Canary Islands, Spain	La Palma Airport
VVI	Santa Cruz, Bolivia	Viru Viru International Airport
SAF	Santa Fe, NM, USA	Santa Fe Municipal Airport
SFN	Santa Fe, Santa Fe, Argentina	Esperanza/Santa Fe Airport
SMX	Santa Maria, CA, USA	Santa Maria Public Airport
SMR	Santa Marta, Colombia	Simon Bolivar Airport
STS	Santa Rosa, CA, USA	Sonoma County Airport
RSA	Santa Rosa, La Pampa, Argentina	Santa Rosa Airport
SDR	Santander, Spain	Santander Airport
STM	Santarem, Para, Brazil	Santarem International Airport
SCQ	Santiago de Compostela, Spain	Santiago de Compostela Airport
SDE	Santiago del Estero, Argentina	Santiago del Estero Airport
SCL	Santiago, Chile	Aeropuerto Comodoro Arturo Merino Benitez
SCU	Santiago, Cuba	Santiago Antonio Maceo Cuba
STI	Santiago, Dominican Republic	Aeropuerto Internacional del Cibao
SDQ	Santo Domingo, Dominican Republic	Las Americas Intl Airport
STD	Santo Domingo, Venezuela	Mayor Humberto Vivas Guerrero
JTR	Santorini/Thira Is, Greece	Santorini Airport
SYX	Sanya, China	Sanya Phoenix Intl Airport
SFL	Sao Filipe, Cape Verde	Sao Filipe Airport
SJP	São Jose do Rio Preto, Brazil	São Jose do Rio Preto Airport
SJK	São Jose dos Campos, Sao Paulo, Brazil	São Jose dos Campos Airport
SLZ	São Luiz, Maranhao, Brazil	Aeroporto Internacional de São Luís
SNE	São Nicolau, Cape Verde	São Nicolau Airport
CGH	São Paulo, São Paulo, Brazil	Aeroporto de São Paulo – Congonhas
GRU	São Paulo, São Paulo, Brazil	Guarulhos International Airport (Governador André Franco Montoro)
VCP	São Paulo Viracopos, Brazil	São Paulo Viracopos Airport
TMS	Sao Tome, Sao Tome and Principe	Sao Tome Airport

CITIES, AIRPORTS AND 3-LETTER IATA CODES ← APPENDIX 2

3-letter IATA Code	City/Country	Airport
CTS	Sapporo, Japan	Chitose Airport
OKD	Sapporo, Japan	Okadama Airport
SJJ	Sarajevo, Bosnia and Herzegowina	Sarajevo Intl Airport
SLK	Saranac Lake, NY, USA	Adirondack Regional Airport
SRQ	Sarasota/Bradenton, FL, USA	Sarasota-Bradenton Intl Airport
VNA	Saravane, Laos	Saravane Airport
YZR	Sarnia, Canada	Sarnia Airport
YXE	Saskatoon, Saskatchewan, Canada	Saskatoon Intl Airport
SUJ	Satu Mare, Romania	Satu Mare Airport
CIU	Sault Ste Marie, MI, USA	Chippewa County Intl Airport
YAM	Sault Ste Marie, Ontario, Canada	Sault Ste Marie Arpt
JMC	Sausalito, CA, USA	Marin County Airport
SAV	Savannah, GA, USA	Savannah/Hilton Head Intl Airport
ZVK	Savannakhet, Laos	Savannakhet Airport
SVL	Savonlinna, Finland	Savonlinna Airport
SVU	Savusavu, Fiji	Savusavu Airport
SCM	Scammon Bay, Alaska, USA	Scammon Bay Airport
YKL	Schefferville, Quebec, Canada	Schefferville Airport
BFF	Scottsbluff, NE, USA	Western Nebraska Regional Airport
LKE	Seattle, WA, USA	Lake Union Sea Plane Base
SEA	Seattle, WA, USA	Seattle Tacoma Intl Airport
BFI	Seattle, WA, USA	Kings County International/ Boeing Field
SEB	Sebha, Libya	Sebha Airport
SRG	Semarang, Indonesia	Yani Airport
SMM	Semporna, Sabah, Malaysia	Semporna Airport
SDJ	Sendai, Japan Sendai	Sendai Airport
DJJ	Sentani, Indonesia	Sentani
ICN	Seoul, South Korea	Incheon International Airport
SEL	Seoul, South Korea	Kimpo International
YZV	Sept	Iles, Quebec, Canada
SRX	Sert, Libya	Sert Airport
SVQ	Sevilla, Spain	Seville Airport
SFA	Sfax, Tunisia	Sfax – Thyna Intl Airport
PVG	Shanghai, China	Pudong Shanghai Airport
SHA	Shanghai, China	Shanghai Intl /Hongqiao/
SNN	Shannon, Ireland	Shannon Airport
SWA	Shantou, China	Santou Airport

GENERAL ENGLISH → FOR AVIATION

3-letter IATA Code	City/Country	Airport
SHJ	Sharjah, United Arab Emirates	Sharjah Intl Airport
SSH	Sharm El Sheikh, Egypt	Sharm El Sheikh Intl Airport
SHW	Sharurah, Saudi Arabia	Sharurah Airport
XFL	Shawinigan, Quebec, Canada	Shawinigan/Via Rail Service
XFM	Shawnigan, British Columbia, Canada	Shawnigan/Via Rail Service
SHE	Shenyang, China	Shenyang Taoxian Intl Airport
SZX	Shenzhen, China Shenzhen	Shenzhen Bao'an Intl Airport
SHR	Sheridan, WY, USA	Sheridan County Airport
LSI	Shetland Islands /Shetland Isd, Scotland, United Kingdom	Sumburgh Airport
LWK	Shetland Islands /Shetland Isd, Scotland, United Kingdom	Tingwall Airport
SJW	Shijiazhuang, China	Shijiazhuang Daguocun Intl Airport
HIL	Shillavo, Ethiopia	Shillavo Airport
SYZ	Shiraz, Iran	Shiraz Airport
SHC	Indaselassie, Ethiopia	Shire Indaselassie Airport
SYO	Shonai, Japan	Shonai Airport
SOW	Show Low, AZ, USA	Show Low Regional Airport
SHV	Shreveport, LA, USA	Shreveport Regional Airport
REP	Siam Reap/Angkor Wat, Cambodia	Siem Reap International Airport
SBZ	Sibiu, Romania	Sibiu Airport
SBW	Sibu, Sarawak, Malaysia	Sibu Airport
SDY	Sidney, MT, USA	Richland Municipal Airport
SAY	Siena, Italy	Siena Airport
IXS	Silchar, India	Silchar Airport
SVC	Silver City, New Mexico, USA	Silver City Airport
SYM	Simao, China	Simao
SIP	Simferopol, Ukraine	Simferopol Intl Airport
SIN	Singapore, Singapore	Changi International Airport
SIR	Sion, Switzerland	Sion Airport
SUX	Sioux City, Iowa, USA	Sioux Gateway International Airport
FSD	Sioux Falls, SD, USA	Sioux Falls Regional Airport
YXL	Sioux Lookout, Ontario, Canada	Sioux Lookout Municipal Airport
JSH	Sitia, Greece	Sitia Airport
SIT	Sitka, AK, USA	Sitka Airport
VAS	Sivas, Turkey	Sivas Airport
SGY	Skagway, AK, USA	Skagway Airport
KDU	Skardu, Pakistan	Skardu Airport
SFT	Skelleftea, Sweden	Skelleftea Airport

CITIES, AIRPORTS AND 3-LETTER IATA CODES ← APPENDIX 2

3-letter IATA Code	City/Country	Airport
JSI	Skiathos, Greece	Skiathos – Alexandros Papadiamantis Airport
SKE	Skien, Norway	Skien Airport
SKU	Skiros, Greece	Skiros Airport
SKP	Skopje, FYROM (Former Yugoslav Republic of Macedonia)	Skopje Airport
SLD	Sliac, Slovakia	Sliac Airport
SXL	Sligo, Ireland	Sligo Airport
MBX	Slivnica/Orehova Vas, Slovenia	Maribor Airport
YSH	Smith Falls, Ontario, Canada	Smith Falls Airport
YYD	Smithers, British Columbia, Canada	Smithers Regional Airport
SNB	Snake Bay, Northern Territory, Australia	Snake Bay Airport
AER	Sochi, Russia	Sochi Airport
SOF	Sofia, Bulgaria	Sofia Intl Airport
SOG	Sogndal, Norway	Sogndal Airport
SHO	Sokcho, South Korea	Seolak Airport
SQH	Son La, Vietnam	Na-San Airport
SGD	Sonderborg, Denmark	Sonderborg Airport
JZH	Songpan Jiuzhai, China	Jiuzhai – Huanglong Airport
RRO	Sorrento, Italy	Sorrento Airport
TZN	South Andros, Bahamas	Congo Town – South Andros Airport
SBN	South Bend, IN, USA	South Bend Regional Airport
XSC	South Caicos, Turks and Caicos Islands	South Caicos Airport
TVL	South Lake Tahoe, CA, USA	South Lake Tahoe Airport
WSN	South Naknek, Alaska, USA	South Naknek Airport
SOU	Southampton, England, United Kingdom	Eastleigh Airport
SOP	Southern Pines, NC, USA	Pinehurst Airport
SPW	Spencer, IA, USA	Spencer Municipal Airport
SPU	Split, Croatia (Hrvatska)	Split Airport
GEG	Spokane, WA, USA	International/Geiger Field
AXP	Spring Point, Bahamas	Spring Point Airport
SPI	Springfield, IL, USA	Capital Airport
SGF	Springfield, MO, USA	Springfield Regional Airport
SXR	Srinagar, India	Srinagar Airport
YAY	St Anthony, Canada	St Anthony Airport
SBH	St Barthelemy, Guadeloupe	
YCM	St Catharines, Ontario, Canada	
STC	St Cloud, MN, USA	Saint Cloud Airport
STX	St Croix Island, VI, USA	
SSB	St Croix Island, VI, USA	Sea Plane Base

GENERAL ENGLISH → FOR AVIATION

3-letter IATA Code	City/Country	Airport
RUN	St Denis De La Reunion, Reunion	Gillot Airport
SGO	St George, Queensland, Australia	St George Airport
GND	St Georges/Grenada, Grenada	Pt Saline Airport
SGU	St George, UT, USA	St George Airport
YSJ	St John, New Brunswick, Canada	Turnbull Field
YYT	St John's, Newfoundland, Canada	St John's International
ANU	St Johns/Antigua, Antigua and Barbuda	VC Bird International
XIM	St Hyacinthe, Quebec, Canada	Saint Hyacinthe/Via Rail Service
SKB	St Kitts, Saint Kitts and Nevis	Golden Rock Airport
YSL	St Leonard, New Brunswick, Canada	St Leonard Airport
STL	St Louis, MO, USA	Lambert St Louis International
UVF	St Lucia, Saint Lucia	Hewanorra Airport
SLU	St Lucia, Saint Lucia	Vigie Field Airport
SXM	St Maarten, Netherlands	Antilles Juliana Airport
SMS	St Marie, Madagascar	St Marie Airport
SFG	St Martin, Netherlands Antilles	Esperance Airport
XIO	St Marys, Ontario, Canada	St Marys/Via Rail Service
STP	St Paul, MN, USA	Downtown Airport
SNP	St Paul Island, Alaska, USA	St Paul Island Airport
PIE	St Petersburg/Clearwater, FL, USA	St Petersburg/Clearwater Intl
SCE	State College, PA, USA	University Park Airport
SHD	Staunton, VA, USA	Shenandoah Valley Regional
SVG	Stavanger, Norway	Stavanger Airport
HDN	Steamboat Springs Hayden, Colorado, USA	Steamboat Springs Hayden/ Yampa Valley Regional Airport
SML	Stella Maris, Bahamas	Bahamas Airport
YJT	Stephenville, Newfoundland, Canada	Stephenville Intl Airport
ARN	Stockholm, Sweden	Arlanda International
BMA	Stockholm, Sweden	Bromma Airport
SCK	Stockton, California, USA	Stockton Airport
SKN	Stokmarknes, Norway	Skagen Airport
YSF	Stony Rapids, Saskatchewan, Canada	Stony Rapids Airport
SYY	Stornoway, Scotland, United Kingdom	Stornoway Airport
SQO	Storuman, Sweden	Storuman Airport
SXB	Strasbourg, France	Strasbourg Intl Airport
XTY	Strathroy, Ontario, Canada	Strathroy/Via Rail Service
SOY	Stronsay, Orkney Islands, Scotland, United Kingdom	Stronsay Airport
YRR	Stuart Island, Canada	Stuart Island Airport
SUE	Sturgeon Bay, WI, USA	Sturgeon Bay Airport
STR	Stuttgart, Germany	Stuttgart Airport

CITIES, AIRPORTS AND 3-LETTER IATA CODES ← APPENDIX 2

3-letter IATA Code	City/Country	Airport
SRE	Sucre, Bolivia	Sucre Airport
YSB	Sudbury, Ontario, Canada	Greater Sudbury Airport
SUL	Sui, Pakistan	Sui Airport
SKZ	Sukkur, Pakistan	Sukkur Airport
YTG	Sullivan Bay, Canada	Sullivan Bay Airport
SWQ	Sumbawa Island, Indonesia	Brang Bidji Airport
NTY	Sun City, South Africa	Pilansberg Airport
SUN	Sun Valley/Hailey, ID, USA	Sun Valley Airport
SDL	Sundsvall, Sweden	Sundsvall/Harnosand Airport
MCY	Sunshine Coast, Queensland, Australia	Sunshine Coast Airport
SUB	Surabaya, Indonesia	Juanda Airport
URT	Surat Thani, Thailand	Surat Thani Airport
SGC	Surgut, Russia	Surgut Airport
SUV	Suva, Fiji Nausori	Nausori Airport
SVJ	Svolvaer, Norway	Helle Airport
SWP	Swakopmund, Namibia	Swakopmund Airport
QSY	Sydney, New South Wales, Australia	Sydney New South Wales Airport
SYD	Sydney, New South Wales, Australia	Sydney/Kingsford Smith Airport
YQY	Sydney, Nova Scotia, Canada	Sydney Municipal Airport
ZYL	Sylhet, Bangladesh	Sylhet Airport
SYR	Syracuse, NY, USA	Hancock International Airport
JSY	Syros Island, Greece	Syros Airport
SZZ	Szczecin, Poland	Solidarity Szczecin – Golenión Airport

	T	
TBT	Tabatinga, Amazonas, Brazil,	Tabatinga International Airport
TBZ	Tabriz, Iran	Tabriz Airport
TUU	Tabuk, Saudi Arabia	Tabuk Airport
TCG	Tacheng, China	Tacheng
TAC	Tacloban, Philippines	Daniel Z. Romualdez
TCQ	Tacna, Peru	Tacna Airport
TAE	Taegu, South Korea	Daegu Intl Airport
TAG	Tagbilaran, Philippines	Tagbilaran Airport
TXG	Taichung, Taiwan	Taichung Airport
TIF	Taif, Saudi Arabia	Taif Airport
TNN	Tainan, Taiwan	Tainan Airport
TPE	Taipei, Taiwan	Taiwan Taoyuan International Airport (formerly Chiang Kai Shek Airport)

GENERAL ENGLISH → FOR AVIATION

3-letter IATA Code	City/Country	Airport
TSA	Taipei, Taiwan	Sonshan Airport
TTT	Taitung, Taiwan	Taitung Airport
TYN	Taiyuan, China	Taiyuan Wusu Intl Airport
TAI	Taiz, Yemen	Al Janad Airport
TAK	Takamatsu, Japan	Takamatsu Airport
TLH	Tallahassee, FL, USA	Tallahassee Regional Airport
TLL	Tallinn, Estonia Ulemiste	Lennant Meri Tallinn Airport
YYH	Taloyak, Canada	Taloyak Airport
TPA	Tampa, FL, USA	Tampa International
TMP	Tampere, Finland	Tampere Pirkkala
TAM	Tampico, Tamaulipas, Mexico	General Francisco Javis Mina Intl Airport
TMW	Tamworth, New South Wales, Australia	Tamworth Regional Airport
TNG	Tangier, Morocco	Boukhalef Airport
TSM	Taos, New Mexico, USA	Taos Regional Apt Airport
TAP	Tapachula, Chiapas, Mexico	Tapachula International
TRK	Tarakan, Indonesia	Juwata Intl Airport
TPP	Tarapoto, Peru	Tarapoto Airport
TRO	Taree, New South Wales, Australia	Taree Airport
TIZ	Tari, Papua New Guinea	Tari Airport
TJA	Tarija, Bolivia	Capitán Oriel Plaza Airport
XFO	Taschereau, Quebec, Canada	Taschereau/Via Rail Service
TAS	Tashkent, Uzbekistan	Tashkent Airport
YTQ	Tasiujuaq, Canada	Tasiujuaq Airport
TAT	Tatry/Poprad, Slovakia	Tatry/Poprad Airport
TAV	Tau, American Samoa	Tau Airport
TUO	Taupo, New Zealand	Taupo Airport
TRG	Tauranga, New Zealand	Tauranga Airport
TVU	Taveuni Island, Fiji	Matei Airport
TBS	Tbilisi, Georgia	Tbilisi Intl Airport
MME	Teesside, England, United Kingdom	Durham Tess Valley Airport
TFF	Tefe, Brazil	Tefé Airport
TGU	Tegucigalpa, Honduras	Toncontin Intl Airport
IKA	Tehran, Imam	Khomeini International Airport
THR	Tehran, Iran	Mehrabad Intl Airport
TLV	Tel Aviv Yafo, Israel	Ben Gurion International
SDV	Tel Aviv, Israel	Sde Dov Airport
TEX	Telluride, CO, USA	Telluride Municipal Airport
TIM	Tembagapura, Indonesia	Tembagapura Airport

CITIES, AIRPORTS AND 3-LETTER IATA CODES ← APPENDIX 2

3-letter IATA Code	City/Country	Airport
TPL	Temple, TX, USA	Draughon – Miller Central Texas Regional Airport
ZCO	Temuco, Chile	Manquehue Airport
TKE	Tenakee, Alaska, United States of America	Tenakee Airport
TFS	Tenerife, Canary Islands, Spain	Reina Sofia Airport
TCI	Tenerife, Canary Islands, Spain	Tenerife Norte Los Rodeos (Metropolitan Area)
TFN	Tenerife, Canary Islands, Spain	Tenerife Norte Los Rodeos
TPQ	Tepic, Nayarit, Mexico	Tepic Intl Airport
TER	Terceira Island, Azores Islands, Portugal	Aeroporto Civil das Lajes
TMJ	Termez, Uzbekistan	Termez Airport
TTE	Ternate, Indonesia	Babullah Airport
YXT	Terrace, British Columbia, Canada	Terrace Airport
HUF	Terre Haute, IN, USA	Terre Haute Intl – Human Field
LSS	Terre de Haut, Guadeloupe	Terre-de-Haut Airport
TEB	Teterboro, New Jersey, United States of America	Teterboro Airport
TXK	Texarkana, AR, USA	Texarkana Regional Airport
TEZ	Tezpur, India	Tezpur Airport
THK	Thakhek, Laos	Thakhek Airport
YQD	The Pas, Manitoba, Canada	The Pas Airport
SKG	Thessaloniki, Greece	Thessaloniki Airport
YTD	Thicket Portage, Manitoba, Canada	Thicket Portage Airport
TVF	Thief River Falls, MN, USA	Thief River Falls Municipal
YTH	Thompson, Manitoba, Canada	Manitoba
YQT	Thunder Bay, Ontario, Canada	Thunder Bay Intl Airport
TIS	Thursday Island, Queensland, Australia	Thursday Island Airport
TSN	Tianjin, China	Tianjin
TIJ	Tijuana, Baja California, Mexico	General Abelardo L. Rodriguez
TIU	Timaru, New Zealand	Timaru Airport
TSR	Timisoara, Romania	Timisoara Airport
YTS	Timmins, Ontario, Canada	Timmins Municipal Airport
TIQ	Tinian, Northern Mariana Islands	Tinian Airport
KTP	Tinson Pen	Kingston Airport, Kingston, Jamaica
TIE	Tippi, Ethiopia	Tippi Airport
TIA	Tirana (Rinas), Albania	Tirana International Airport Nene Tereza
TRE	Tiree, Scotland, United Kingdom	Tiree Island Airport
TGM	Tirgu Mures, Romania	Tirgu Mures Airport
TRZ	Tiruchirapally, India	Tiruchirapally Intl Airport
TIV	Tivat, Yugoslavia	Tivat Airport

GENERAL ENGLISH → FOR AVIATION

3-letter IATA Code	City/Country	Airport
TAB	Tobago, Tobago, Trinidad and Tobago	Arthur Napoleon Raymond Robinson Intl Airport
TOB	Tobruk, Libya	Tobruk Airport
YAZ	Tofino, British Columbia, Canada	Tofino Airport
TOG	Togiak, Alaska, USA	Togiak Airport
OOK	Toksook Bay, AK, USA	Toksook Bay Airport
TKN	Tokunoshima, Japan	Tokunoshima Airport
TKS	Tokushima, Japan	Tokushima Airport
NRT	Tokyo, Japan	Narita
TOL	Toledo, OH, USA	Toledo Express Airport
TLC	Toluca, Mexico	Toluca Airport
TMG	Tomanggong, Malaysia	Tomanggong Airport
TEN	Tongren, China	Tongren Airport
TWB	Toowoomba, Queensland, Australia	Toowoomba Airport
FOE	Topeka, KS, USA	Forbes Field
YTZ	Toronto, Ontario, Canada	Toronto
YYZ	Toronto, Ontario, Canada	Lester B Pearson International Airport
TRC	Torreon, Coahuila, Mexico	Francisco Sanabria Intl Airport
EIS	Tortola/Beef Island, Virgin Islands (British)	Beef Island – Tortola Airport
TTB	Tortoli, Italy	Tortoli Airport
TTJ	Tottori, Japan	Tottori Airport
TLN	Toulon, France	Toulon Airport
TLS	Toulouse, France	Toulouse – Blagnac Airport
TUF	Tours, France	Val de Loire Airport
TSV	Townsville, Queensland, Australia	Townsville Airport
TOY	Toyama, Japan	Toyama Airport
TZX	Trabzon, Turkey	Trabzon Airport
TST	Trang, Thailand	Trang Airport
TPS	Trapani, Sicily, Italy	Vincenzo Chiport Trapani – Birgi
TVC	Traverse City, MI, USA	Cherry Capital Airport
TCB	Treasure Cay, Bahamas	Treasure Cay Airport
REL	Trelew, Chubut, Argentina	Trelew
TTN	Trenton, NJ, USA	Trenton – Mercer Airport
TSF	Treviso, Italy	Treviso Airport
TRS	Trieste, Italy	Trieste – Friuli Venezia Gichia Airport
TDD	Trinidad, Bolivia	Trinidad Airport
TIP	Tripoli, Libya	Idris Airport

CITIES, AIRPORTS AND 3-LETTER IATA CODES ← APPENDIX 2

3-letter IATA Code	City/Country	Airport
TRV	Trivandrum, India	Trivandrum International Airport
THN	Trollhattan, Sweden	Trollhattan Airport
TMT	Trombetas, Brazil	Trombetas Airport
TOS	Tromso, Norway	Tromso Airport, Langnes
TRD	Trondheim, Norway	Trondheim Vaernes
TRU	Trujillo, Peru	Trujillo Airport
TKK	Truk, Caroline Islands, Micronesia	Chuck Intl Airport
XLZ	Truro, Nova Scotia, Canada	Truro Nova Scotia Airport
TSZ	Tsetserleg, Arkhangai, Mongolia	Tsetserleg Airport
TSJ	Tsushima, Japan	Tsushima Airport
TUS	Tucson, AZ, USA	Tucson International Airport
TUC	Tucuman, Tucuman, Argentina	Benjamin Matienzo
TUR	Tucurui, Brazil	Tucurui Airport
TUG	Tuguegarao, Philippines	Tuguegarao Airport
TUL	Tulsa, OK, USA	Tulsa International Airport
TBP	Tumbes, Peru	Cap – FAP Pedro Canga Rodríguez Airport
TUN	Tunis, Tunisia	Tunis Carthage Intl Airport
WTL	Tuntutuliak, Alaska, USA	Tuntutuliak Airport
TNK	Tununak, Alaska	Tununak Airport
TXN	Tunxi, China	Tunxi Airport
TUP	Tupelo, MS, USA	Tupelo Regional Airport
TUI	Turaif, Saudi Arabia	Turaif Airport
TUK	Turbat Airport	Turbat Airport
TRN	Turin, Italy	Turin Airport
TKU	Turku, Finland	Turku Airport
TCL	Tuscaloosa, AL, USA	Tuscaloosa Regional Airport
TGZ	Tuxtla Gutierrez, Chiapas, Mexico	Ángel Albino Corzo Intl Airport
TBB	Tuyhoa, VIetnam	Tuyhoa Airport
TWF	Twin Falls, ID, USA	Twin Falls City Couny Airport
TWA	Twin Hills, Alaska, USA	Twin Hills Airport
TYR	Tyler, TX, USA	Pounds Field
PAM	Tyndall Air Force Base	Panama City, Florida, USA
TJM	Tyumen, Russia	Tyumen Airport

	U	
QUB	Ubari, Libya	Ubari Airport
UBJ	Ube, Japan	Yamaguchi Ube Airport
UBA	Uberaba, Brazil	Uberaba Airport

GENERAL ENGLISH → FOR AVIATION

3-letter IATA Code	City/Country	Airport
UDI	Uberlândia, Brazil	Gomes Airport
UBP	Ubon Ratchathani, Thailand	Ubon Ratchathani Airport
UDR	Udaipur, India	Udaipur
UTH	Udon Thani, Thailand	Udon Thani Intl Airport
UFA	Ufa, Russia	Ufa Airport
UPG	Ujung Pandang, Indonesia	Sultan Hasanuddin Intl Airport
ULO	Ulaangom, Uvs, Mongolia	Ulaangom Airport
ULN	Ulan Bator, Mongolia	Chinggis Khaan Intl Airport
UUD	Ulan Ude, Russia	Ulan Ude Airport
ULZ	Uliastai, Zavkhan, Mongolia	Uliastai, Airport
USN	Ulsan, South Korea	Usan Airport
ULD	Ulundi, South Africa	Ulundi Airport
ULY	Ulyanovsk, Russia	Ulyanoysk East Airport
UME	Umea, Sweden	Umea Airport
YUD	Umiujaq, Canada	Umiujaq Airport
UTT	Umtata, South Africa	Umtata Airport
UNA	Una, Brazil	Una Airport
UNK	Unalakleet, Alaska, USA	Unalakleet Airport
UNI	Union Island, Saint Vincent and The Grenadines	Union Island Airport
UTN	Upington, South Africa	Upington Airport
UGC	Urgench, Uzbekistan	Urgench Airport
UPN	Uruapan, Michoacan, Mexico	Uruapan Airport (Licenciado y General Ignácio López Rayón Intl Airport)
URC	Urumqi, China	Urumqi Dicuopu
USH	Ushuaia, Tierra Del Fuego, Argentina	Ushuaia. Islas Malvinas Airport
UCA	Utica, NY, USA	Oneida County Airport
UDJ	Uzhgorod, Ukraine	Uzhgorod Airport

	V	
VAA	Vaasa, Finland	Vaasa Airport
BDQ	Vadodara, India	Vadodara Airport
VDS	Vadso, Norway	Vadso Airport
EGE	Vail/Eagle, CO, USA	Eagle County Regional
YVO	Val D'Or, Canada	Val D'Or Airport
VDZ	Valdez, AK, USA	Valdez Airport
ZAL	Valdivia, Chile	Pichoy Airport
VLD	Valdosta, GA, USA	Valdosta Regional
VLC	Valencia, Spain	Valencia
VLN	Valencia, Venezuela	Arturo Michelena Intl Airport

CITIES, AIRPORTS AND 3-LETTER IATA CODES ← APPENDIX 2

3-letter IATA Code	City/Country	Airport
VLL	Valladolid, Spain	Valladolid Airport
VUP	Valledupar, Colombia	Afonso Lopez Pumarejo Airport
VPS	Valparaiso, FL, USA	Fort Walton Beach
VDE	Valverde, El Hierro, Canary Islands, Spain	El Hierro Airport
VAN	Van, Turkey	Van Airport
CXH	Vancouver, British Columbia, Canada	Vancouver Harbour Airport
YVR	Vancouver, British Columbia, Canada	Vancouver International
VAI	Vanimo, Papua New Guinea	Vanimo Airport
VNE	Vannes, France	Vannes
VRA	Varadero, Cuba	Juan Gualberto Gomez Airport
VNS	Varanasi, India	Babatpur – Varanasi Airport
VRK	Varkaus, Finland	Varkaus Airport
VAR	Varna, Bulgaria	Varna Airport
VST	Vasteras, Sweden	Hasslo Airport
VAV	Vava'U, Tonga	Vava'U Airport
VXO	Vaxjo, Sweden	Vaxjo Airport
VCE	Venice, Italy	Venice – Marco Polo Airport
VER	Veracruz, Veracruz, Mexico	Las Bajadas/General Heriberto Jara
VRB	Vero Beach, FL, USA	Vero Beach Municipal Airport
VRN	Verona, Italy	Verona Villafranca Airport
VEY	Vestmannaeyjar, Iceland	Vestmannaeyjar Airport
VHY	Vichy, France	Vichy – Charmeil Airport
YYJ	Victoria, British Columbia, Canada	Victoria International Airport
YWH	Victoria, British Columbia, Canada	Victoria Inner Harbour Airport
VCT	Victoria, TX, USA	Victoria Regional Airport
VFA	Victoria Falls, Zimbabwe	Victoria Falls Airport
VDM	Viedma, Argentina	Viedma Airport
VIE	Vienna, Austria	Veinna Intl Airport
LVT	Vientiane, Laos	Vientiane Airport
VQS	Vieques, Puerto Rico	Vieques Airport
VGO	Vigo, Spain	Vigo Airport
VLG	Villa Gesell, Buenos Aires, Argentina	Villa Gesell Airport
VSA	Villahermosa, Tabasco, Mexico	Carlos Perez Airport
VHM	Vilhelmina, Sweden	VIlhelmina Airport
VNO	Vilnius, Lithuania	Vilnius Airport
VII	Vinh City, Vietnam	Vinh City Airport
VIJ	Virgin Gorda, Virgin Islands (British)	Virgin Gorda Airport
VIS	Visalia, CA, USA	Visalia Municipal Airport

3-letter IATA Code	City/Country	Airport
VBY	Visby, Sweden	Visby Airport
VTZ	Vishakhapatnam, India	Vishakhapatnam Airport
VIX	Vitória, Espírito Santo, Brazil	Aeroporto de Vitória – Eurico de Aguias Sales
VIT	Vitoria, Spain	Vitoria Airport
VDC	Vitória da Conquista, Brazil	Vitória da Conquista Airport
VVO	Vladivostok, Russia	Vladivostok Airport
SKS	Vojens Lufthavn, Denmark	Jojens Airport
VOG	Volgograd, Russia	Volgograd Airport

	W	
YWK	Wabush, Newfoundland, Canada	Wabush Municipal
ACT	Waco, TX, USA	Madison Cooper
WAE	Wadi Ad Dawasir, Saudi Arabia	Wadi Ad Dawasir Airport
WGA	WaggaWagga, New South Wales, Australia	Forest Hill – WaggaWagga Airport
NTQ	Wajima, Japan	Wajima Airport
WKJ	Wakkanai, Japan	Wakkanai Airport
WGE	Walgett, New South Wales, Australia	Walgett Airport
ALW	Walla Walla, WA, USA	Walla Walla Regional Airport
WVB	Walvis Bay, South Africa	Walvis Bay Airport
WKA	Wanaka, New Zealand	Wanaka Airport
WAG	Wanganui, New Zealand	Wanganui Airport
WXN	Wanxian, China	Wanxian Airport
WAW	Warsaw, Poland Okecie	Warsaw Frederic Chopin Airport
IAD	Washington, DC, USA	Dulles Airport
DCA	Washington, DC, USA R	Ronald Reagan National Airport
IAD	Washington, DC, USA	Washington Dulles International
YKQ	Waskaganish, Quebec, Canada	Waskaganish Airport
WAT	Waterford, Ireland	Waterford Airport
ALO	Waterloo, IA, USA	Waterloo Municipal Airport
ART	Watertown, NY, USA	Watertown Airport
ATY	Watertown, SD, USA	Watertown Regional Airport
YQH	Watson Lake, Yukon Territory, Canada	Watson Lake Airport
CWA	Wausau, WI, USA	Central Wisconsin Airport
YXZ	Wawa, Ontario, Canada	Wawa Airport
TBN	Waynesville	Ft Leonard Wood, MO, USA
EJH	Wedjh, Saudi Arabia	Wedjh Airport

CITIES, AIRPORTS AND 3-LETTER IATA CODES ← APPENDIX 2

3-letter IATA Code	City/Country	Airport
NRN	Weeze, Germany	Niederrhein Airport
WEH	Weihai, China	Weihai Airport
WEI	Weipa, Australia	Weipa Airport
WLG	Wellington, New Zealand	Wellington Intl Airport
EAT	Wenatchee, WA, USA	Pangborn Memorial Field
ENV	Wendover, Utah, USA	Wendover Airport
WNZ	Wenzhou, China	Wenzhou Yongqiang Airport
PBI	West Palm Beach, FL, USA	Palm Beach International Airport
WYS	West Yellowstone, Montana, USA	West Yellowstone Airport
GWT	Westerland, Germany	Westerland – Sylt Airport
WST	Westerly, Rhode Island, USA	Westerly Airport
WSZ	Westport, New Zealand	Westport Airport
WSX	Westsound, Washington, USA	Westsound Airport
WWK	Wewak, Papua New Guinea	Wewak
XFQ	Weymont, Quebec, Canada	Weymont/Via Rail Service
WHK	Whakatane, New Zealand	Whakatane Airport
WRE	Whangarei, New Zealand	Whangarei Airport
YWS	Whistler, Canada	Whistler Airport
HPN	White Plains, NY, USA	Westchester County Airport
YWR	White River, Ontario, Canada	White River Airport
YXY	Whitehorse, Yukon Territory, Canada	Erik Nielsen Whitehorse Intl Airport
WYA	Whyalla, Australia	Ahyalla Airport
ICT	Wichita, KS, USA	Wichita MidContinent Airport
SPS	Wichita Falls, TX, USA	Wichita Falls Municipal
WIC	Wick, Scotland, United Kingdom	Wick Airport
AVP	Wilkes Barre/Scranton, PA, USA	WilkesBarre/Scranton Intl Airport
CUR	Willemstad/Curacao Island, Netherlands Antilles	Aeropuerto Hato
AZA	Mesa, Arizona, USA	Williams Gateway Airport
YWL	Williams Lake, British Columbia, Canada	Williams Lake Airport
IPT	Williamsport, PA, USA	Williamsport Regional Airport
ISN	Williston, ND, USA	Sloulin Field International Airport
ILM	Wilmington, NC, USA	Wilmington Intl Airport
ILG	Wilmington/New Castle County, DE, USA	New Castle Airport
ERS	Windhoek, Namibia	Eros Airport
WDH	Windhoek, Namibia	Hosea Kutako International Airport (formerly Jg Strijdom airport)
YQG	Windsor, Ontario, Canada	Windsor International

GENERAL ENGLISH → FOR AVIATION

3-letter IATA Code	City/Country	Airport
YWG	Winnipeg, Manitoba, Canada	Winnipeg International
INT	Winston, Salem, NC, USA	Smith Reynolds
WIN	Winton, Queensland, Australia	Winton Airport
OLF	Wolf Point, MT, USA	Wolf Point Intl Airport
WJU	Wonju, Republic of Korea	Wonju Airport
UMR	Woomera, South Australia, Australia	Woomera Airfield
ORH	Worcester, MA, USA	Worcester Regional Airport
WRL	Worland, WY, USA	Worland Municipal Airport
WRG	Wrangell, Alaska, USA	Wrangell Airport
WRI	Wrightstown NJ USA	McGuire Air Force Base
WRO	Wroclaw, Poland	Wroclaw – Copernicus Airport
WUH	Wuhan, China	Wuhan Airport
WUS	Wuyishan, China	Wuyishan Airport
XWY	Wyoming, Ontario, Canada	Wyoming / Via Rail Service

	X	
XIY	Xi An, China	Xi'An Xianyang Intl Airport
XMN	Xiamen, China	Xiamen International
XFN	Xiangfan, China	Xiangfan Airport
XIL	Xilinhot, China	Xilinhot Airport
XNN	Xining, China	Xining Airport
XUZ	Xuzhou, China	Xuzhou Guanjin Airport

	Y	
YKM	Yakima, WA, USA	Yakima Air Terminal
YAK	Yakutat, Alaska, USA	Yakutat Airport
YKS	Yakutsk, Russia	Yakutsk Airport
GAJ	Yamagata, Japan	Yamagata Airport
YNB	Yanbo, Saudi Arabia	Yanbo Airport
YNZ	Yancheng, China	Yancheng Airport
RGN	Yangon, Myanmar	Mingaladon Airport
YNY	Yangyang, Republic of Korea	Yangyang Airport
YNJ	Yanji, China	Yanji
YNT	Yantai, China	Laishan
NSI	Yaounde, Cameroon	Yaounde Nsimalen Intl Airport
YAP	Yap, Caroline Islands, Micronesia	Yap Intl Airport
YQI	Yarmouth, Nova Scotia, Canada	Yarmouth Airport
AZD	Yazd, Iran	Yazd Airport
YEC	Yechon, South Korea Yechon	Yechon Airport
YZF	Yellowknife, Northwest Territories, Canada	Yellowknife

CITIES, AIRPORTS AND 3-LETTER IATA CODES ← APPENDIX 2

3-letter IATA Code	City/Country	Airport
COD	Yellowstone, Cody, Wyoming, USA	Yellowstone Regional Airport
EVN	Yerevan, Armenia	Zvartnots Intl Airport
YBP	Yibin, China	Yibin Caiba Airport
YIH	Yichang, China	Yichang Airport
INC	Yinchuan, China	Yinchuan Airport
YIN	Yining, China	Yining Airport
YIW	Yiwu, China	Yiwu Airport
JOG	Yogyakarta, Indonesia	
YGJ	Yonago, Japan	Yonago Airport
RSU	Yosu, South Korea	Yosu Airport
YNG	Youngstown, OH, USA Y	Youngstown Municipal Airport
YIP	Ypsilanti/Detroit, MI, USA	Willow Run Airport, Ypsilanti
YUM	Yuma, AZ, USA	Yuma International Airport
YMS	Yurimaguas, Peru	Yurimaguas Airport
UUS	Yuzhno	Sakhalinsk, Russia, Yuzno

	Z	
ZCL	Zacatecas, Zacatecas, Mexico	General Leobardo C. Ruiz Intl Airport
ZAD	Zadar, Croatia	Zadar Airport
ZAG	Zagreb, Croatia (Hrvatska)	Zagreb Airport
ZAH	Zahedan, Iran	Zahedan Intl Airport
ZTH	Zakinthos, Greece	Zakinthos Intl Airport
ZAM	Zamboanga, Philippines	Zamboanga Airport
ZNZ	Zanzibar, Tanzania	Kisauni Zanzibar Intl Airport or Kisaumi Airport
OZH	Zaporozhye, Ukraine	Zaporozhye Airport
ZAZ	Zaragoza, Spain	Zaragoza Airport
ZHA	Zhanjiang, China	Zhanjiang Airport
ZAT	Zhaotong, China	Zhaotong Airport
CGO	Zhengzhou, China	Zhengzhou Xinzheng Intl Airport
PZH	Zhob, Pakistan	Zhob Airport
HSN	Zhoushan, China	Zhoushan Airport
ZUH	Zhuhai, China	Zhuhai Airport
IEG	Zielona Gora, Poland	Zielona Gora Airport
ZRH	Zurich, Switzerland	Zurich Airport
ZQW	Zweibruecken, Germany	Zweibruecken Airport

Este livro foi impresso na
LIS GRÁFICA E EDITORA LTDA.
Rua Felício Antônio Alves, 370 – Bonsucesso
CEP 07175-450 – Guarulhos – SP
Fone: (11) 3382-0777 – Fax: (11) 3382-0778
lisgrafica@lisgrafica.com.br – www.lisgrafica.com.br